Summerhill

A RADICAL APPROACH TO CHILD REARING

Children of the future Age
Reading this indignant page,
Know that in a former time
Love! sweet Love! was thought a crime.

WILLIAM BLAKE

SUMMERHILL

A RADICAL APPROACH TO CHILD REARING

By A. S. NEILL

With a Foreword by Erich Fromm

HART PUBLISHING COMPANY

New York City

TO HAROLD H. HART

I hope you will get as much credit (or blame) for this book as I will. You have acted, not as a publisher, but as a believer in what Summerhill has done and is doing.

Your patience has amazed me. To sort out thousands of words from four of my earlier books, to edit them and combine them with new material—this has been a formidable task.

In your visits to the school, you showed that your chief concern was to tell America about something you saw and loved and believed in. Here you were part of the school. You saw all the fundamentals and rightly ignored what did not matter, for example, the untidiness of happy children.

I hereby elect you an honorary pupil of Summerhill.

A. S. Neill

October 30, 1959
Summerhill, Leiston, Suffolk, England

A Foreword by Erich Fromm

I

During the eighteenth century, the ideas of freedom, democracy, and self-determination were proclaimed by progressive thinkers; and by the first half of the 1900's these ideas came to fruition in the field of education. The basic principle of such self-determination was the replacement of authority by freedom, to teach the child *without the use of force* by appealing to his curiosity and spontaneous needs, and thus to get him interested in the world around him. This attitude marked the beginning of progressive education and was an important step in human development.

But the results of this new method were often disappointing. In recent years, an increasing reaction against progressive education has set in. Today, many people believe the theory itself erroneous and that it should be thrown overboard. There is a strong movement afoot for more and more discipline, and even a campaign to permit physical punishment of pupils by public school teachers.

Perhaps the most important factor in this reaction is the remarkable success in teaching achieved in the Soviet Union. There the old-fashioned methods of authoritarianism are applied in full strength; and the results, as far as *knowledge* is concerned, seem to indicate that we had better revert to the old disciplines and forget about the freedom of the child.

Is the idea of education without force wrong? Even if the idea itself is not wrong, how can we explain its relative failure?

I believe the idea of freedom for children was *not* wrong, but the idea of freedom has almost always been perverted. To discuss this matter clearly we must first understand the nature of freedom; and to do this we must differentiate between *overt authority* and *anonymous authority*.*

Overt authority is exercised directly and explicitly. The person in authority frankly tells the one who is subject to him, "You must do this. If you do not, certain sanctions will be applied against you." Anonymous authority tends to hide that force is being used. Anonymous authority pretends that there is *no* authority, that all is done with the consent of the individual. While the teacher of the past said to Johnny, "You must do this. If you don't, I'll punish you"; today's teacher says, "I'm sure you'll *like* to do this." Here, the sanction for disobedience is not corporal punishment, but the suffering face of the parent, or what is worse, conveying the feeling of not being "adjusted," of not acting as the crowd acts. Overt authority used physical force; anonymous authority employs psychic manipulation.

The change from the overt authority of the nineteenth century to the anonymous authority of the twentieth was determined by the organizational needs of our modern industrial society. The concentration of capital led to the formation of giant enterprises managed by hierarchically organized bureaucracies. Large conglomerations of workers and clerks work together, each individual a part of a vast organized production machine, which in order to run at all, must run smoothly and without interruption. The individual worker becomes merely a cog in this machine. In such a production organization, the individual is managed and manipulated.

And in the sphere of consumption (in which the individual allegedly expresses his free choice) he is likewise managed and manipulated. Whether it be the consumption of food, clothing, liquor, cigarettes, movies or television programs, a powerful sug-

---

* A more detailed analysis of the problem of authority can be found in E. Fromm, *Escape from Freedom*, Rinehart and Co. Inc., New York, 1941.

gestion apparatus is at work with two purposes: first, to constantly increase the individual's appetite for new commodities; and secondly, to direct these appetites into the channels most profitable for industry. Man is transformed into the consumer, the eternal suckling, whose one wish is to consume more and "better" things.

Our economic system must create men who fit its needs; men who cooperate smoothly; men who *want* to consume more and more. Our system must create men whose tastes are standardized, men who can be easily influenced, men whose needs can be anticipated. Our system needs men who *feel* free and independent but who are nevertheless willing to do what is expected of them, men who will fit into the social machine without friction, who can be guided without force, who can be led without leaders, and who can be directed without any aim except the one to "make good." * It is not that authority has disappeared, nor even that it has lost in strength, but that it has been transformed from the overt authority of force to the anonymous authority of persuasion and suggestion. In other words, in order to be adaptable, modern man is obliged to nourish the illusion that everything is done with his consent, even though such consent be extracted from him by subtle manipulation. His consent is obtained, as it were, behind his back, or behind his consciousness.

The same artifices are employed in progressive education. The child is forced to swallow the pill, but the pill is given a sugar coating. Parents and teachers have confused true nonauthoritarian education with *education by means of persuasion and hidden coercion*. Progressive education has been thus debased. It has failed to become what it was intended to be and has never developed as it was meant to.

---

* For a more detailed analysis of the influence of our industrial system on the character structure of the individual, see E. Fromm, *The Sane Society,* Rinehart and Co. Inc., New York, 1955.

II

A. S. Neill's system is a radical approach to child rearing. In my opinion, his book is of great importance because it represents the *true* principle of education without fear. In Summerhill School authority does not mask a system of manipulation.

Summerhill does not expound a theory; it relates the actual experience of almost 40 years. The author contends that "freedom works."

The principles underlying Neill's system are presented in this book simply and unequivocally. They are these in summary.

1. Neill maintains a firm faith "in the goodness of the child." He believes that the average child is not born a cripple, a coward, or a soulless automaton, but has full potentialities to love life and to be interested in life.

2. The aim of education—in fact the aim of life—is to work joyfully and to find happiness. Happiness, according to Neill, means being interested in life; or as I would put it, responding to life not just with one's brain but with one's whole personality.

3. In education, intellectual development is not enough. Education must be both intellectual *and* emotional. In modern society we find an increasing separation between intellect and feeling. The experiences of man today are mainly experiences of thought rather than an immediate grasp of what his heart feels, his eyes see, and his ears hear. In fact, this separation between intellect and feeling has led modern man to a near schizoid state of mind in which he has become almost incapable of experiencing anything except in thought.

4. Education must be geared to the psychic needs and capacities of the child. The child is not an altruist. He does not yet love in the sense of the mature love of an adult. It is an error to expect something from a child which he can show only in a

ALTRUISM- Regard for and devoted to the interests of others

hypocritical way. Altruism develops *after* childhood.

5. Discipline, dogmatically imposed, and punishment create fear; and fear creates hostility. This hostility may not be conscious and overt, but it nevertheless paralyzes endeavor and authenticity of feeling. The extensive disciplining of children is harmful and thwarts sound psychic development.

6. *Freedom does not mean license.* This very important principle, emphasized by Neill, is that respect for the individual must be mutual. A teacher does not use force against a child, nor has a child the right to use force against a teacher. A child may not intrude upon an adult just because he is a child, nor may a child use pressure in the many ways in which a child can.

7. Closely related to this principle is the need for true sincerity on the part of the teacher. The author says that never in the 40 years of his work in Summerhill has he lied to a child. Anyone who reads this book will be convinced that this statement, which might sound like boasting, is the simple truth.

8. Healthy human development makes it necessary that a child eventually cut the primary ties which connect him with his father and mother, or with later substitutes in society, and that he become truly independent. He must learn to face the world as an individual. He must learn to find his security not in any symbiotic attachment, but in his capacity to grasp the world intellectually, emotionally, artistically. He must use all his powers to find union with the world, rather than to find security through submission or domination.

9. Guilt feelings primarily have the function of binding the child to authority. Guilt feelings are an impediment to independence; they start a cycle which oscillates constantly between rebellion, repentance, submission, and new rebellion. Guilt, as it is felt by most people in our society, is not primarily a reaction

to the voice of conscience, but essentially an awareness of disobedience against authority and fear of reprisal. It does not
matter whether such punishment is physical or a withdrawal of
love, or whether one simply is made to feel an outsider. All such
guilt feelings create fear; and fear breeds hostility and hypocrisy.

10. Summerhill School does not offer religious education. This,
however, does not mean that Summerhill is not concerned
with what might be loosely called the basic humanistic values.
Neill puts it succinctly: "The battle is not between believers in
theology and nonbelievers in theology; it is between believers
in human freedom and believers in the suppression of human
freedom." The author continues, "Some day a new generation
will not accept the obsolete religion and myths of today. When
the new religion comes, it will refute the idea of man's being
born in sin. A new religion will praise God by making men
happy."

Neill is a critic of present-day society. He emphasizes that the
kind of person we develop is a mass-man. "We are living in
an insane society" and "most of our religious practices are
sham." Quite logically, the author is an internationalist, and
holds a firm and uncompromising position that readiness for
war is a barbaric atavism of the human race.

Indeed, Neill does not try to educate children to fit well into
the existing order, but endeavors to rear children who will become happy human beings, men and women whose values are
not to *have* much, not to *use* much, but to *be* much. Neill is a
realist; he can see that even though the children he educates
will not necessarily be extremely successful in the worldly sense,
they will have acquired a sense of genuineness which will effec-
tually prevent their becoming misfits or starving beggars. The
author has made a decision between full human development

ATAVISM. Reversion to a more primitive type.

and full market-place success—and he is uncompromisingly honest in the way he pursues the road to his chosen goal.

III

Reading this book, I have felt greatly stimulated and encouraged. I hope many other readers will. This is not to say that I agree with every statement the author makes. Certainly most readers will not read this book as if it were the Gospel, and I am sure that the author, least of all, would want this to happen.

I might indicate two of my main reservations. I feel that Neill somewhat underestimates the importance, pleasure, and authenticity of an intellectual in favor of an artistic and emotional grasp of the world. Furthermore, the author is steeped in the assumptions of Freud; and as I see it, he somewhat overestimates the significance of sex, as Freudians tend to do. Yet I retain the impression that the author is a man with such realism, and such a genuine grasp of what goes on in a child, that these criticisms refer more to some of his formulations than to his actual approach to the child.

I stress the word "realism" because what strikes me most in the author's approach is his capacity to *see*, to discern fact from fiction, not to indulge in the rationalizations and illusions by which most people live, and by which they block authentic experience.

Neill is a man with a kind of courage rare today, the courage to believe in what he sees, and to combine realism with an unshakable faith in reason and love. He maintains an uncompromising reverence for life, and a respect for the individual. He is an experimenter and an observer, not a dogmatist who has an egotistic stake in what he is doing. He mixes education with therapy, but for him therapy is not a separate matter to solve some special "problems," but simply the process of demonstrating to the child that life is there to be grasped, and not to run away from.

It will be clear to the reader that the experiment about which this book reports is necessarily one which cannot be repeated many times in our present-day society. This is so not only because it depends on being carried out by an extraordinary person like Neill, but also because few parents have the courage and independence to care more for their children's happiness than for their "success." But this fact by no means diminishes the significance of this book.

Even though no school like Summerhill exists in the United States today, any parent can profit by reading this book. These chapters will challenge him to rethink his own approach to his child. He will find that Neill's way of handling children is quite different from what most people sneeringly brush aside as "permissive." Neill's insistence on a certain balance in the child-parent relationship—*freedom without license*—is the kind of thinking that can radically change home attitudes.

The thoughtful parent will be shocked to realize the extent of pressure and power that he is unwittingly using against the child. This book should provide new meanings for the words *love, approval, freedom*.

Neill shows uncompromising respect for life and freedom and a radical negation of the use of force. Children reared by such methods will develop within themselves the qualities of reason, love, integrity, and courage, which are the goals of the Western humanistic tradition.

If it can happen once in Summerhill, it can happen everywhere—*once the people are ready for it*. Indeed there are no problem children as the author says, but only "problem parents" and a "problem humanity." I believe Neill's work is a seed which will germinate. In time, his ideas will become generally recognized in a new society in which man himself and his unfolding are the supreme aim of all social effort.

Contents

Foreword by Erich Fromm   ix

A Word of Introduction by the Author   xxiii

I. SUMMERHILL SCHOOL

The Idea of Summerhill   3
A Look at Summerhill   13
Summerhill Education vs. Standard Education   24
What Happens to Summerhill Graduates   29
Private Lessons at Summerhill   35
Self-Government   45
Coeducation   56
Work   59
Play   62
Theater   66
Dancing and Music   71
Sports and Games   73
Report of the British Government Inspectors   75
Notes on His Majesty's Inspectors' Report   86
The Future of Summerhill   89

II. CHILD REARING

The Unfree Child	95
The Free Child	104
Love and Approval	117
Fear	124
Inferiority and Fantasy	133
Destructiveness	138
Lying	146
Responsibility	152
Obedience and Discipline	155
Rewards and Punishment	162
Defecation and Toilet Training	172
Food	177
Health and Sleep	182
Cleanliness and Clothing	184
Toys	188
Noise	190
Manners	192
Money	198
Humor	200

III. SEX

Sex Attitudes	205
Sex Instruction	218
Masturbation	223
Nudity	229
Pornography	231
Homosexuality	234
Promiscuity, Illegitimacy, and Abortion	236

IV. RELIGION AND MORALS

Religion	241
Moral Instruction	247
Influencing the Child	255
Swearing and Cursing	259
Censorship	263

V. CHILDREN'S PROBLEMS

Cruelty and Sadism	269
Criminality	272
Stealing	276
Delinquency	282
Curing the Child	289
The Road to Happiness	293

VI. PARENTS' PROBLEMS

Love and Hate	301
Spoiling the Child	306
Power and Authority	309
Jealousy	317
Divorce	323
Parental Anxiety	325
Parental Awareness	331

VII. QUESTIONS AND ANSWERS

In General	343
About Summerhill	348
About Child Rearing	355
About Sex	370

About Religion 374
About Psychology 376
About Learning 379

INDEX 380

Summerhill

A RADICAL APPROACH TO CHILD REARING

Your children are not your children.
They are the sons and daughters of Life's longing for itself.
They come through you but not from you,
And though they are with you yet they belong not to you.

You may give them your love but not your thoughts,
For they have their own thoughts.
You may house their bodies but not their souls,
For their souls dwell in the house of tomorrow, which you cannot visit, not even in your dreams.
You may strive to be like them, but seek not to make them like you,
For life goes not backward nor tarries with yesterday.

You are the bows from which your children as living arrows are sent forth.

. . . .

Let your bending in the archer's hand be for gladness.

KAHLIL GIBRAN

A Word of Introduction

In psychology, no man knows very much. The inner forces of human life are still largely hidden from us.

Since Freud's genius made it alive, psychology has gone far; but it is still a new science, mapping out the coast of an unknown continent. Fifty years hence, psychologists will very likely smile at our ignorance of today.

Since I left education and took up child psychology, I have had all sorts of children to deal with—incendiaries, thieves, liars, bed-wetters, and bad-tempered children. Years of intensive work in child training has convinced me that I know comparatively little of the forces that motivate life. I am convinced, however, that parents who have had to deal with only their own children know much less than I do.

It is because I believe that a difficult child is nearly always made difficult by wrong treatment at home that I dare address parents.

What is the province of psychology? I suggest the word *curing*. But what kind of curing? I do not want to be cured of my habit of choosing the colors orange and black; nor do I want to be cured of smoking; nor of my liking for a bottle of beer. No teacher has the right to cure a child of making noises on a drum. The only curing that should be practiced is the curing of unhappiness.

The difficult child is the child who is unhappy. He is at war with himself; and in consequence, he is at war with the world.

The difficult adult is in the same boat. No happy man ever disturbed a meeting, or preached a war, or lynched a Negro. No happy woman ever nagged her husband or her children. No happy man ever committed a murder or a theft. No happy employer ever frightened his employees.

All crimes, all hatreds, all wars can be reduced to unhappiness. This book is an attempt to show how unhappiness arises, how it ruins human lives, and how children can be reared so that much of this unhappiness will never arise.

More than that, this book is the story of a place—Summerhill —where children's unhappiness is cured and, more important, where children are reared in happiness.

ONE

SUMMERHILL SCHOOL

The Idea of Summerhill

This is a story of a modern school—Summerhill.

Summerhill was founded in the year 1921. The school is situated within the village of Leiston, in Suffolk, England, and is about one hundred miles from London.

Just a word about Summerhill pupils. Some children come to Summerhill at the age of five years, and others as late as fifteen. The children generally remain at the school until they are sixteen years old. We generally have about twenty-five boys and twenty girls.

The children are divided into three age groups: The youngest range from five to seven, the intermediates from eight to ten, and the oldest from eleven to fifteen.

Generally we have a fairly large sprinkling of children from foreign countries. At the present time (1960) we have five Scandinavians, one Hollander, one German and one American.

The children are housed by age groups with a house mother for each group. The intermediates sleep in a stone building, the seniors sleep in huts. Only one or two older pupils have rooms for themselves. The boys live two or three or four to a room, and so do the girls. The pupils do not have to stand room inspection and no one picks up after them. They are left free. No one tells them what to wear: they put on any kind of costume they want to at any time.

Newspapers call it a *Go-as-you-please School* and imply that it is a gathering of wild primitives who know no law and have no manners.

It seems necessary, therefore, for me to write the story of Summerhill as honestly as I can. That I write with a bias is natural;

yet I shall try to show the demerits of Summerhill as well as its merits. Its merits will be the merits of healthy, free children whose lives are unspoiled by fear and hate.

Obviously, a school that makes active children sit at desks studying mostly useless subjects is a bad school. It is a good school only for those who believe in *such* a school, for those uncreative citizens who want docile, uncreative children who will fit into a civilization whose standard of success is money.

Summerhill began as an experimental school. It is no longer such; it is now a demonstration school, for it demonstrates that freedom works.

When my first wife and I began the school, we had one main idea: *to make the school fit the child*—instead of making the child fit the school.

I had taught in ordinary schools for many years. I knew the other way well. I knew it was all wrong. It was wrong because it was based on an adult conception of what a child should be and of how a child should learn. The other way dated from the days when psychology was still an unknown science.

Well, we set out to make a school in which we should allow children freedom to be themselves. In order to do this, we had to renounce all discipline, all direction, all suggestion, all moral training, all religious instruction. We have been called brave, but it did not require courage. All it required was what we had—a complete belief in the child as a good, not an evil, being. For almost forty years, this belief in the goodness of the child has never wavered; it rather has become a final faith.

My view is that a child is innately wise and realistic. If left to himself without adult suggestion of any kind, he will develop as far as he is capable of developing. Logically, Summerhill is a place in which people who have the innate ability and wish to be scholars will be scholars; while those who are only fit to sweep the streets will sweep the streets. But we have not produced a street cleaner so far. Nor do I write this snobbishly, for I would rather see a school produce a happy street cleaner than a neurotic scholar.

What is Summerhill like? Well, for one thing, lessons are optional. Children can go to them or stay away from them—for years if they want to. There *is* a timetable—but only for the teachers.

The children have classes usually according to their age, but sometimes according to their interests. We have no new methods of teaching, because we do not consider that teaching in itself matters very much. Whether a school has or has not a special method for teaching long division is of no significance, for long division is of no importance except to those who *want* to learn it. And the child who *wants* to learn long division *will* learn it no matter how it is taught.

Children who come to Summerhill as kindergarteners attend lessons from the beginning of their stay; but pupils from other schools vow that they will never attend any beastly lessons again at any time. They play and cycle and get in people's way, but they fight shy of lessons. This sometimes goes on for months. The recovery time is proportionate to the hatred their last school gave them. Our record case was a girl from a convent. She loafed for three years. The average period of recovery from lesson aversion is three months.

Strangers to this idea of freedom will be wondering what sort of madhouse it is where children play all day if they want to. Many an adult says, "If I had been sent to a school like that, I'd never have done a thing." Others say, "Such children will feel themselves heavily handicapped when they have to compete against children who have been made to learn."

I think of Jack who left us at the age of seventeen to go into an engineering factory. One day, the managing director sent for him.

"You are the lad from Summerhill," he said. "I'm curious to know how such an education appears to you now that you are mixing with lads from the old schools. Suppose you had to choose again, would you go to Eton or Summerhill?"

"Oh, Summerhill, of course," replied Jack.

"But what does it offer that the other schools don't offer?"

Jack scratched his head. "I dunno," he said slowly; "I think it gives you a feeling of complete self-confidence."

"Yes," said the manager dryly, "I noticed it when you came into the room."

"Lord," laughed Jack, "I'm sorry if I gave you that impression."

"I liked it," said the director. "Most men when I call them into the office fidget about and look uncomfortable. You came in as my equal. By the way, what department did you say you would like to transfer to?"

This story shows that learning in itself is not as important as personality and character. Jack failed in his university exams because he hated book learning. But his lack of knowledge about *Lamb's Essays* or the French language did not handicap him in life. He is now a successful engineer.

All the same, there is a lot of learning in Summerhill. Perhaps a group of our twelve-year-olds could not compete with a class of equal age in handwriting or spelling or fractions. But in an examination requiring originality, our lot would beat the others hollow.

We have no class examinations in the school, but sometimes I set an exam for fun. The following questions appeared in one such paper:

Where are the following:—Madrid, Thursday Island, yesterday, love, democracy, hate, my pocket screwdriver (alas, there was no helpful answer to that one).

Give meanings for the following: (the number shows how many are expected for each)—Hand (3) . . . only two got the third right—the standard of measure for a horse. Brass (4) . . . metal, cheek, top army officers, department of an orchestra. Translate Hamlet's To-be-or-not-to-be speech into Summerhillese.

These questions are obviously not intended to be serious, and the children enjoy them thoroughly. Newcomers, on the whole, do not rise to the answering standard of pupils who have become acclimatized to the school. Not that they have less brain power, but rather because they have become so accustomed to work in a serious groove that any light touch puzzles them.

This is the play side of our teaching. In all classes much work is done. If, for some reason, a teacher cannot take his class on the appointed day, there is usually much disappointment for the pupils.

David, aged nine, had to be isolated for whooping cough. He cried bitterly. "I'll miss Roger's lesson in geography," he protested. David had been in the school practically from birth, and he had definite and final ideas about the necessity of having his lessons given to him. David is now a lecturer in mathematics at London University.

A few years ago someone at a General School Meeting (at which all school rules are voted by the entire school, each pupil and each staff member having one vote) proposed that a certain culprit should be punished by being banished from lessons for a week. The other children protested on the ground that the punishment was too severe.

My staff and I have a hearty hatred of all examinations. To us, the university exams are anathema. But we cannot refuse to teach children the required subjects. Obviously, as long as the exams are in existence, they are our master. Hence, the Sum-

ANATHEMA- a curse -

merhill staff is always qualified to teach to the set standard.

Not that many children want to take these exams; only those going to the university do so. And such children do not seem to find it especially hard to tackle these exams. They generally begin to work for them seriously at the age of fourteen, and they do the work in about three years. Of course they don't always pass at the first try. The more important fact is that they try again.

Summerhill is possibly the happiest school in the world. We have no truants and seldom a case of homesickness. We very rarely have fights—quarrels, of course, but seldom have I seen a stand-up fight like the ones we used to have as boys. I seldom hear a child cry, because children when free have much less hate to express than children who are downtrodden. Hate breeds hate, and love breeds love. Love means approving of children, and that is essential in any school. You can't be on the side of children if you punish them and storm at them. Summerhill is a school in which the child knows that he is approved of.

Mind you, we are not above and beyond human foibles. I spent weeks planting potatoes one spring, and when I found eight plants pulled up in June, I made a big fuss. Yet there was a difference between my fuss and that of an authoritarian. My fuss was about potatoes, but the fuss an authoritarian would have made would have dragged in the question of morality—right and wrong. I did not say that it was wrong to steal my spuds; I did not make it a matter of good and evil—I made it a matter of *my spuds*. They were *my* spuds and they should have been left alone. I hope I am making the distinction clear.

Let me put it another way. To the children, I am no authority to be feared. I am their equal, and the row I kick up about my spuds has no more significance to them than the row a boy may kick up about his punctured bicycle tire. It is quite safe to have a row with a child when you are equals.

Now some will say: "That's all bunk. There can't be equality. Neill is the boss; he is bigger and wiser." That is indeed true. I am the boss, and if the house caught fire the children would run to me. They know that I am bigger and more knowledgeable, but that does not matter when I meet them on their own ground, the potato patch, so to speak.

When Billy, aged five, told me to get out of his birthday party because I hadn't been invited, I went at once without hesitation —just as Billy gets out of my room when I don't want his company. It is not easy to describe this relationship between teacher and child, but every visitor to Summerhill knows what I mean when I say that the relationship is ideal. One sees it in the attitude to the staff in general. Rudd, the chemistry man, is Derek. Other members of the staff are known as Harry, and Ulla, and Pam. I am Neill, and the cook is Esther.

In Summerhill, everyone has equal rights. No one is allowed to walk on my grand piano, and I am not allowed to borrow a boy's cycle without his permission. At a General School Meeting, the vote of a child of six counts for as much as my vote does.

But, says the knowing one, in practice of course the voices of the grownups count. Doesn't the child of six wait to see how you vote before he raises his hand? I wish he sometimes would, for too many of my proposals are beaten. Free children are not easily influenced; the absence of fear accounts for this phenomenon. Indeed, the absence of fear is the finest thing that can happen to a child.

Our children do not fear our staff. One of the school rules is that after ten o'clock at night there shall be quietness on the upper corridor. One night, about eleven, a pillow fight was going on, and I left my desk, where I was writing, to protest against the row. As I got upstairs, there was a scurrying of feet and the corridor was empty and quiet. Suddenly I heard a disappointed voice say, "Humph, it's only Neill," and the fun began again at once. When I explained that I was trying to write a book downstairs, they showed concern and at once agreed to chuck the noise. Their scurrying came from the suspicion that their bedtime officer (one of their own age) was on their track.

I emphasize the importance of this absence of fear of adults. A child of nine will come and tell me he has broken a window with a ball. He tells me, because he isn't afraid of arousing wrath or moral indignation. He may have to pay for the window, but he doesn't have to fear being lectured or being punished.

There was a time some years back when the School Government resigned, and no one would stand for election. I seized the opportunity of putting up a notice: "In the absence of a government, I herewith declare myself Dictator. Heil Neill!" Soon there were mutterings. In the afternoon Vivien, aged six, came to me and said, "Neill, I've broken a window in the gym."

I waved him away. "Don't bother me with little things like that," I said, and he went.

A little later he came back and said he had broken two windows. By this time I was curious, and asked him what the great idea was.

"I don't like dictators," he said, "and I don't like going without my grub." (I discovered later that the opposition to dictatorship had tried to take itself out on the cook, who promptly shut up the kitchen and went home.)

"Well," I asked, "what are you going to do about it?"

"Break more windows," he said doggedly.

"Carry on," I said, and he carried on.

When he returned, he announced that he had broken seventeen windows. "But mind," he said earnestly, "I'm going to pay for them."

"How?"

"Out of my pocket money. How long will it take me?"

I did a rapid calculation. "About ten years," I said.

He looked glum for a minute; then I saw his face light up. "Gee," he cried, "I don't have to pay for them at all."

"But what about the private property rule?" I asked, "The windows are my private property."

"I know that but there isn't any private property rule now. There isn't any government, and the government makes the rules."

It may have been my expression that made him add, "But all the same I'll pay for them."

But he didn't have to pay for them. Lecturing in London shortly afterward, I told the story; and at the end of my talk, a young man came up and handed me a pound note "to pay for the young devil's windows." Two years later, Vivien was still telling people of his windows and of the man who paid for them. "He must have been a terrible fool, because he never even saw me."

Children make contact with strangers more easily when fear is unknown to them. English reserve is, at bottom, really fear; and that is why the most reserved are those who have the most wealth. The fact that Summerhill children are so exceptionally friendly to visitors and strangers is a source of pride to me and my staff.

We must confess, however, that many of our visitors are people of interest to the children. The kind of visitor most unwelcome to them is the teacher, especially the earnest teacher, who wants to see their drawing and written work. The most welcome visitor is the one who has good tales to tell—of adventure and travel or, best of all, of aviation. A boxer or a good tennis player is surrounded at once, but visitors who spout theory are left severely alone.

The most frequent remark that visitors make is that they cannot tell who is staff and who is pupil. It is true: the feeling of unity is that strong when children are approved of. There is no deference to a teacher as a teacher. Staff and pupils have the same food and have to obey the same community laws. The children would resent any special privileges given to the staff.

When I used to give the staff a talk on psychology every week, there was a muttering that it wasn't fair. I changed the plan and made the talks open to everyone over twelve. Every Tuesday night, my room is filled with eager youngsters who not only listen but give their opinions freely. Among the subjects the children have asked me to talk about have been these: The Inferiority Complex, The Psychology of Stealing, The Psychology of the Gangster, The Psychology of Humor, Why Did Man Become a Moralist?, Masturbation, Crowd Psychology. It is obvious that such children will go out into life with a broad clear knowledge of themselves and others.

The most frequent question asked by Summerhill visitors is, "Won't the child turn round and blame the school for not making him learn arithmetic or music?" The answer is that young Freddy Beethoven and young Tommy Einstein will refuse to be kept away from their respective spheres.

The function of the child is to live his own life—not the life that his anxious parents think he should live, nor a life according to the purpose of the educator who thinks he knows what is best. All this interference and guidance on the part of adults only produces a generation of robots.

You cannot *make* children learn music or anything else without to some degree converting them into will-less adults. You fashion them into accepters of the *status quo*—a good thing for a society that needs obedient sitters at dreary desks, standers in shops, mechanical catchers of the 8:30 suburban train—a society, in short, that is carried on the shabby shoulders of the scared little man—the scared-to-death conformist.

A Look at Summerhill

Let me describe a typical day in Summerhill. Breakfast is from 8:15 to 9. The staff and pupils carry their breakfast from the kitchen across to the dining room. Beds are supposed to be made by 9:30, when lessons begin.

At the beginning of each term, a timetable is posted. Thus, Derek in the laboratory may have Class I on Monday, Class II on Tuesday, and so on. I have a similar timetable for English and mathematics; Maurice for geography and history. The younger children (aged seven to nine) usually stay with their own teacher most of the morning, but they also go to Science or the Art Room.

No pupil is compelled to attend lessons. But if Jimmy comes to English on Monday and does not make an appearance again until Friday of the following week, the others quite rightly object that he is holding back the work, and they may throw him out for impeding progress.

Lessons go on until one, but the kindergarteners and juniors lunch at 12:30. The school has to be fed in two relays. The staff and seniors sit down to lunch at 1:30.

Afternoons are completely free for everyone. What they all do in the afternoon I do not know. I garden, and seldom see youngsters about. I see the juniors playing gangsters. Some of the seniors busy themselves with motors and radios and drawing and painting. In good weather, seniors play games. Some tinker about in the workshop, mending their bicycles or making boats or revolvers.

Tea is served at four. At five, various activities begin. The juniors like to be read to. The middle group likes work in the Art

Room—painting, linoleum cuts, leather work, basket making. There is usually a busy group in the pottery; in fact, the pottery seems to be a favorite haunt morning and evening. The oldest group works from five onward. The wood and metal workshop is full every night.

On Monday nights, the pupils go to the local movie at their parents' expense. When the program changes on Thursday, those who have the money go again.

On Tuesday night, the staff and seniors hear my talk on psychology. At the same time the juniors have various reading groups. Wednesday night is dance night. Dance records are selected from a great pile. The children are all good dancers, and some visitors say that they feel inferior dancing with them. On Thursday night, there's nothing special on. The seniors go to the movies in Leiston or Aldeburgh. Friday is left for any special event, such as rehearsing for a play.

Saturday night is our most important one, for it is General School Meeting night. Dancing usually follows. During the winter months, Sunday is theater evening.

There is no timetable for handiwork. There are no set lessons in woodworking. Children make what they want to. And what they want to make is nearly always a toy revolver or gun or boat or kite. They are not much interested in elaborate joints of the dovetail variety; even the older boys do not care for difficult carpentry. Not many of them take an interest in my own hobby —hammered brasswork—because you can't attach much of a fantasy to a brass bowl.

On a good day you may not see the boy gangsters of Summerhill. They are in far corners intent on their deeds of derring-do. But you will see the girls. They are in or near the house, and never far away from the grownups.

You will often find the Art Room full of girls painting and making bright things with fabrics. In the main, however, I think that the small boys are more creative; at least I never hear a boy say he is bored because he doesn't know what to do, whereas I sometimes hear girls say that.

Possibly I find the boys more creative than the girls because the school may be better equipped for boys than for girls. Girls of ten and over have little use for a workshop with iron and wood. They have no desire to tinker with engines, nor are they attracted by electricity or radio. They have their art work, which includes pottery, cutting linoleum blocks and painting, and sewing work, but for some that is not enough. Boys are just as keen on cooking as girls are. The girls and boys write and produce their own plays, make their own costumes and scenery. Generally, the acting talent of the pupils is of a high standard, because the acting is sincere and not show-offish.

The girls seem to frequent the chemical lab just as often as the boys do. The workshop is about the only place that does not attract girls from nine up.

The girls take a less active part in school meetings than the boys do, and I have no ready explanation for this fact.

Up to a few years ago, girls were apt to come late to Summerhill; we had lots of failures from convents and girls' schools. I never consider such a child a true example of a free education. These girls who came late were usually children of parents who had no appreciation of freedom, for if they had had, their girls would not have been problems. Then when the girl was cured here in Summerhill of her special failing, she was whisked off by her parents to "a nice school where she will be educated." But in recent years we have been getting girls from homes that believe in Summerhill. A fine bunch they are, too, full of spirit and originality and initiative.

We have lost girls occasionally because of financial reasons; sometimes when their brothers were kept on at expensive private schools. The old tradition of making the son the important one in the family dies hard. We have lost both girls and boys through the possessive jealousy of the parents, who feared that the children might transfer to the school their loyalty toward home.

Summerhill has always had a bit of a struggle to keep going. Few parents have the patience and faith to send their children to a school in which the youngsters can play as an alternative to learning. Parents tremble to think that at twenty-one their son may not be capable of earning a living.

Today, Summerhill pupils are mostly children whose parents want them brought up without restrictive discipline. This is a most happy circumstance, for in the old days I would have the son of a die-hard who sent his lad to me in desperation. Such parents had no interest at all in freedom for children, and secretly they must have considered us a crowd of lunatic cranks. It was very difficult to explain things to those die-hards.

I recall the military gentleman who thought of enrolling his nine-year-old son as a pupil.

"The place seems all right," he said, "but I have one fear. My boy may learn to masturbate here."

I asked him why he feared this.

"It will do him so much harm," he said.

"It didn't do you or me much harm, did it?" I said pleasantly. He went off rather hurriedly with his son.

Then there was the rich mother who, after asking me questions for an hour, turned to her husband and said, "I can't decide whether to send Marjorie here or not."

"Don't bother," I said. "I have decided for you. I'm not taking her."

I had to explain to her what I meant. "You don't really believe in freedom," I said. "If Marjorie came here, I should waste half my life explaining to you what it was all about, and in the end you wouldn't be convinced. The result would be disastrous for

Marjorie, for she would be perpetually faced with the awful doubt: Which is right, home or school?"

The ideal parents are those who come down and say, "Summerhill is the place for our kids; no other school will do."

When we opened the school, the difficulties were especially grave. We could only take children from the upper and middle classes because we had to make ends meet. We had no rich man behind us. In the early days of the school, a benefactor, who insisted on <u>anonymity</u>, helped us through one or two bad times; and later one of the parents made generous gifts—a new kitchen, a radio, a new wing on our cottage, a new workshop. He was the ideal benefactor, for he set no conditions and asked for nothing in return. "Summerhill gave my Jimmy the education I wanted for him," he said simply, for James Shand was a true believer in freedom for children.

But we have never been able to take the children of the very poor. That is a pity, for we have had to confine our study to only the children of the middle class. And sometimes it is difficult to see child nature when it is hidden behind too much money and expensive clothes. When a girl knows that on her twenty-first birthday she will come into a substantial amount of money, it is not easy to study child nature in her. Luckily, however, most of the present and past pupils of Summerhill have not been spoiled by wealth; all of them know that they must earn a living when they leave school.

In Summerhill, we have chambermaids from the town who work for us all day but who sleep at their own homes. They are young girls who work hard and well. In a free atmosphere where they are not bossed, they work harder and better than maids do who are under authority. They are excellent girls in every way. I have always felt ashamed of the fact that these girls have to work hard because they were born poor, whereas I have had spoiled girls from well-to-do homes who had not the energy to make their own beds. But I must confess that I myself hated to make my bed. My lame excuse that I had so much else to do did not impress the children. They jeered at my defense that you can't expect a general to pick up rubbish.

I have suggested more than once that the adults in Summerhill are no paragons of virtue. We are human like everyone else, and our human frailties often come into conflict with our theories. In the average home, if a child breaks a plate, father or mother makes a fuss—the plate becoming more important than the child. In Summerhill, if a maid or a child drops a pile of plates, I say nothing and my wife says nothing. Accidents are accidents. But if a child borrows a book and leaves it out in the rain, my wife gets angry because books mean much to her. In such a case, I am personally indifferent, for books have little value for me. On the other hand, my wife seems vaguely surprised when I make a fuss about a ruined chisel. I value tools, but tools mean little to her.

In Summerhill, our life is one of giving all the time. Visitors wear us out more than the children do, for they also want us to give. It may be more blessed to give than to receive, but it certainly is more exhausting.

Our Saturday night General Meetings, alas, show the conflict between children and adults. That is natural, for to have a community of mixed ages and for everyone to sacrifice all to the young children would be to completely spoil these children. The adults make complaints if a gang of seniors keeps them awake by laughing and talking after all have gone to bed. Harry complains that he spent an hour planing a panel for the front door, went to lunch, and came back to find that Billy had converted it into a shelf. I make accusations against the boys who borrowed my soldering outfit and didn't return it. My wife makes a fuss because three small children came after supper and said they were hungry and got bread and jam, and the pieces of bread were found lying in the hallway the next morning. Peter reports sadly that a gang threw his precious clay at each other in the pottery room. So it goes on, the fight between the adult point of view and the juvenile lack of awareness. But the fight never degenerates into personalities; there is no feeling of bitterness against the individual. This conflict keeps Summerhill very much alive. There is always something happening, and there isn't a dull day in the whole year.

Luckily, the staff is not too possessive, though I admit it hurts me when I have bought a special tin of paint at three pounds a gallon and then find that a girl has taken the precious stuff to paint an old bedstead. I am possessive about my car and my typewriter and my workshop tools, but I have no feeling of possession about people. If you are possessive about people, you ought not to be a schoolmaster.

The wear and tear of materials in Summerhill is a natural process. It could be obviated only by the introduction of fear. The wear and tear of psychic forces cannot be obviated in any way, for children ask and must be given. Fifty times a day my sitting room door opens and a child asks a question: "Is this movie night?" "Why don't I get a P.L. [Private Lesson]?" "Have you seen Pam?" "Where's Ena?" It is all in a day's work, and I do not feel any strain at the time, though we have no real private life, partly because the house is not a good one for a school—not good from the adult's point of view, for the children are always on top of us. But by the end of term, my wife and I are thoroughly fatigued.

One noteworthy fact is that members of the staff seldom lose their tempers. That says as much for the children as for the staff. Really, they are delightful children to live with, and the occasions for losing one's temper are very few. If a child is free to approve of himself, he will not usually be hateful. He will not see any fun in trying to make an adult lose his temper.

We had one woman teacher who was oversensitive to criticism, and the girls teased her. They could not tease any other member of the staff, because no other member would react. You can only tease people who have dignity.

Do Summerhill children exhibit the usual aggression of ordinary children? Well, every child has to have some aggression in order to force his way through life. The exaggerated aggression we see in unfree children is an overprotest against hate that has been shown toward them. At Summerhill where no child feels he is hated by adults, aggression is not so necessary. The aggressive children we have are invariably those whose homes give them no love and understanding.

When I was a boy at a village school, bloody noses were at least a weekly phenomenon. Aggression of the fighting type is hate; and youngsters full of hate need to fight. When children are in an atmosphere in which hate is eliminated, they do not show hate.

I think that the Freudian emphasis on aggression is due to the study of homes and schools *as they are*. You cannot study canine psychology by observing the retriever on a chain. Nor can you dogmatically theorize about human psychology when humanity is on a very strong chain—one fashioned by generations of life-haters. I find that in the freedom of Summerhill aggression does not appear in anything like the same strength in which it appears in strict schools.

At Summerhill, however, freedom does not mean the abrogation of common sense. We take every precaution for the safety of the pupils. The children may bathe only when there is a life-saver present for every six children; no child under eleven may cycle on the street alone. These rules come from the children themselves, voted in a General School Meeting.

But there is no law about climbing trees. Climbing trees is a part of life's education; and to prohibit all dangerous undertakings would make a child a coward. We prohibit climbing on roofs, and we prohibit air guns and other weapons that might wound. I am always anxious when a craze for wooden swords begins. I insist that the points be covered with rubber or cloth, but even then I am always glad when the craze is over. It is not easy to draw the line between realistic carefulness and anxiety.

I have never had favorites in the school. Of course I have always liked some children better than others, but I have managed to keep from revealing it. Possibly the success of Summerhill has been in part because the children feel that they are all treated alike and treated with respect. I fear the existence in any school of a sentimental attitude toward the pupils; it is so easy to make your geese swans, to see a Picasso in a child who can splash color about.

In most schools where I have taught, the staff room was a little hell of intrigue, hate, and jealousy. Our staff room is a happy place. The spites so often seen elsewhere are absent. Under freedom, adults acquire the same happiness and good will that the pupils acquire. Sometimes, a new member of our staff will react to freedom very much as children react: he may go unshaved, stay abed too long of mornings, even break school laws. Luckily, the living out of complexes takes a much shorter time for adults than it does for children.

On alternate Sunday nights, I tell the younger children a story about their own adventures. I have done it for years. I have taken them to Darkest Africa, under the sea, and over the clouds. Some time ago, I made myself die. Summerhill was taken over by a strict man called Muggins. He made lessons compulsory. If you even said *Dash,* you got caned. I pictured how they all meekly obeyed his orders.

Those three- to eight-year-olds got furious with me. "We didn't. We all ran away. We killed him with a hammer. Think we would stand a man like that?"

In the end, I found I could satisfy them only by coming to life again and kicking Mr. Muggins out the front door. These were mostly small children who had never known a strict school, and their reaction of fury was spontaneous and natural. A world in which the schoolmaster was not on their side was an appalling one for them to think of—not only because of their experience of Summerhill but also because of their experience at home where Mommy and Daddy were also on their side.

An American visitor, a professor of psychology, criticized our school on the grounds that it is an island, that it is not fitting into a community, and that it is not part of a larger social unit. My answer is this: If I were to found a school in a small town, attempting to make it a part of the community, what would happen? Out of a hundred parents, what percentage would approve of free choice in attending lessons? How many would approve of a child's right to masturbate? From the word go, I should have to compromise with what I believe to be truth.

Summerhill *is* an island. It has to be an island, because its parents live in towns miles apart, in countries overseas. Since it is impossible to collect all the parents together in the town of Leiston, Suffolk, Summerhill cannot be a part of Leiston's cultural and economic and social life.

I hasten to add that the school is not an island to Leiston town. We have many contacts with local people, and the relationship on both sides is a friendly one. Yet, fundamentally, we are not a part of the community. I would never think of asking the editor of the local newspaper to publish success stories about my old pupils.

We play games with the town children, but our educational aims are far apart. Not having any religious affiliation, we have no connection with religious bodies in the town. If Summerhill were part of the town community center, it would be obliged to give religious teaching to its pupils.

I have the distinct feeling that my American friend did not realize what his criticism meant. I take it that it meant: Neill is only a rebel against society; his system can do nothing to weld society into a harmonious unit, cannot bridge the gulf between child psychology and the social ignorance of child psychology, between life and anti-life, school and home. My answer is that I am not an active proselytizer of society: I can only convince society that it is necessary for it to rid itself of its hate and its punishment and its mysticism. Although I write and say what I think of society, if I tried to reform society *by action,* society would kill me as a public danger.

If, for example, I tried to form a society in which adolescents would be free to have their own natural love life, I should be ruined if not imprisoned as an immoral seducer of youth. Hating compromise as I do, I have to compromise here, realizing that my primary job is not the reformation of society, but the bringing of happiness to some few children.

Summerhill Education vs. Standard Education

I hold that the aim of life is to find happiness, which means to find interest. Education should be a preparation for life. Our culture has not been very successful. Our education, politics, and economics lead to war. Our medicines have not done away with disease. Our religion has not abolished usury and robbery. Our boasted humanitarianism still allows public opinion to approve of the barbaric sport of hunting. The advances of the age are advances in mechanism—in radio and television, in electronics, in jet planes. New world wars threaten, for the world's social conscience is still primitive.

If we feel like questioning today, we can pose a few awkward questions. Why does man seem to have many more diseases than animals have? Why does man hate and kill in war when animals do not? Why does cancer increase? Why are there so many suicides? So many insane sex crimes? Why the hate that is anti-Semitism? Why Negro hating and lynching? Why backbiting and spite? Why is sex obscene and a leering joke? Why is being a bastard a social disgrace? Why the continuance of religions that have long ago lost their love and hope and charity? Why, a thousand whys about our vaunted state of civilized eminence!

I ask these questions because I am by profession a teacher, one who deals with the young. I ask these questions because those so often asked by teachers are the unimportant ones, the ones about school subjects. I ask what earthly good can come out of discussions about French or ancient history or what not when these subjects don't matter a jot compared to the larger question of life's natural fulfillment—of man's inner happiness.

How much of our education is real doing, real self-expression? Handwork is too often the making of a pin tray under the eye of an expert. Even the Montessori system, well-known as a system of directed play, is an artificial way of making the child learn by doing. It has nothing creative about it.

In the home, the child is always being taught. In almost every home, there is always at least one ungrown-up grownup who rushes to show Tommy how his new engine works. There is always someone to lift the baby up on a chair when baby wants to examine something on the wall. Every time we show Tommy how his engine works we are stealing from that child the joy of life—the joy of discovery—the joy of overcoming an obstacle. Worse! We make that child come to believe that he is inferior, and must depend on help.

Parents are slow in realizing how unimportant the learning side of school is. Children, like adults, learn what they want to learn. All prize-giving and marks and exams sidetrack proper personality development. Only pedants claim that learning from books is education.

Books are the least important apparatus in a school. All that any child needs is the three R's; the rest should be tools and clay and sports and theater and paint and freedom.

Most of the school work that adolescents do is simply a waste of time, of energy, of patience. It robs youth of its right to play and play and play; it puts old heads on young shoulders.

When I lecture to students at teacher training colleges and universities, I am often shocked at the ungrownupness of these lads and lasses stuffed with useless knowledge. They know a lot; they shine in dialectics; they can quote the classics—but in their outlook on life many of them are infants. For they have been taught *to know,* but have not been allowed *to feel.* These students are friendly, pleasant, eager, but something is lacking— the emotional factor, the power to subordinate thinking to feeling. I talk to these of a world they have missed and go on missing. Their textbooks do not deal with human character, or with love, or with freedom, or with self-determination. And so the system goes on, aiming only at standards of book learning—goes on separating the head from the heart.

It is time that we were challenging the school's notion of work. It is taken for granted that every child should learn mathematics, history, geography, some science, a little art, and certainly literature. It is time we realized that the average young child is not much interested in any of these subjects.

I prove this with every new pupil. When told that the school is free, every new pupil cries, "Hurrah! You won't catch me doing dull arithmetic and things!"

I am not decrying learning. But learning should come after play. And learning should not be deliberately seasoned with play to make it palatable.

Learning is important—but not to everyone. Nijinsky could not pass his school exams in St. Petersburg, and he could not enter the State Ballet without passing those exams. He simply could not learn school subjects—his mind was elsewhere. They faked an exam for him, giving him the answers with the papers —so a biography says. What a loss to the world if Nijinsky had had to really pass those exams!

Creators learn what they want to learn in order to have the tools that their originality and genius demand. We do not know how much creation is killed in the classroom with its emphasis on learning.

I have seen a girl weep nightly over her geometry. Her mother wanted her to go to the university, but the girl's whole soul was artistic. I was delighted when I heard that she had failed her college entrance exams for the seventh time. Possibly, the mother would now allow her to go on the stage as she longed to do.

Some time ago, I met a girl of fourteen in Copenhagen who had spent three years in Summerhill and had spoken perfect English here. "I suppose you are at the top of your class in English," I said.

She grimaced ruefully. "No, I'm at the bottom of my class, because I don't know English grammar," she said. I think that disclosure is about the best commentary on what adults consider education.

Indifferent scholars who, under discipline, scrape through college or university and become unimaginative teachers, mediocre doctors, and incompetent lawyers would possibly be good mechanics or excellent bricklayers or first-rate policemen.

We have found that the boy who cannot or will not learn to read until he is, say, fifteen is always a boy with a mechanical bent who later on becomes a good engineer or electrician. I should not dare dogmatize about girls who never go to lessons, especially to mathematics and physics. Often such girls spend much time with needlework, and some, later on in life, take up dressmaking and designing. It is an absurd curriculum that makes a prospective dressmaker study quadratic equations or Boyle's Law.

Caldwell Cook wrote a book called *The Play Way,* in which he told how he taught English by means of play. It was a fascinating book, full of good things, yet I think it was only a new way of bolstering the theory that learning is of the utmost importance. Cook held that learning was so important that the pill should be sugared with play. This notion that unless a child is learning something the child is wasting his time is nothing less than a curse—a curse that blinds thousands of teachers and most school inspectors. Fifty years ago the watchword was "Learn through doing." Today the watchword is "Learn through playing." Play is thus used only as a means to an end, but to what good end I do not really know.

If a teacher sees children playing with mud, and he thereupon improves the shining moment by holding forth about river-bank erosion, what end has he in view? What child cares about river erosion? Many so-called educators believe that it does not matter what a child learns as long as he is *taught* something. And, of course, with schools as they are—just mass-production factories—what can a teacher do but teach something and come to believe that teaching, in itself, matters most of all?

When I lecture to a group of teachers, I commence by saying that I am not going to speak about school subjects or discipline or classes. For an hour my audience listens in rapt silence; and after the sincere applause, the chairman announces that I am ready to answer questions. At least three-quarters of the questions deal with subjects and teaching.

I do not tell this in any superior way. I tell it sadly to show how the classroom walls and the prisonlike buildings narrow the teacher's outlook, and prevent him from seeing the true essentials of education. His work deals with the part of a child that is above the neck; and perforce, the emotional, vital part of the child is foreign territory to him.

I wish I could see a bigger movement of rebellion among our younger teachers. Higher education and university degrees do not make a scrap of difference in confronting the evils of society. A learned neurotic is not any different than an unlearned neurotic.

In all countries, capitalist, socialist, or communist, elaborate schools are built to educate the young. But all the wonderful labs and workshops do nothing to help John or Peter or Ivan surmount the emotional damage and the social evils bred by the pressure on him from his parents, his schoolteachers, and the pressure of the coercive quality of our civilization.

What Happens to Summerhill Graduates

A parent's fear of the future affords a poor prognosis for the health of his children. This fear, oddly enough, shows itself in the desire that his children should learn more than he has learned. This kind of parent is not content to leave Willie to learn to read when he wants to, but nervously fears that Willie will be a failure in life unless he is pushed. Such parents cannot wait for the child to go at his own rate. They ask, If my son cannot read at twelve, what chance has he of success in life? If he cannot pass college entrance exams at eighteen, what is there for him but an unskilled job? But I have learned to wait and watch a child make little or no progress. I never doubt that in the end, if not molested or damaged, he will succeed in life.

Of course, the philistine can say, "Humph, so you call a truck driver a success in life!" My own criterion of success is the *ability to work joyfully and to live positively*. Under that definition, most pupils in Summerhill turn out to be successes in life.

Tom came to Summerhill at the age of five. He left at seventeen, without having in all those years gone to a single lesson. He spent much time in the workshop making things. His father and mother trembled with apprehension about his future. He never showed any desire to learn to read. But one night when he was nine, I found him in bed reading *David Copperfield*.

"Hullo," I said, "who taught you to read?"

"I taught myself."

Some years later, he came to me to ask, "How do you add a half and two-fifths?" and I told him. I asked if he wanted to know any more. "No thanks," he said.

Later on, he got work in a film studio as a camera boy. When he was learning his job, I happened to meet his boss at a dinner party, and I asked how Tom was doing.

"The best boy we ever had," the employer said. "He never walks—he runs. And at week-ends, he is a damned nuisance, for on Saturdays and Sundays he won't stay away from the studio."

There was Jack, a boy who could not learn to read. No one could teach Jack. Even when he asked for a reading lesson, there was some hidden obstruction that kept him from distinguishing between *b* and *p, l* and *k*. He left school at seventeen without the ability to read.

Today, Jack is an expert toolmaker. He loves to talk about metalwork. He can read now; but so far as I know, he mainly reads articles about mechanical things—and sometimes he reads works on psychology. I do not think he has ever read a novel; yet he speaks perfectly grammatical English, and his general knowledge is remarkable. An American visitor, knowing nothing of his story, said to me, "What a clever lad Jack is!"

Diane was a pleasant girl who went to lessons without much interest. Her mind was not academic. For a long time, I wondered what she would do. When she left at sixteen, any inspector of schools would have pronounced her a poorly educated girl. Today, Diane is demonstrating a new kind of cookery in London. She is highly skilled at her work; and more important, she is *happy* in it.

One firm demanded that its employees should have at least passed the standard college entrance exams. I wrote to the head of the firm concerning Robert, "This lad did not pass any exams, for he hasn't got an academic head. But he has got guts." Robert got the job.

Winifred, aged thirteen, a new pupil, told me that she hated all subjects, and shouted with joy when I told her she was free to do exactly as she liked. "You don't even have to come to school if you don't want to," I said.

She set herself to have a good time, and she had one—for a few weeks. Then I noticed that she was bored.

"Teach me something," she said to me one day; "I'm bored stiff."

"Righto!" I said cheerfully, "what do you want to learn?"

"I don't know," she said.

"And I don't either," said I, and I left her.

Months passed. Then she came to me again. "I am going to pass the college entrance exams," she said, "and I want lessons from you."

Every morning she worked with me and other teachers, and she worked well. She confided that the subjects did not interest her much, but the aim *did* interest her. Winifred found herself by being allowed to be herself.

It is interesting to know that free children take to mathematics. They find joy in geography and in history. Free children cull from the offered subjects only those which interest them. Free children spend most time at other interests—woodwork, metalwork, painting, reading fiction, acting, playing out fantasies, playing jazz records.

Tom, aged eight, was continually opening my door and asking, "By the way, what'll I do now?" No one would tell him what to do.

Six months later, if you wanted to find Tom you went to his room. There you always found him in a sea of paper sheets. He spent hours making maps. One day a professor from the University of Vienna visited Summerhill. He ran across Tom and asked him many questions. Later the professor came to me and said, "I tried to examine that boy on geography, and he talked of places I never heard of."

But I must also mention the failures. Barbel, Swedish, fifteen, was with us for about a year. During all that time, she found no work that interested her. She had come to Summerhill too late. For ten years of her life, teachers had been making up her mind for her. When she came to Summerhill, she had already lost all initiative. She was bored. Fortunately, she was rich and had the promise of a lady's life.

I had two Yugoslavian sisters, eleven and fourteen. The school failed to interest them. They spent most of their time making rude remarks about me in Croatian. An unkind friend used to translate these for me. Success would have been miraculous in this case, for the only common speech we had was art and music. I was very glad when their mother came for them.

Over the years we have found that Summerhill boys who are going in for engineering do not bother to take the matriculation exams. They go straight to practical training centers. They have a tendency to see the world before they settle down to university work. One went around the world as a ship's steward. Two boys took up coffee farming in Kenya. One boy went to Australia, and one even went to remote British Guiana.

Derrick Boyd is typical of the adventurous spirit that a free education encourages. He came to Summerhill at the age of eight and left after passing his university exams at eighteen. He wanted to be a doctor, but his father could not afford to send him to the university at the time. Derrick thought he would fill in the waiting time by seeing the world. He went to the London docks and spent two days trying to get a job—any job—even as a stoker. He was told that too many real sailors were unemployed, and he went home sadly.

Soon a schoolmate told him of an English lady in Spain who wanted a chauffeur. Derrick seized the chance, went to Spain, built the lady a house or enlarged her existing house, drove her all over Europe, and then went to the university. The lady decided to help him with his university fees. After two years, the lady asked him to take a year off to drive her to Kenya and build her a house there. Derrick finished his medical studies in Capetown.

Larry, who came to us about the age of twelve, passed university exams at sixteen and went out to Tahiti to grow fruit. Finding this a poorly paid occupation, he took to driving a taxi. Later he went to New Zealand, where I understand he did all sorts of jobs, including driving another taxi. He then entered Brisbane University. Some time ago, I had a visit from the dean of that university, who gave an admiring account of Larry's doings. "When we had vacation and the students went home," he said, "Larry went out to work as a laborer at a sawmill." He is now a practicing physician in Essex, England.

Some old boys, it is true, have not shown enterprise. For obvious reasons, I cannot describe them. Our successes are always those whose homes were good. Derrick and Jack and Larry had parents who were completely in sympathy with the school, so that the boys never had that most tiresome of conflicts: Which is right, home or school?

Has Summerhill produced any geniuses? No, so far no geniuses; perhaps a few creators, not famous as yet; a few bright artists; some clever musicians; no successful writer that I know of; an excellent furniture designer and cabinetmaker; some actors and actresses; some scientists and mathematicians who may yet do original work. I think that for our numbers—about forty-five pupils in the school at one time—a generous proportion has gone into some kind of creative or original work.

However, I have often said that one generation of free children does not prove anything much. Even in Summerhill some children get a guilty conscience about not learning enough lessons. It could not be otherwise in a world in which examinations are the gateways to some professions. And also, there is usually an Aunt Mary who exclaims, "Eleven years old and you can't read properly!" The child feels vaguely that the whole outside environment is anti-play and pro-work.

Speaking generally, the method of freedom is almost sure with children under twelve, but children over twelve take a long time to recover from a spoon-fed education.

Private Lessons at Summerhill

In the past, my main work was not teaching but the giving of "Private Lessons." Most of the children required psychological attention, but there were always some who had just come from other schools, and the private lessons were intended to hasten their adaption to freedom. If a child is all tied up inside, he cannot adapt himself to being free.

The P.Ls. were informal talks by the fireside. I sat with a pipe in my mouth, and the child could smoke, too, if he liked. The cigarette was often the means of breaking the ice.

Once I asked a boy of fourteen to come and have a chat with me. He had just come to Summerhill from a typical private school. I noticed that his fingers were yellow with nicotine, so I took out my pack of cigarettes and offered it to him. "Thanks," he stammered, "but I don't smoke, sir."

"Take one, you damned liar," I said with a smile, and he took one. I was killing two birds with one stone. Here was a boy to whom headmasters were stern, moral disciplinarians to be cheated every time. By offering him a cigarette, I was showing that I approved of his smoking. By calling him a damned liar, I was meeting him on his own level. At the same time, I was attacking his authority complex by showing him that a headmaster could swear easily and cheerfully. I wish I could have photographed his facial expression during that first interview.

He had been expelled from his previous school for stealing. "I hear you are a bit of a crook," I said. "What's your best way of swindling the railway company?"

"I never tried to swindle it, sir."

"Oh," I said, "that won't do. You must have a try. I know lots of ways," and I told him a few. He gaped. This surely was a madhouse he had come to. The principal of the school telling him how to be a better crook? Years later, he told me that that interview was the biggest shock of his life.

What kind of children needed P.L.s? The best answer will be a few illustrations.

Lucy, the kindergarten teacher, comes to me and says that Peggy seems very unhappy and antisocial. I say, "Righto, tell her to come and have a P.L." Peggy comes to my sitting room.

"I don't want a P.L.," she says, as she sits down. "They are just silly."

"Absolutely," I agree. "Waste of time. We won't have one."

She considers this. "Well," she says slowly, "I don't mind a tiny wee one." By this time, she has placed herself on my knee. I ask her about her Daddy and Mommy and especially about her little brother. She says he is a very silly little ass.

"He must be," I agree. "Do you think that Mommy likes him better than she likes you?"

"She likes us both the same," she says quickly, and adds, "She says that, anyway."

Sometimes the fit of unhappiness has arisen from a quarrel with another child. But more often it is a letter from home that has caused the trouble, perhaps a letter saying that a brother or sister has a new doll or a bike. The end of the P.L. is that Peggy goes out quite happily.

With newcomers it was not so easy. When we got a child of eleven who had been told that babies are brought by the doctor, it took hard work to free the child from lies and fears. For naturally, such a child had a guilt sense toward masturbation, and that sense of guilt had to be destroyed if the child was to find happiness.

Most small children did not require regular P.Ls. The ideal circumstance under which to have regular sessions is when a child *demands* a P.L. Some of the older ones demanded P.Ls.; sometimes, but rarely, a young child did too.

Charlie, aged sixteen, felt much inferior to lads of his own age. I asked him when he felt most inferior, and he said when the kids were bathing, because his penis was much smaller than anybody else's. I explained to him how his fear came about. He was the youngest child in a family of six sisters, all much older than he. There was a gulf of ten years between him and the youngest sister. The household was a feminine one. The father was dead, and the big sisters did all the bossing. Hence, Charlie identified himself with the feminine in life, so that he, too, could have power.

After about ten P.Ls., Charlie stopped coming to me. I asked him why. "Don't need P.Ls. now," he said cheerfully; "my tool is as big as Bert's now."

But there was more involved than that in the short course of therapy. Charlie had been told that masturbation would make him impotent when he was a man, and his fear of impotence had affected him physically. His cure was also due to the elimination of his guilt complex and of the silly lie about impotence. Charlie left Summerhill a year or two later. He is now a fine, healthy, happy man who will get on in life.

Sylvia had a stern father who never praised her. On the contrary, he criticized and nagged her all day long. Her one desire in life was to get father's love. She sat in her room and wept bitterly as she told her story. Hers was a difficult case to help. Analysis of the daughter could not change the father. There was no solution for Sylvia until she became old enough to get away from home. I warned her that there was a danger that she might marry the wrong man merely to escape from the father.

"What sort of wrong man?" she asked.

"A man like your father, one who will treat you sadistically," I said.

Sylvia was a sad case. At Summerhill, she was a social, friendly girl who offended no one. At home she was said to be a devil. Obviously, it was the father who needed analysis—not the daughter.

Another insoluble case was that of little Florence. She was illegitimate, and she didn't know it. My experience tells me that every illegitimate child knows unconsciously that he is illegitimate. Florence assuredly knew that there was some mystery behind her. I told the mother that the only cure for her daughter's hate and unhappiness was to tell her the truth.

"But, Neill, I daren't. It wouldn't make any difference to me. But if I tell her, she won't keep it to herself, and my mother will cut her out of her will."

Well, well, we'll just have to wait till the grandmother's gone before Florence can be helped, I'm afraid. You can do nothing if a vital truth has to be kept dark.

An old boy of twenty came back to stay with us for a time, and he asked me for a few P.Ls.

"But I gave you dozens when you were here," I said.

"I know," he said sadly, "dozens that I didn't really care for, but now I feel I want them."

Nowadays, I don't give regular therapy. With the average child, when you have cleared up the birth and masturbation question and shown how the family situation has created hates and jealousies, there is nothing more to be done. Curing a neurosis in a child is a matter of the release of emotion, and the cure will not be furthered in any way by expounding psychiatric theories to the child and telling him that he has a complex.

I recall a boy of fifteen whom I tried to help. For weeks he sat silent at our P.Ls., answering only in monosyllables. I decided to be drastic, and at his next P.L. I said to him: "I'm going to tell you what I think of you this morning. You're a lazy, stupid, conceited, spiteful fool."

"Am I?" he said, red with anger. "Who do you think you are anyway?" From that moment, he talked easily and to the point.

Then there was George, a boy of eleven. His father was a small tradesman in a village near Glasgow. The boy was sent to me by his doctor. George's problem was one of intense fear. He feared to be away from home, even at the village school. He screamed in terror when he had to leave home. With great difficulty, his father got him to come to Summerhill. He wept and clung to his father so that the father could not return home. I suggested to the father that he stay for a few days.

I had already had the case history from the doctor, whose comments were, in my estimation, correct and most useful. The question of getting the father to return home was becoming acute. I tried to talk to George, but he wept and sobbed that he wanted to go home. "This is just a prison," he sobbed. I went on talking and ignored his tears.

"When you were four," I said, "your little brother was taken to the infirmary and they brought him back in a coffin. (*Increased sobbing.*) Your fear of leaving home is that the same thing will happen to you—you'll go home in a coffin. (*Louder sobs.*) But that's not the main point, George, my boy: *you killed your brother!*"

Here he protested violently, and threatened to kick me.

"You didn't *really* kill him, George, but you thought that he got more love from your mother than you got; and sometimes, you wished he would die. When he *did* die, you had a terrible guilty conscience, because you thought that *your* wishes had killed him, and that God would kill you in punishment for your guilt if you went away from home."

His sobbing ceased. Next day, although he made a scene at the station, he let his father go home.

George did not get over his homesickness for some time. But

the sequel was that in eighteen months he insisted on traveling home for the vacation—alone, crossing London from station to station by himself. He did the same on his way back to Summerhill.

More and more I come to the conclusion that therapy is not necessary when children can live out their complexes in freedom. But in a case like that of George, freedom would not have been enough.

In the past I have given P.Ls. to thieves and have seen resulting cures, but I have had thieves who refused to come to P.Ls. Yet after three years of freedom, these boys were also cured.

At Summerhill, it is love that cures; it is approval and the freedom to be true to oneself. Of our forty-five children, only a small fraction receive P.Ls. I believe more and more in the therapeutic effect of creative work. I would have the children do more handiwork, dramatics, and dancing.

Let me make clear that I gave P.Ls. only for emotional release. If a child were unhappy, I gave him a P.L. But if he couldn't learn to read or if he hated mathematics, I did not try to cure him with analytic treatment. Sometimes, in the course of a P.L., it came out that the inability to learn to read dated from Mommy's constant promptings to be "a nice, clever boy like your brother" or that the hatred of arithmetic came from dislike of a previous teacher of arithmetic.

Naturally, I am the father symbol for all the children; and my wife is the mother symbol. Socially, my wife fares worse than I do, for she gets all the unconscious hate of mother displaced on her by the girls, while I get their love. The boys give their love of their mother to my wife and hatred of their father to me. Boys do not express hate so easily as girls. That is due to their being able to deal so much more with things than with people. An angry boy kicks a ball while a girl spits catty words at a mother symbol.

But to be fair, I must say that it is only during a certain period that girls are catty and difficult to live with—the preadolescent and the first-year-of-adolescence period. And not all girls go through this stage. Much depends on their previous school and, more still, on the mother's attitude toward authority.

In the P.Ls., I pointed out relationships between reactions to home and school. Any criticism of me I translated as one of father. Any accusation against my wife I showed to be one against mother. I tried to keep analysis objective; to enter into subjective depths would have been unfair to the children.

There were occasions, naturally, when a subjective explanation was necessary, as in the case of Jane. Jane, aged thirteen, went round the school telling various children that Neill wanted to see them.

I had a stream of callers—"Jane says you want me." I told Jane later that sending others to me meant that she wanted to come herself.

What was the technique of a P.L.? I had no set method. Sometimes, I began with a question, "When you look in the mirror, do you like your face?" The answer was always no.

"What part of your face do you hate most?" The invariable answer was, "My nose."

Adults give the same reply. The face is the person as far as the outside world is concerned. We think of faces when we think of people, and we look at faces when we talk to people. So that the face becomes the outside picture of the inner self. When a child says he dislikes his face, he means he dislikes his personality. My next step was to leave the face and to go on to the self.

"What do you hate most in yourself?" I asked.

Usually, the answer was a physical one. "My feet are too big." "Too fat." "Too little." "My hair."

I never gave an opinion—never agreed that he or she was fat or lean. Nor did I force things. If the body was of interest, we talked about it until there was nothing more to be said. Then we went on to the personality.

I often gave an exam. "I am going to write down a few things," I would say, "and examine you in them. You give yourself the mark you think you deserve. For example, I'll ask you what percentage out of a hundred you would give yourself for, say, ability at games or for bravery and so on." And the exam began.

Here is one given to a boy of fourteen.

Good looks: "Oh, not so good, about 45 per cent."

Brains: "Um, 60."

Bravery: "25."

Loyalty: "I don't let my pals down—80."

Musicality: "Zero."

Handiwork: (*Mumbled answer unclear.*)

Hate: "That's too difficult. No, I can't answer that one."

Games: "66."

Social feeling: "90."

Idiocy: "Oh, about 190 per cent."

Naturally, the child's answers allowed an opportunity for discussion. I found it best to begin with the ego since it awakened interest. Then, when we later went on to the family, the child talked easily and with interest.

With young children, the technique was more spontaneous. I followed the child's lead. Here is a typical first P.L. with a six-year-old girl named Margaret. She comes into my room and says, "I want a P.L."

"Righto," I say.

She sits down in an easy chair.

"What is a P.L.?" she asks.

"It isn't anything to eat," I say, "but somewhere in this

pocket I have a caramel. Ah, here it is." And I give her the candy.

"Why do you want a P.L.?" I ask.

"Evelyn had one, and I want one too."

"Good. You begin it. What do you want to talk about?"

"I've got a dolly. (*Pause.*) Where did you get that thing on the mantelpiece? (*She obviously does not want to wait for an answer.*) Who was in this house before you came?"

Her questions point to a desire to know some vital truth, and I have a good suspicion that it is the truth about birth.

"Where do babies come from?" I ask suddenly.

Margaret gets up and marches to the door.

"I hate P.Ls.," she says, and departs. But a few days later, she asks for another P.L.—and so we progress.

Little Tommy, aged six, also did not mind P.Ls. as long as I refrained from mentioning "rude" things. For the first three sessions he went out indignantly, and I knew why. I knew that only rude things really interested him. He was one of the victims of the masturbation prohibition.

Many children never got P.Ls. They did not want them. These were the children who had been properly brought up without parental lies and lectures.

Therapy does not cure at once. The treated person does not benefit much for some time, usually about a year. Hence, I never felt pessimistic about older pupils who left school in what we might describe as a half-baked psychological condition.

Tom was sent to us because he had been a failure at his school. I gave him a year's intensive P.Ls. and there was no apparent result. When he left Summerhill, he looked as if he would be a failure all through life. But a year later, his parents wrote that he had suddenly decided to be a doctor and was studying hard at the university.

Bill seemed a more hopeless case. His P.Ls. took three years.

He left school, apparently, an aimless youth of eighteen. He drifted about from job to job for over a year, and then he decided to be a farmer. All reports I've heard say that he is doing well and is keen on his work.

P.Ls. were really a re-education. Their object was to lop off all complexes resulting from morality and fear.

A free school like Summerhill could be run without P.Ls. They merely speed up the process of re-education by beginning with a good spring cleaning before the summer of freedom.

Self-Government

Summerhill is a self-governing school, democratic in form. Everything connected with social, or group, life, including punishment for social offenses, is settled by vote at the Saturday night General School Meeting.

Each member of the teaching staff and each child, regardless of his age, has one vote. My vote carries the same weight as that of a seven-year-old.

One may smile and say, "But your voice has more value, hasn't it?" Well, let's see. Once I got up at a meeting and proposed that no child under sixteen should be allowed to smoke. I argued my case: a drug, poisonous, not a real appetite in children, but mostly an attempt to be grown up. Counterarguments were thrown across the floor. The vote was taken. I was beaten by a large majority.

The sequel is worth recording. After my defeat, a boy of sixteen proposed that no one under twelve should be allowed to smoke. He carried his motion. However, at the following weekly meeting, a boy of twelve proposed the repeal of the new smoking rule, saying, "We are all sitting in the toilets smoking on the sly just like kids do in a strict school, and I say it is against the whole idea of Summerhill." His speech was cheered, and that meeting repealed the law. I hope I have made it clear that my voice is not always more powerful than that of a child.

Once, I spoke strongly about breaking the bedtime rules, with the consequent noise and the sleepy heads that lumbered around the next morning. I proposed that culprits should be fined all their pocket money for each offense. A boy of fourteen proposed that there should be a penny reward per hour for everyone staying up after his or her bedtime. I got a few votes, but he got a big majority.

Summerhill self-government has no bureaucracy. There is a different chairman at each meeting, appointed by the previous chairman, and the secretary's job is voluntary. Bedtime officers are seldom in office for more than a few weeks.

Our democracy makes laws—good ones, too. For example, it is forbidden to bathe in the sea without the supervision of lifeguards, who are always staff members. It is forbidden to climb on the roofs. Bedtimes must be kept or there is an automatic fine. Whether classes should be called off on the Thursday or on the Friday preceding a holiday is a matter for a show of hands at a General School Meeting.

The success of the meeting depends largely on whether the chairman is weak or strong, for to keep order among forty-five vigorous children is no easy task. The chairman has power to fine noisy citizens. Under a weak chairman, the fines are much too frequent.

The staff takes a hand, of course, in the discussions. So do I; although there are a number of situations in which I must remain neutral. In fact, I have seen a lad charged with an offense get away with it on a complete alibi, although he had privately confided to me that he had committed the offense. In a case like this, I must always be on the side of the individual.

I, of course, participate like anyone else when it comes to casting my vote on any issue or bringing up a proposal of my own. Here is a typical example. I once raised the question of whether football should be played in the lounge. The lounge is under my office, and I explained that I disliked the noise of football while I was working. I proposed that indoor football be forbidden. I was supported by some of the girls, by some older boys, and by most of the staff. But my proposal was not carried, and that meant my continuing to put up with the noisy scuffle of feet below my office. Finally, after much public disputation at several meetings, I did carry by majority approval the abolition of football in the lounge. And this is the way the minority generally gets its rights in our school democracy; it keeps demanding them. This applies to little children as much as it does to adults.

On the other hand, there are aspects of school life that do not come under the self-government regime. My wife plans the arrangements for bedrooms, provides the menu, sends out and pays bills. I appoint teachers and ask them to leave if I think they are not suitable.

The function of Summerhill self-government is not only to make laws but to discuss social features of the community as well. At the beginning of each term, rules about bedtime are made by vote. You go to bed according to your age. Then questions of general behavior come up. Sports committees have to be elected, as well as an end-of-term dance committee, a theater committee, bedtime officers, and downtown officers who report any disgraceful behavior out of the school boundaries.

The most exciting subject ever brought up is that of food. I have more than once waked up a dull meeting by proposing that second helpings be abolished. Any sign of kitchen favoritism in the matter of food is severely handled. But when the kitchen brings up the question of wasting food, the meeting is not much interested. The attitude of children toward food is essentially a personal and self-centered one.

In a General School Meeting, all academic discussions are avoided. Children are eminently practical and theory bores them. They like concreteness, not abstraction. I once brought forward a motion that swearing be abolished by law, and I gave my reason. I had been showing a woman around with her little boy, a prospective pupil. Suddenly from upstairs came a very strong adjective. The mother hastily gathered up her son and went off in a hurry. "Why," I asked at a meeting, "should my income suffer because some fathead swears in front of a prospective parent? It isn't a moral question at all; it is purely financial. You swear and I lose a pupil."

My question was answered by a lad of fourteen. "Neill is talking rot," he said. "Obviously, if this woman was shocked, she didn't believe in Summerhill. Even if she had enrolled her boy, the first time he came home saying damn or hell, she would have taken him out of here." The meeting agreed with him, and my proposal was voted down.

A General School Meeting often has to tackle the problem of bullying. Our community is pretty hard on bullies; and I notice that the school government's bullying rule has been underlined on the bulletin board: *"All cases of bullying will be severely dealt with."* Bullying is not so rife in Summerhill, however, as in strict schools, and the reason is not far to seek. Under adult discipline, the child becomes a hater. Since the child cannot express his hatred of adults with impunity, he takes it out on smaller or weaker boys. But this seldom happens in Summerhill. Very often, a charge of bullying when investigated amounts to the fact that Jenny called Peggy a lunatic.

Sometimes a case of stealing is brought up at the General School Meeting. There is never any punishment for stealing, but there is always reparation. Often children will come to me and say, "John stole some coins from David. Is this a case for psychology, or shall we bring it up?"

If I consider it a case for psychology, requiring individual attention, I tell them to leave it to me. If John is a happy, normal boy who has stolen something inconsequential, I allow charges to be brought against him. The worst that happens is that he is docked all of his pocket money until the debt is paid.

How are General School Meetings run? At the beginning of each term, a chairman is elected for one meeting only. At the end of the meeting he appoints his successor. This procedure is followed throughout the term. Anyone who has a grievance, a charge, or a suggestion, or a new law to propose brings it up.

Here is a typical example: Jim took the pedals from Jack's bicycle because his own cycle is in disrepair, and he wanted to go away with some other boys for a week-end trip. After due consideration of the evidence, the meeting decides that Jim must replace the pedals, and he is forbidden to go on the trip.

The chairman asks, "Any objections?"

Jim gets up and shouts that there jolly well are! Only his adjective isn't exactly "jolly." "This isn't fair!" he cries. "I didn't know that Jack ever used his old crock of a bike. It has been kicking about among the bushes for days. I don't mind shoving his pedals back, but I think the punishment unfair. I don't think I should be cut out of the trip."

Follows a breezy discussion. In the debate, it transpires that Jim usually gets a weekly allowance from home, but the allowance hasn't come for six weeks, and he hasn't a bean. The meeting votes that the sentence be quashed, and it is duly quashed.

But what to do about Jim? Finally it is decided to open a subscription fund to put Jim's bike in order. His schoolmates chip in to buy him pedals for his bike, and he sets off happily on his trip.

Usually, the School Meeting's verdict is accepted by the culprit. However, if the verdict is unacceptable, the defendant may appeal, in which case the chairman will bring up the matter once again at the very end of the meeting. At such an appeal, the matter is considered more carefully, and generally the original verdict is tempered in view of the dissatisfaction of the defendant. The children realize that if the defendant feels he has been unfairly judged, there is a good chance that he actually has been.

No culprit at Summerhill ever shows any signs of defiance or hatred of the authority of his community. I am always surprised at the docility our pupils show when punished.

One term, four of the biggest boys were charged at the General School Meeting with doing an illegal thing—selling various articles from their wardrobes. The law forbidding this had been passed on the ground that such practices are unfair to the parents who buy the clothes and unfair as well to the school, because when children go home minus certain wearing apparel, the parents blame the school for carelessness. The four boys were punished by being kept on the grounds for four days and being sent to bed at eight each night. They accepted the sentence without a murmur. On Monday night, when everyone had gone to the town movies, I found Dick, one of the culprits, in bed reading.

"You are a chump," I said. "Everyone has gone to the movies. Why don't you get up?"

"Don't try to be funny," he said.

This loyalty of Summerhill pupils to their own democracy is amazing. It has no fear in it, and no resentment. I have seen a boy go through a long trial for some antisocial act, and I have seen him sentenced. Often, the boy who has just been sentenced is elected chairman for the next meeting.

The sense of justice that children have never ceases to make me marvel. And their administrative ability is great. As education, self-government is of infinite value.

Certain classes of offenses come under the automatic fine rule. If you ride another's bike without permission, there is an automatic fine of sixpence. Swearing in town (but you can swear as much as you like on the school grounds), bad behavior in the movies, climbing on roofs, throwing food in the dining room—these and other infractions of rules carry automatic fines.

Punishments are nearly always fines: hand over pocket money for a week or miss a movie.

An oft-heard objection to children acting as judges is that they punish too harshly. I find it not so. On the contrary, they are very lenient. On no occasion has there been a harsh sentence at Summerhill. And invariably the punishment has some relation to the crime.

Three small girls were disturbing the sleep of others. Punishment: they must go to bed an hour earlier every night for a week. Two boys were accused of throwing clods at other boys. Punishment: they must cart clods to level the hockey field.

Often the chairman will say, "The case is too silly for words," and decide that nothing should be done.

When our secretary was tried for riding Ginger's bike without permission, he and two other members of the staff who had also ridden it were ordered to push each other on Ginger's bike ten times around the front lawn.

Four small boys who climbed the ladder that belonged to the builders who were erecting the new workshop were ordered to climb up and down the ladder for ten minutes straight.

The meeting never seeks advice from an adult. Well, I can remember only one occasion when it was done. Three girls had raided the kitchen larder. The meeting fined them their pocket money. They raided the kitchen again that night and the meeting fined them a movie. They raided it once more, and the meeting was graveled what to do. The chairman consulted me. "Give them tuppence reward each," I suggested. "What? Why, man, you'll have the whole school raiding the kitchen if we do that." "You won't," I said. "Try it."

He tried it. Two of the girls refused to take the money; and all three were heard to declare that they would never raid the larder again. They didn't—for about two months.

Priggish behavior at meetings is rare. Any sign of priggishness is frowned upon by the community. A boy of eleven, a strong exhibitionist, used to get up and draw attention to himself by making long involved remarks of obvious irrelevance. At least he tried to, but the meeting shouted him down. The young have a sensitive nose for insincerity.

At Summerhill we have proved, I believe, that self-government works. In fact, the school that has no self-government should not be called a progressive school. It is a compromise school. You cannot have freedom unless children feel completely free to govern their own social life. When there is a boss, there is no real freedom. This applies even more to the benevolent boss than to the disciplinarian. The child of spirit can rebel against the hard boss, but the soft boss merely makes the child impotently soft and unsure of his real feelings.

Good self-government in a school is possible only when there is a sprinkling of older pupils who like a quiet life and fight the indifference or opposition of the gangster age. These older youngsters are often outvoted, but it is they who really believe in and want self-government. Children up to, say, twelve, on the other hand, will not run good self-government on their own, because they have not reached the social age. Yet at Summerhill, a seven-year-old rarely misses a General Meeting.

One spring we had a spate of bad luck. Some community-minded seniors had left us after passing their college entrance exams, so that there were very few seniors left in the school. The vast majority of the pupils were at the gangster stage and age. Although they were social in their speeches, they were not old enough to run the community well. They passed any amount of laws and then forgot them and broke them. The few older pupils left were, by some chance, rather individualist, and tended to live their own lives in their own groups, so that the staff was figuring too prominently in attacking the breaking of the school rules. Thus it came about that at a General School Meeting I felt compelled to launch a vigorous attack on the seniors for being not antisocial but asocial, breaking the bedtime rules by sitting up far too late and taking no interest in what the juniors were doing in an antisocial way.

Frankly, younger children are only mildly interested in government. Left to themselves, I question whether younger children would ever form a government. Their values are not our values, and their manners are not our manners.

Stern discipline is the easiest way for the adult to have peace and quiet. Anyone can be a drill sergeant. What the ideal alternative method of securing a quiet life is I do not know. Our Summerhill trials and errors certainly fail to give the adults a quiet life. On the other hand they do not give the children an overnoisy life. Perhaps the ultimate test is happiness. By this criterion, Summerhill has found an excellent compromise in its self-government.

Our law against dangerous weapons is likewise a compromise. Air guns are forbidden. The few boys who want to have air guns in the school hate the law; but in the main, they conform to it. When they are a minority, children do not seem to feel so strongly as adults do.

In Summerhill, there is one perennial problem that can never be solved; it might be called the problem of *the individual vs. the community.* Both staff and pupils get exasperated when a gang of little girls led by a problem girl annoy some people, throw water on others, break the bedtime laws, and make themselves a perpetual nuisance. Jean, the leader, is attacked in a General Meeting. Strong words are used to condemn her misuse of freedom as license.

A visitor, a psychologist, said to me: "It is all wrong. The girl's face is an unhappy one; she has never been loved, and all this open criticism makes her feel more unloved than ever. She needs love, not opposition."

"My dear woman," I replied, "we *have* tried to change her with love. For weeks, we rewarded her for being antisocial. We have shown her affection and tolerance, and she has not reacted. Rather, she has looked on us as simpletons, easy marks for her aggression. We cannot sacrifice the entire community to one individual."

I do not know the complete answer. I know that when Jean is fifteen, she will be a social girl and not a gang leader. I pin my faith on public opinion. No child will go on for years being disliked and criticized. As for the condemnation by the school meeting, one simply cannot sacrifice other children to one problem child.

Once, we had a boy of six who had a miserable life before he came to Summerhill. He was a violent bully, destructive and full of hate. The four- and five-year-olds suffered and wept. The community had to do something to protect them; and in doing so, it had to be against the bully. The mistakes of two parents could not be allowed to react on other children whose parents had given them love and care.

On a very few occasions, I have had to send a child away because the others were finding the school a hell because of him. I say this with regret, with a vague feeling of failure, but I could see no other way.

Have I had to alter my views on self-government in these long years? On the whole, no. I could not visualize Summerhill without it. It has always been popular. It is our show piece for visitors. But that, too, has its drawbacks, as when a girl of fourteen whispered to me at a meeting, "I meant to bring up about girls blocking the toilets by putting sanitary napkins in them, but look at all these visitors." I advised her to damn the visitors and bring the matter up—which she did.

The educational benefit of practical civics cannot be over-emphasized. At Summerhill, the pupils would fight to the death for their right to govern themselves. In my opinion, one weekly General School Meeting is of more value than a week's curriculum of school subjects. It is an excellent theater for practicing public speaking, and most of the children speak well and without self-consciousness. I have often heard sensible speeches from children who could neither read nor write.

I cannot see an alternative method to our Summerhill democracy. It may be a fairer democracy than the political one, for children are pretty charitable to each other, and have no vested interests to speak of. Moreover, it is a more genuine democracy because laws are made at an open meeting, and the question of uncontrollable elected delegates does not arise.

After all, it is the broad outlook that free children acquire that makes self-government so important. Their laws deal with essentials, not appearances. The laws governing conduct in the town are the compromise with a less free civilization. "Downtown"—the outside world—wastes its precious energy in worrying over trifles. As if it matters in the scheme of life whether you wear dressy clothes or say hell. Summerhill, by getting away from the outward nothings of life, can have and does have a community spirit that is in advance of its time. True, it is apt to call a spade a damn shovel, but any ditchdigger will tell you with truth that a spade *is* a damn shovel.

Coeducation

In most schools there is a definite plan to separate boys from girls, especially in their sleeping quarters. Love affairs are not encouraged. They are not encouraged in Summerhill either—but neither are they discouraged.

In Summerhill, boys and girls are left alone. Relations between the sexes appear to be very healthy. One sex will not grow up with any illusions or delusions about the other sex. Not that Summerhill is just one big family, where all the nice little boys and girls are brothers and sisters to one another. If that were so, I would become a rabid anti-coeducationist at once.

Under real coeducation—not the kind where boys and girls sit in class together but live and sleep in separate houses—shameful curiosity is almost eliminated. There are no Peeping Toms in Summerhill. There is far less anxiety about sex than at other schools.

Every now and again an adult comes to the school, and asks, "But don't they all sleep with each other?" And when I answer that they do not, he or she cries, "But why not? At their age, I would have had a hell of a good time!"

It is this type of person who assumes that if boys and girls are educated together, they must necessarily indulge in sexual license. To be sure, such people do not say that this thought underlies their objections. Instead, they rationalize by saying that boys and girls have different capacities for learning, and therefore should not have lessons together.

Schools should be coeducational because life is coeducational. But coeducation is feared by many parents and teachers because of the danger of pregnancy. Indeed, I am told that not a few principals of coed schools spend sleepless nights worrying over that possibility.

Conditioned children of both sexes are often incapable of loving. This news may be comforting to those who fear sex; but to youth in general, the inability to love is a great human tragedy.

When I asked a few adolescents from a famous private coed school if there were any love affairs in their school, the answer was no. Upon expressing surprise, I was told, "We sometimes have a friendship between a boy and a girl, but it is never a love affair." Since I saw some handsome lads and some pretty girls on that campus, I knew that the school was imposing an anti-love ideal on the pupils and that its highly moral atmosphere was inhibiting sex.

I once asked the principal of a progressive school, "Have you any love affairs in the school?"

"No," he replied gravely. "But then, we never take problem children."

Those against coeducation may object that the system makes boys effeminate and girls masculine. But deep down is the moral fear, actually a jealous fear. Sex with love is the greatest pleasure in the world, and it is repressed because it *is* the greatest pleasure. All else is evasion.

The reason that I entertain no fears that the older pupils at Summerhill who have been here since early childhood might indulge in sexual license is because I know that I am not dealing with children who have a repressed, and therefore unnatural, interest in sex.

Some years ago, we had two pupils arrive at the same time: a boy of seventeen from a boy's private school and a girl of sixteen from a girl's private school. They fell in love with each other and were always together. I met them late one night and I stopped them. "I don't know what you two are doing," I said, "and morally I don't care, for it isn't a moral question at all. But economically I do care. If you, Kate, have a kid, my school will be ruined."

I went on to expand upon this theme. "You see," I said, "you have just come to Summerhill. To you it means freedom to do what you like. Naturally, you have no special feeling for the school. If you had been here from the age of seven, I'd never have had to mention the matter. You would have such a strong attachment to the school that you *would* think of the consequences to Summerhill." It was the only possible way to deal with the problem. Fortunately, I never had to speak to them again on the subject.

Work

In Summerhill, we used to have a community law that pro-vided that every child over twelve and every member of the staff must do two hours of work each week on the grounds. The pay was a token pay of a nickel an hour. If you did not work, you were fined a dime. A few, teachers included, were content to pay the fines. Of those who worked, most had their eyes on the clock. There was no play component in the work, and therefore the work bored everyone. The law was re-examined, and the children abolished it by an almost unanimous vote.

A few years ago, we needed an infirmary in Summerhill. We decided to build one ourselves—a proper building of brick and cement. None of us had ever laid a brick, but we started in. A few pupils helped to dig the foundations and knocked down some old brick walls to get the bricks. But the children demanded payment. We refused to pay wages. In the end, the infirmary was built by the teachers and visitors. The job was just too dull for children, and to their young minds the need for the sanatorium too remote. They had no self-interest in it. But some time later when they wanted a bicycle shed, they built one all by themselves without any help from the staff.

I am writing of children—not as we adults think they should be—but as they really are. Their community sense—their sense of social responsibility—does not develop until the age of eighteen or more. Their interests are immediate, and the future does not exist for them.

I have never yet seen a lazy child. What is called laziness is either lack of interest or lack of health. A healthy child cannot be idle; he has to be doing something all day long. Once I knew a very healthy lad who was considered a lazy fellow. Mathematics did not interest him, but the school curriculum demanded that he learn mathematics. Of course, he didn't want to study mathematics, and so his math teacher thought he was lazy.

I read recently that if a couple who were out for an evening were to dance every dance they would be walking twenty-five miles. Yet they would feel little or no fatigue because they would be experiencing pleasure all evening long—assuming that their steps agreed. So it is with a child. The boy who is lazy in class will run miles during a football game.

I find it impossible to get youths of seventeen to help me plant potatoes or weed onions, although the same boys will spend hours souping up motor engines, or washing cars, or making radio sets. It took me a long time to accept this phenomenon. The truth began to dawn on me one day when I was digging my brother's garden in Scotland. I didn't enjoy the job, and it came to me suddenly that what was wrong was that I was digging a garden that meant nothing to me. And my garden means nothing to the boys, whereas their bikes or radios mean a lot to them. True altruism is a long time in coming, and it never loses its factor of selfishness.

Small children have quite a different attitude toward work than teen-agers have. Summerhill juniors, ranging from age three to eight, will work like Trojans mixing cement or carting sand or cleaning bricks; and they will work with no thought of reward. They identify themselves with grownups and their work is like a fantasy worked out in reality.

However, from the age of eight or nine until the age of nineteen or twenty, the desire to do manual labor of a dull kind is just not there. This is true of most children; there are individual children, of course, who remain workers from early childhood right on through life.

Altruism - unselfish concern for the welfare of others

The fact is that we adults exploit children far too often. "Marion, run down to the mail box with this letter." Any child hates to be made use of. The average child dimly realizes that he is fed and clothed by his parents without any effort on his part. He feels that such care is his natural right, but he realizes that on the other hand he is expected and obliged to do a hundred menial tasks and many disagreeable chores, which the parents themselves evade.

I once read about a school in America that was built by the pupils themselves. I used to think that this was the ideal way. It isn't. If children built their own school, you can be sure that some gentleman with a breezy, benevolent authority was standing by, lustily shouting encouragement. When such authority is not present, *children simply do not build schools.*

My own opinion is that a sane civilization would not ask children to work until at least the age of eighteen. Most boys and girls would do a lot of work before they reached eighteen, but such work would be play for them, and probably uneconomical work from the viewpoint of the parents. I feel depressed when I think of the gigantic amount of work students have to do to prepare for exams. I understand that in prewar Budapest nearly fifty per cent of the students broke down physically or psychologically after their matriculation exams.

The reason we here in Summerhill keep getting such good reports about the industrious performance of our old pupils on responsible jobs is that these boys and girls have lived out their self-centered fantasy stage in Summerhill. As young adults they are able to face the realities of life without any unconscious longing for the play of childhood.

Play

Summerhill might be defined as a school in which play is of the greatest importance. Why children and kittens play I do not know. I believe it is a matter of energy.

I am not thinking of play in terms of athletic fields and organized games; I am thinking of play in terms of fantasy. Organized games involve skill, competition, teamwork; but children's play usually requires no skill, little competition, and hardly any teamwork. Small children will play gangster games with shooting or sword play. Long before the motion picture era, children played gang games. Stories and movies will give a direction to some kind of play, but the fundamentals are in the hearts of all children of all races.

At Summerhill the six-year-olds play the whole day long—play with fantasy. To a small child, reality and fantasy are very close to each other. When a boy of ten dressed himself up as a ghost, the little ones screamed with delight; they knew it was only Tommy; they had seen him put on that sheet. But as he advanced on them, they one and all screamed in terror.

Small children live a life of fantasy and they carry this fantasy over into action. Boys of eight to fourteen play gangsters and are always bumping people off or flying the skies in their wooden airplanes. Small girls also go through a gang stage, but it does not take the form of guns and swords. It is more personal. Mary's gang objects to Nellie's gang, and there are rows and hard words. Boys' rival gangs are only play enemies. Small boys are thus more easy to live with than small girls.

I have not been able to discover where the borderline of fantasy begins and ends. When a child brings a doll a meal on a tiny toy plate, does she really believe for the moment that the doll is alive? Is a rocking horse a real horse? When a boy cries "Stick 'em up" and then fires, does he think or feel that his is a real gun? I am inclined to think that children do imagine that their toys are real, and only when some insensitive adult butts in and reminds them of their fantasy do they come back to earth with a plop. No sympathetic parent will ever break up a child's fantasy.

Boys do not generally play with girls. Boys play gangsters, and play tag; they make huts in trees; they dig holes and trenches.

Girls seldom organize any play. The time-honored game of playing teacher or doctor is unknown among free children, for they feel no need to mimic authority. Smaller girls play with dolls; but older girls seem to get the most fun out of contact with people, not things.

We have often had mixed hockey teams. Card games and other indoor games are usually mixed.

Children love noise and mud; they clatter on stairs; they shout like louts; they are unconscious of furniture. If they are playing a game of touch, they would walk over the Portland Vase if it happened to be in their way—walk over it without seeing it.

Mothers, too often, do not play enough with their babies. They seem to think that putting a soft teddy bear in the carriage with the baby solves things for an hour or two, forgetting that babies want to be tickled and hugged.

Granting that childhood is playhood, how do we adults generally react to this fact? We *ignore* it. We forget all about it —because play, to us, is a waste of time. Hence we erect a large city school with many rooms and expensive apparatus for teaching; but more often than not, all we offer to the play instinct is a small concrete space.

One could, with some truth, claim that the evils of civilization are due to the fact that no child has ever had enough play. To put it differently, every child has been hothoused into an adult long before he has reached adulthood.

The adult attitude toward play is quite arbitrary. We, the old, map out a child's timetable: Learn from nine till twelve and then an hour for lunch; and again lessons until three. If a free child were asked to make a timetable, he would almost certainly give to play many periods and to lessons only a few.

Fear is at the root of adult antagonism to children's play. Hundreds of times I have heard the anxious query, "But if my boy plays all day, how will he ever learn anything; how will he ever pass exams?" Very few will accept my answer, "If your child plays all he wants to play, he will be able to pass college entrance exams after two years' intensive study, instead of the usual five, six, or seven years of learning in a school that discounts play as a factor in life."

But I always have to add, "That is—if he ever *wants* to pass the exams!" He may want to become a ballet dancer or a radio engineer. She may want to be a dress designer or a children's nurse.

Yes, fear of the child's future leads adults to deprive children of their right to play. There is more in it than that, however. There is a vague moral idea behind the disapproval of play, a suggestion that being a child is not so good, a suggestion voiced in the admonition to young adults, "Don't be a kid."

Parents who have forgotten the yearnings of their childhood —forgotten how to play and how to fantasy—make poor parents. When a child has lost the ability to play, he is psychically dead and a danger to any child who comes in contact with him.

Teachers from Israel have told me of the wonderful community centers there. The school, I'm told, is part of a community whose primary need is hard work. Children of ten, one teacher told me, weep if—as a punishment—they are not allowed to dig the garden. If I had a child of ten who wept because he was forbidden to dig potatoes, I should wonder if he were mentally defective. Childhood is playhood; and any community system that ignores that truth is educating in a wrong way. To me the Israeli method is sacrificing young life to economic needs. It may be necessary; but I would not dare to call that system ideal community living.

It is intriguing, yet most difficult, to assess the damage done to children who have not been allowed to play as much as they wanted to. I often wonder if the great masses who watch professional football are trying to live out their arrested play interest by identifying with the players, playing by proxy as it were. The majority of our Summerhill graduates does not attend football matches, nor is it interested in pageantry. I believe few of them would walk very far to see a royal procession. Pageantry has a childish element in it; its color, formalism, and slow movement have some suggestion of toyland and dressed-up dolls. That may be the reason that women seem to love pageantry more than men do. As people get older and more sophisticated, they seem to be attracted less and less by pageantry of any kind. I doubt if generals and politicians and diplomats get anything out of state processions except boredom.

There is some evidence that children brought up freely and with the maximum of play do not tend to become mass-minded. Among old Summerhillians, the only ones who can easily and enthusiastically cheer in a crowd are the ones who came from the homes of parents with Communist leanings.

Theater

During the winter, Sunday night at Summerhill is acting night. The plays are always well attended. I have seen six successive Sunday nights with a full dramatic program. But sometimes after a wave of dramatics there will not be a performance for a few weeks.

The audience is not too critical. It behaves well—much better than most London audiences do. We seldom have catcalls or feet thumping or whistling.

The Summerhill theater is a converted squash-rackets court, which holds about a hundred people. It has a movable stage; that is, it is made of boxes that can be piled up into steps and platforms. It has proper lighting with elaborate dimming devices and spotlights. There is no scenery—only gray curtains. When the cue is *Enter villagers through gap in hedge,* the actors push the curtain aside.

The tradition of the school is that only plays written in Summerhill are performed. And the unwritten code is that a play written by a teacher is performed only if there is a dearth of children's plays. The cast makes its own costumes, too, and these are usually exceptionally well done. Our school dramas tend toward comedy and farce rather than tragedy; but when we have a tragedy, it is well done—sometimes beautifully done.

Girls write plays more than boys do. Small boys often produce their own plays; but usually the parts are not written out. They hardly need to be, for the main line of each character is always "Stick 'em up!" In these plays the curtain is always rung down on a set of corpses, for small boys are by nature thorough and uncompromising.

Daphne, a girl of thirteen, used to give us Sherlock Holmes plays. I remember one about a constable who ran away with the sergeant's wife. With the aid of the sleuth and, of course, "My Dear Watson" the sergeant tracked the wife to the constable's lodgings. There a remarkable sight met their eyes. The constable lay on a sofa with his arm around the faithless wife, while a bevy of demimonde women danced sinuous dances in the middle of the room. *The constable was in evening dress.* Daphne always brought high life into her dramas.

Girls of fourteen or so sometimes write plays in verse, and these are often good. Of course, not all the staff and children write plays.

There is a strong aversion to plagiarism. When, some time ago, a play was dropped from the program and I had to write one hastily as a stopgap, I wrote on the theme of one of W. W. Jacob's stories. There was an outcry of "Copycat! Swindler!"

Summerhill children do not like dramatized stories. Nor do they want the usual highbrow stuff so common in other schools. Our crowd never acts Shakespeare; but sometimes I write a Shakespearean skit as, for example, Julius Caesar with an American gangster setting—the language a mixture of Shakespeare and a detective story magazine.

Mary brought the house down when as Cleopatra she stabbed everyone on the stage; and then, looking at the blade of her knife, read aloud the words "stainless steel," and plunged the knife into her breast.

The acting ability of the pupils is of a high standard. Among Summerhill pupils there is no such thing as stage fright. The little children are a delight to see; they live their parts with complete sincerity. The girls act more readily than the boys. Indeed, boys under ten seldom act at all except in their own gangster plays; and some children never get to act nor have any desire to do so.

We discovered in our long experience that the worst actor is he who acts in life. Such a child can never get away from himself and is self-conscious on the stage. Perhaps self-conscious is the wrong term, for it means being conscious that others are conscious of you.

Acting is a necessary part of education. It is largely exhibitionism; but at Summerhill when acting becomes only exhibitionism, an actor is not admired.

As an actor, one must have a strong power of identifying oneself with others. With adults, this identification is never unconscious; adults know they are play-acting. But I question if small children really do know. Quite often, when a child enters and his cue is, "Who are you?" instead of answering, "I am the abbey ghost!" he will answer, "I'm Peter."

In one of the plays written for the very youngest, there was a dinner scene with real viands. It took the prompter some time and concern to get the actors to move on to the next scene. The children went on tucking in the food with complete indifference to the audience.

Acting is one method of acquiring self-confidence. But some children who never act tell me that they hate the performances because they feel so inferior. Here is a difficulty for which I have found no solution. Such a child generally finds another line of endeavor in which he can show superiority. The difficult case is that of the girl who loves acting but can't act. It says much for the good manners of the school that such a girl is seldom left out of a cast.

Boys and girls of thirteen and fourteen refuse to take any part that involves making love, but the small children will play any part easily and gladly. The seniors who are over fifteen will play love parts if they are comedy parts. Only one or two seniors will take a serious love part. Love parts cannot be well played until one has experienced love. Yet children who have never known grief in real life may act splendidly in a sorrowful part. I have seen Virginia break down at rehearsals and weep while playing a sad part. That is accounted for by the fact that every child has known grief in imagination In fact, death enters early into every child's fantasies.

Plays for children ought to be at the level of the children. It is wrong to make children do classical plays which are far away from their real fantasy life. Their plays, like their reading, should be for their age. Summerhill children seldom read Scott or Dickens or Thackeray, because today's children belong to an age of movies. When a child goes to the movies, he gets a story as long as *Westward Ho* in an hour and a quarter—a story that would take him days to read, a story without all the dull descriptions of people and landscapes. So in their plays children do not want a story of Elsinore; they want a story of their own environment.

Although Summerhill children perform the plays that they themselves write, they nevertheless, when given the opportunity, respond enthusiastically to really fine drama. One winter I read a play to the seniors once a week. I read all of Barrie, Ibsen, Strindberg, Chekhov, some of Shaw and Galsworthy, and some modern plays like *The Silver Cord* and *The Vortex*. Our best actors and actresses liked Ibsen.

The seniors are interested in stage techniques and take an original view of it. There is a time-honored trick in playwriting of never allowing a character to leave the stage without his making an excuse for doing so. When a dramatist wanted to get rid of the father so that the wife and daughter could tell each other what an ass he was, old father obligingly got up, and remarking, "Well, I'd better go and see if the gardener has planted those cabbages," he shuffled out. Our young Summerhill playwrights have a more direct technique. As one girl said to me, "In real life you go out of a room without saying anything about why you are going." You *do,* and you do on the Summerhill stage, too.

Summerhill specializes in a certain branch of dramatic art which we call spontaneous acting. I set acting tasks like the following: *Put on an imaginary overcoat; take it off again and hang it on a peg. Pick up a bunch of flowers and find a thistle among them. Open a telegram that tells you your father (or mother) is dead. Take a hasty meal at a railroad restaurant and be on tenterhooks lest the train leave without you.*

Sometimes the acting is a "talkie." For example, I sit down at a table and announce that I am an immigration officer at Harwich. Each child has to have an imaginary passport and must be prepared to answer my questions. That is good fun.

Again, I am a film producer interviewing a prospective cast, or a businessman seeking a secretary. Once I was a man who had advertised for an amanuensis. None of the children knew what the word meant. One girl acted as if it meant a manicurist and this afforded some good comedy.

Spontaneous acting is the creative side of a school theater—is the vital side. Our theater has done more for creativity than anything else in Summerhill. Anyone can act in a play, but everyone cannot write a play. The children must realize, even if dimly, that their tradition of performing only original, homegrown plays encourages creativity rather than reproduction and imitation.

Dancing and Music

On with the dance—but it must be danced according to the rules. And the strange thing is that the crowd will accept the rules as a crowd, while at the same time the individuals composing the crowd may be unanimous in hating the rules.

To me a London ballroom symbolizes what England is. Dancing, which should be an individual and creative pleasure, is reduced to a stiff walk. One couple dances just like another couple. Crowd conservatism prevents most dancers from being original. Yet the joy of dancing is the joy of invention. When invention is left out, dancing becomes mechanical and dull. English dancing fully expresses the English fear of emotion and originality.

If there is no room for freedom in such a pleasure as dancing, how can we expect to find it in the more serious aspects of life? If one dare not invent his own dance steps, it is unlikely that he will be tolerated if he dares to invent his own religious, educational, or political steps!

At Summerhill, every program includes dances. These are always arranged and performed by the girls, and they do them well. They do not dance to classical music; it is always jazz. We had one ballet to Gershwin's *An American in Paris* music. I wrote the story and the girls interpreted it in dance. I have seen worse dances on the London stage.

Dancing serves as an excellent outlet for unconscious sex interest. I say *unconscious* because a girl may be a beauty, but if she is a bad dancer, she will not have many dance partners.

Nearly every night our private living room is filled with children. We often play phonograph records and here disagreements arise. The children want Duke Ellington and Elvis Presley and I hate the stuff. I like Ravel and Stravinsky and Gershwin. Sometimes I get fed up with jazz and lay down the law, saying that since it is my room I'll play what I want to play.

The *Rosenkavalier* trio or the *Meistersinger* quintet will clear the room. But then, few children like classical music or classical paintings. We make no attempt to lead them to higher tastes —whatever that may mean.

Actually, it does not matter to one's happiness in life whether one loves Beethoven or hot jazz. Schools would have more success if they included jazz in the curriculum and left out Beethoven. At Summerhill, three boys, inspired by jazz bands, took up musical instruments. Two of them bought clarinets and one chose a trumpet. On leaving school, they all went to study at the Royal Academy of Music. Today, they are all playing in orchestras which play classical music exclusively. I like to think that the reason for this advance in musical taste is that when they were at Summerhill each was permitted to hear Duke Ellington *and* Bach, or any other composer for that matter.

Sports and Games

In most schools, sports are compulsory. Even the watching of matches is compulsory. In Summerhill, games are, like lessons, optional.

One boy was in the school for ten years and didn't play a game, and he was never asked to play a game. But most of the children love games. The juniors do not organize games. They play gangsters or red Indians; they build tree huts and do all the things that small children usually do. Not having reached the cooperative stage, they should not have games organized for them. Organized play and sports come naturally at the right time.

At Summerhill, our chief games are hockey in the winter and tennis in the summer. One difficulty with children is to get good teamwork in tennis doubles. They take teamwork for granted in hockey; but often two tennis players act as individuals instead of as a single unit. Teamwork comes more easily about the age of seventeen.

Swimming is very popular with all ages. The beach at Sizewell is not a good beach for children, for the tide seems always to be full. The long stretches of sand with rocks and pools so dear to children are not to be found on our coast.

We have no artificial gymnastics in the school, nor do I think them necessary. The children get all the exercise they need in their games, swimming, dancing, and cycling. I question if free children would go to a gym class. Our indoor games are table tennis, chess, cards.

The younger children have a paddling pool, a sand pit, a seesaw and swings. The sand pit is always filled with grubby children on a warm day; and the younger ones are always complaining that the bigger children come and use their sand pit. It appears that we shall have to have a sand pit for the seniors. The sand and mud-pie era lives on longer than we thought it did.

We have had debates and wranglings about our inconsistency in giving prizes for sports. The inconsistency lies in our resolute refusal to introduce prizes or marks into the school curriculum. The argument against rewards is that a thing should be done for its own sake, not for the reward; and that is indeed true. So we are sometimes asked why it is right to give a prize for tennis, but wrong to give one for geography. I suppose the answer is that a game of tennis is naturally competitive and consists in beating the other fellow. The study of geography is not. If I know geography, I don't really care if the other fellow knows less or more geography than I do. I know that children *want* prizes for games, and they don't want them for school subjects —at least not in Summerhill. In Summerhill, at any rate, we do not turn our sports winners into heroes. Because Fred is captain of the hockey team does not give his voice added weight in a General School Meeting.

Sports in Summerhill are in their proper place. A boy who never plays a game is never looked down upon and never considered an inferior. "Live and let live" is a motto that finds its ideal expression when children are free to be themselves. I, myself, have little interest in sports, but I am keenly interested in good sportsmanship. If Summerhill teachers had urged, "Come on, lads, get on the field!" sports in Summerhill would have become a perverted thing. Only under freedom to play or not to play can one develop true sportsmanship.

Report of the British Government Inspectors

MINISTRY OF EDUCATION

Report by H. M. Inspectors

on the

Summerhill School,

Leiston, Suffolk East

Inspected on

20th and 21st June, 1949

MINISTRY OF EDUCATION
CURZON STREET
LONDON, W. 1.

IND: 38B/6/8.

This School is famous throughout the world as one in which educational experiment is conducted on revolutionary lines and in which the published theories of its Head Master, widely known and discussed, are put into practice. The task of inspecting it proved to be exacting and interesting, exacting because of the wide difference in practice between this School and others with which the inspectors were familiar, and interesting because of the opportunity offered of trying to assess, and not merely to observe, the value of the education given.

All the children in the School are boarders and the annual fee is £120. In spite of the low salaries paid to the staff, which will be referred to later, the Head Master finds it difficult to run the School at this figure which he is reluctant to increase in view of what he knows about the financial circumstances of the parents. Although the fee is low, compared with that at many independent boarding schools and the staffing ratio is high, the inspectors were a little surprised at the financial difficulties of which the Head Master complained. Only a close scrutiny of accounts and expenses could show whether costs could be cut without loss and it might be a good plan to invite such a scrutiny from some independent and experienced source. In the meantime it may be said that whatever else is deficient, the children are well and plentifully fed.

The principles upon which the School is conducted are well known to the readers of the Head Master's books. Some have gained wide acceptance since they were first declared, some are exerting a widening influence in schools generally while others are regarded with suspicion and abhorrence by the majority of teachers and parents. While the inspectors tried to follow their normal custom of assessing what is being done in an objective manner, it appears to them impossible to report fairly on the School without some reference to its principles and aims, whether they accept them personally or not.

The main principle upon which the School is run is freedom. This freedom is not quite unqualified. There is a number of laws concerned with safety of life and limb made by the children but approved by the Head Master only if they are sufficiently stringent. Children, for instance, cannot bathe except in the presence of two members of the staff who are lifesavers. The younger children cannot go out of the school grounds without the escort of older ones. These, and similar regulations, are categorical, and transgressors are punished by a system of fines. But the degree of freedom allowed to the children is very much greater than the inspectors had seen in any other school, and the freedom is real. No child, for instance, is obliged to attend any lessons. As will be revealed later, the majority do attend for the most part regularly, but one pupil was actually at this School for 13 years without once attending a lesson and is now an expert toolmaker and precision instrument maker. This extreme case is mentioned to show that the freedom given to children is genuine and is not withdrawn as soon as its results become awkward. The School, however, is not run on anarchist principles. Laws are made by a school parliament which meets regularly under the chairmanship of a child and is attended by any staff and child who wish. This assembly has unlimited power of discussion and apparently fairly wide ones of legislation. On one occasion it discussed the dismissal of a teacher, showing, it is understood, excellent judgment in its opinions. But such an event is rare, and normally the parliament is concerned with the day-to-day problems of living in a community.

The inspectors were able to attend a session on the first day of the inspection. The principal matters under discussion were the enforcement of the bedtime regulations made by the parliament and the control of entry into the kitchen at unauthorized times. These problems were discussed with great vigor and freedom of comment, in a reasonably orderly fashion and without respect of persons. Although it seemed that a good deal of time was spent on some rather fruitless lines of argument, the Inspectors were disposed to agree with the Head Master that the experience of learning how to organize their own affairs was more valuable to the children than the time lost.

It is evident that the majority of parents and teachers would be most hesitant to grant complete freedom in the matter of sex. Many who would agree with the Head Master up to a point would part company with him there. They would, perhaps, have no difficulty in accepting his view that sex knowledge should be freely given, that sex should be separated from guilt and that many long-accepted inhibitions have done infinite harm, but they would, in a mixed school, take more precautions than he does. It is, obviously, exceedingly difficult to comment fairly upon the results of not doing so. In any community of adolescents sexual feelings must be present and they will certainly not be removed by being surrounded by taboos. They are, in fact, likely to be inflamed. At the same time, as the Head Master agrees, complete freedom to express them is not possible even if it is desirable. All that can safely be said here is that it would be difficult to find a more natural, open-faced, unself-conscious collection of boys and girls, and disasters which some might have expected to occur have not occurred in all the twenty-eight years of the School's existence.

One other highly controversial matter must be mentioned here, the absence of any kind of religious life or instruction. There is no ban on religion, and if the school parliament decided to introduce it, it would presumably be introduced. Similarly, if an individual wanted it, nothing would be done to hinder him. The children all come from families which do not accept orthodox Christian doctrines, and in fact no desire for religion has ever been expressed. Without doing any violence to the term it may safely be said that many Christian principles are put into practice in this School and that there is much in it of which any Christian can approve. The effects of the complete absence of religious instruction could obviously not be judged in a two days' inspection.

It seemed necessary to write this introductory account of the School before proceeding to the more usual material of a report. It is against this background of real freedom that the organization and activities of the School must be viewed.

ORGANIZATION

There are 70 children between the ages of 4 and 16. They live in four separate buildings which will be described in the section on premises. In this section their education in the narrower sense of the word will be described. There are six Forms organized very loosely according to age but with considerable weighting according to ability. These Forms meet according to a quite ordinary and orthodox timetable of five 40-minute periods on five mornings a week. They have definite places of meeting and definite teachers to teach them. Where they differ from similar Forms in ordinary schools is that there is not the slightest guarantee that everyone, or indeed anyone, will turn up. The inspectors were at much pains to discover what in fact happened, both by attending classes and by inquiry. It appears that attendance increases in regularity as the children grow older and that once a child has decided to attend a particular class he usually does so regularly. It was much more difficult to discover whether the balance of work and subjects was a good one. As many of the children take the School Certificate, their choice is controlled by examination requirements as the examination approaches; but the younger ones are completely free to choose. On the whole the results of this system are unimpressive. It is true that the children work with a will and an interest that is most refreshing, but their achievements are rather meager. This is not, in the inspectors' opinion, an inevitable result of the system, but rather of the system working badly. Among its causes appears to be:

1. The lack of a good teacher of juniors who can supervise and integrate their work and activities.

2. The quality of the teaching generally. The teaching of infants is, as far as could be judged, enlightened and effective and there is some good teaching in the upper Forms, but the lack of a good junior teacher who can inspire and stimulate the 8, 9 and 10 year olds is most apparent. Some surprisingly old-fashioned and formal methods are in use, and when the children reach the age at which they are ready for advanced work they suffer from considerable disadvantages and present their teachers with severe problems. The teaching of the older children is a good deal better and in one or two cases really good.

3. The children lacked guidance. It is commendable that a fifteen-year-old girl should decide that she would like to learn French and German, two languages that she had previously neglected, but to allow her to attempt this task in two periods for German and three for French a week is surely a little irresponsible. The child's progress was slow in spite of her admirable determination and she ought to have been allowed much more time. It appears to the inspectors that some kind of tutorial system might be developed to assist children in planning their work.

4. Lack of privacy. "Summerhill is a difficult place in which to study." The words are the Head Master's. It is a hive of activity and there is much to capture the attention and interest. No

child has a room to himself and there are no rooms specifically set apart for quiet study. A determined person could no doubt always find somewhere, but the necessary degree of determination is rare. Few children remain in the School beyond the age of 16 though there is nothing to prevent them. There are and have been some extremely able and intelligent children at Summerhill and it must be doubted whether, academically, it is giving them all that they need.

At the same time there is some excellent work done wherever the quality of the teaching is good. The Art is outstanding. It was difficult to detect any significant difference between the painting of Summerhill children and that of children from many much more traditional schools, but by any standard the work was good. Some good craft work in great variety was to be seen. The installation of a kiln was going on during the inspection and the pots awaiting first firing were excellent in form. The provision of a treadle-loom would allow another craft which has made promising beginnings to develop.

A good deal of creative written work is done, including a Wall Newspaper, and plays which are written and acted every term. A good deal was heard of these plays, but it is apparently not customary to preserve the scripts so it was not possible to judge of their quality. Recently a performance of *Macbeth* was given in the small School theater, all the sets and dresses being home-made. It was interesting to learn that this was decided upon by the children against the wishes of the Head Master who prefers them to act plays of their own writing.

Physical Education is carried on in accordance with the principles of the School. There are no compulsory games or physical training. Football, cricket, and tennis are all played with enthusiasm, football it is understood with considerable skill owing to the presence on the staff of an expert. The children arrange matches with other schools in the town. On the day visited there was a cricket match against the neighboring modern school, in which Summerhill had decided not to play their best player having learned that their opponents' best player was ill.

A great deal of time is spent out of doors, and the children lead an active, healthy life and look like it. Only a close and expert investigation could reveal how much, if anything, they lose from the absence of more formal Physical Education.

PREMISES

The School is situated in grounds which give ample scope for recreation. The main building, which was formerly a private house, provides for school purposes a hall, a dining room, sick rooms, an art room, a small craft room and the girls' dormitories. The youngest children sleep in a cottage, where their classroom is also situated. The dormitories for the other boys and the remaining classrooms are in huts in the garden, where are also the bedrooms of some members of the staff. All these rooms have doors opening directly to the garden. The classrooms are small, though not unsuitable, as the teaching is done in small groups. One of the dormitories represents a notable building effort by the boys and staff: it was built as a sanatorium for which apparently no use has arisen. The sleeping accommodation is somewhat primitive when judged by normal standards, but it is understood that the health record of the School is good, and the provision may be regarded as satisfactory. There are sufficient bathrooms available.

While these garden premises are at first sight unusually primitive and public, they do in fact seem to be eminently well suited for creating the atmosphere of a permanent holiday camp which is an important feature of the School. Moreover they gave the opportunity of seeing how the children pursued their studies entirely undisturbed by the many visitors, who were present on the day of the inspection.

STAFF

The staff are paid £8 a month with board and lodging. To find men and women who not only believe in the principles of the School but are sufficiently mature and well balanced to be able to live on equal terms with children, who are well qualified academically and highly skilled as teachers and then to persuade them to work for £8 a month, must be a considerable task for the Head Master. Service at Summerhill is not a recommendation in many quarters, and the necessary combination of conviction, disinterestedness, character and ability is rare. It has already been pointed out that the staff are not equal to all the demands, yet they are very much better than the staff of many independent schools paying much higher salaries. They include an M.A. (Hons.) Edinburgh in English, an M.A. and B.Sc. of Liverpool, a Cambridge Wrangler, a F.A. (Hons.) London in French and German, and a Cambridge B.A. in History. Four have teacher's qualifications. This does not include the teachers of art and crafts who have foreign qualifications and are among the best on the staff.

While they need strengthening here and there, the present staff is far from being weak and if, by attendance at courses and visits of observation, they could widen and refresh their experience and bring themselves up to date, they could give a very good account of themselves. At the same time it is too much to hope that a salary of £96 a year can go on attracting to this School the teachers that it needs and it seems clear that this difficulty will have to be squarely faced.

The Head Master is a man of deep conviction and sincerity. His faith and patience must be inexhaustible. He has the rare power of being a strong personality without dominating. It is impossible to see him in his School without respecting him even if one disagrees with or even dislikes some of his ideas. He has a sense of humor, a warm humanity and a strong common sense which would make him a good Head Master anywhere, and his happy family life is shared with the children who are presumably as capable of profiting by example as any others.

He takes a broad view of education as the means of learning how to live abundantly and, though he would admit the force of some at least of the criticisms in this Report, he would feel that his School must stand or fall rather by the kind of children that it allows its pupils to grow into, than by the specific skills and abilities that it teaches them. On this basis of evaluation it may be said:

1. That the children are full of life and zest. Of boredom and apathy there was no sign. An atmosphere of contentment and tolerance pervades the School. The affection with which it is regarded by its old pupils is evidence of its success. An average number of 30 attend the end-of-term plays and dances, and many make the School their headquarters during the holidays.

It may be worth noting at this point that, whereas in its early days the School was attended almost entirely by "problem" children, the intake is now from a fairly normal cross-section of the population.

2. That the children's manners are delightful. They may lack, here and there, some of the conventions of manners, but their friendliness, ease and naturalness, and their total lack of shyness and self-consciousness made them very easy, pleasant people to get on with.

3. That initiative, responsibility and integrity are all encouraged by the system and that, so far as such things can be judged, they are in fact being developed.

4. That such evidence as is available does not suggest that the products of Summerhill are unable to fit into ordinary society when they leave School. Information such as follows does not of course tell the whole story but it indicates that Summerhill edu-

cation is not necessarily hostile to worldly success. Old pupils have become a Captain in the R.E.M.E. [Royal Electrical/Mechanical Engineers], a Battery Q.M.S. [Quartermaster Sergeant], a bomber pilot and Squadron Leader, a Nursery Nurse, an Air Hostess, a clarinet player in the Grenadier Guards Band, a Beit Fellow of the Imperial College, a ballet dancer at Sadler's Wells, a radio operator and contributor of short stories to an important national daily newspaper, and a market research investigator with a big firm. They have taken the following degrees etc., among others: F.A. Hons. Econ. Cambridge; Scholar Royal College of Art; B.Sc., 1st Class Hons. Physics, London; B.A. Hons. History, Cambridge; B.A., 1st Class Hons. Modern Language, Manchester.

5. The Head Master's educational views make this School an exceptionally suitable place for the type of education in which such fundamental work is based on children's interests and in which class work is not unduly governed by examination requirements. To have created a situation in which academic education of the most intelligent kind could flourish is an achievement, but in fact it is not flourishing and a great opportunity is thus being lost. With better teaching at all stages, and above all the junior stage, it might be made to flourish, and an experiment of profound interest be given its full chance to prove itself.

There remains in the mind some doubts both about principles and about methods. A closer and longer acquaintance with the School would perhaps remove some of these and possibly intensify others. What cannot be doubted is that a piece of fascinating and valuable educational research is going on here which it would do all educationists good to see.

Notes on His Majesty's Inspectors' Report

We were indeed lucky to have two broad-minded inspectors sent to us. We dropped "mister" straightaway. During the two days' visit, we had quite a few friendly arguments.

I felt that school inspectors were accustomed to picking up a French book in front of a class and quizzing the class to find out what the pupils knew. I reasoned that that kind of training and experience would be of little use in inspecting the worth of a school in which lessons were not the prime criterion. I said to one of the inspectors, "You really can't inspect Summerhill because our criteria are happiness, sincerity, balance and sociability." He grinned and said they'd have a go at it anyway. And both our inspectors made a remarkable adaptation, and obviously enjoyed themselves in the process.

Odd things struck them. Said one, "What a delightful shock it is to enter a classroom and find the children not taking any notice of you, after years of seeing classes jump to attention." Yes, we were lucky to have the two of them.

But to the report itself: "the inspectors were a little surprised at the financial difficulties. . . ." The answer lies mostly in bad debts, yet that is not the whole story. The report mentions an annual fee of £120, but since then we have tried to cope with high prices throughout the years by raising the average annual fee to about £250 (about $700). This does not allow anything for repairs to the buildings, for purchasing new apparatus, and so on. For one thing, damages are heavier in Summerhill than in a disciplined school. Summerhill children are allowed to go through their gangster period, and consequently more furniture is destroyed.

The report says that we have seventy children. Today, we are down to forty-five, a fact that offsets to some extent the rise in fees.

The report speaks of the poor teaching of our juniors. We have always had that difficulty. Even with an excellent teacher, it is difficult to get through the ordinary public school work if only for the reason that the children are free to do other things. If children in a public school at the age of ten or twelve could climb trees or dig holes instead of going to lessons, their standards would be like ours. But we accept the fact that our boys and girls will have a period during which there must be a lower standard of learning, because we think that play is of greater importance during this period in their lives than learning.

Even if we assume that the backwardness in lessons of our juniors is important, it is still true that a year later these same juniors, then turned seniors, passed the Oxford exams with very good grades. These pupils were examined in a total of 39 subjects, an average of 6½ subjects for each pupil. The results were 24 *Very Good,* which is better than 70 per cent. In all the 39 exams, there was only one failure. The handicap of not being up to regular school standard when a boy is a junior in Summerhill does not necessarily mean that such a pupil will be at a low standard when he is a senior.

For my part I have always liked late starters. I have seen quite a few bright children who could recite Milton at four blossom forth as drunkards and loafers at twenty-four. I like to meet the man who at the age of fifty-three says he doesn't quite know what he is to be in life. I have a hunch that the boy who knows at seven just what he wants to be may be an inferior who will have a conservative attitude to life later on.

The report says: "To have created a situation in which academic education of the most intelligent kind could flourish is an achievement; but in fact, it is not flourishing and a great opportunity is thus being lost." That is the only paragraph in which the two inspectors did not rise above their academic preoccupations. Our system flourishes when a child *wants* an academic education, as our exam results show. But perhaps the inspectors' paragraph means that better junior teaching would result in more children *wanting* to take matriculation exams.

Is it not time that we put academic education in its place? Academic education too often tries to make a silk purse out of a sow's ear. I wonder what an academic education would have done for some of our old Summerhill pupils—a dress designer, a hairdresser, a male ballet dancer, some musicians, some children's nurses, some mechanics, some engineers, and half a dozen artists.

Yet it is a fair report, a sincere one, a generous one. I am publishing it simply because it is good that the reading public should see a view of Summerhill that is not my own. Note that the report does not carry any form of official recognition by the Ministry of Education. Personally, I do not mind; but recognition would have been welcome because of two factors: the teachers would have come under the State Superannuation Scheme, and parents would have a better chance of getting aid from local Councils.

I should like to put on record the fact that Summerhill has never had any difficulty with the Ministry of Education. Any inquiry, any visit of mine to the Ministry, has been met with courtesy and friendliness. My only setback came when the Minister refused permission for a Scandinavian parent to import and erect prefabs, free of charge, just after the war.

When I think of the authoritative interest taken by European governments in private schools, I am glad I live and work in a country that allows so much scope to private venture. I show tolerance of children; the Ministry shows tolerance of my school. I am content.

The Future of Summerhill

Now that I am in my seventy-sixth year, I feel that I shall not write another book about education, for I have little new to say. But what I have to say has something in my favor; I have not spent the last forty years writing down *theories* about children. Most of what I have written has been based on observing children, living with them. True, I have derived inspiration from Freud, Homer Lane, and others; but gradually, I have tended to drop theories when the test of reality proved them invalid.

It is a queer job that of an author. Like broadcasting, an author sends out some sort of message to people he does not see, people he cannot count. My public has been a special one. What might be called the official public knows me not. The British Broadcasting Company would never think of inviting me to broadcast on education. No university, my own of Edinburgh included, would ever think of offering me an honorary degree. When I lecture to Oxford and Cambridge students, no professor, no don comes to hear me. I think I am rather proud of these facts, feeling that to be acknowledged by the officials would suggest that I was out-of-date.

At one time, I resented the fact that *The London Times* would never publish any letter I sent in; but today, I feel their refusal is a compliment.

I am not claiming that I have gotten away from the wish for recognition; yet age brings changes—especially changes in values. Recently I lectured to seven hundred Swedes, packing a hall built for six hundred, and I had no feeling of elation or conceit. I thought I was really indifferent until I asked myself the question, "How would you have felt if the audience had consisted of ten?" The answer was "damned annoyed," so that if positive pride is lacking, negative chagrin is not.

Ambition dies with age. Recognition is a different matter. I do not like to see a book with the title of, say, *The History of Progressive Schools* when such a book ignores my work. I have never yet met anyone who was honestly indifferent to recognition.

There is a comical aspect about age. For years I have been trying to reach the young—young students, young teachers, young parents—seeing age as a brake on progress. Now that I am old— one of the Old Men I have preached against so long—I feel differently. Recently, when I talked to three hundred students in Cambridge, I felt myself the youngest person in the hall. I *did*. I said to them: "Why do you need an old man like me to come and tell *you* about freedom?" Nowadays, I do not think in terms of youth and age. I feel that years have little to do with one's thinking. I know lads of twenty who are ninety, and men of sixty who are twenty. I am thinking in terms of freshness, enthusiasm, of lack of conservatism, of deadness, of pessimism.

I do not know if I have mellowed or not. I suffer fools less gladly than I used to do, am more irritated by boring conversations, and less interested in people's personal histories. But then, I've had far too many imposed on me these last thirty years. I also find less interest in things, and seldom want to buy anything. I haven't looked in a clothes shop window for years. And even my beloved tool shops in Euston Road do not attract me nowadays.

If I have now reached the stage when children's noise tires me more than it used to, I cannot say that age has brought impatience. I can still see a child do all the wrong things, live out all the old complexes, knowing that in good time the child will be a good citizen. Age lessens fear. But age also lessens courage. Years ago, I could easily tell a boy who threatened to jump from a high window if he did not get his own way, to go on and jump. I am not so sure I could do so today.

A question that is often put to me is, "But isn't Summerhill a one-man show? Could it carry on without you?" Summerhill is by no means a one-man show. In the day-by-day working of the school, my wife and the teachers are just as important as I am. *It is the idea of noninterference with the growth of the child and non-pressure on the child that has made the school what it is.*

Is Summerhill known throughout the world? Hardly. And only to a comparative handful of educators. Summerhill is best known in Scandinavia. For thirty years, we have had pupils from Norway, Sweden, Denmark—sometimes twenty at a time. We have also had pupils from Australia, New Zealand, South Africa, and Canada. My books have been translated into many languages, including Japanese, Hebrew, Hindustani, and Gujarati. Summerhill has had some influence in Japan. Over thirty years ago, we had a visit from Seishi Shimoda, an outstanding educator. All his translations of my books have sold rather well; and I hear that teachers in Tokyo meet to discuss our methods. Mr. Shimoda again spent a month with us in 1958. A principal of a school in the Sudan tells me that Summerhill is of great interest to some teachers there.

I put down these facts about translations, visits, and correspondence without illusions. Stop a thousand people in Oxford Street and ask them what the word Summerhill conveys to them. Very likely none of them would know the name. One should cultivate a sense of humor about one's importance or lack of it.

I do not think that the world will use the Summerhill method of education for a very long time—if it ever uses it. The world may find a better way. Only an empty windbag would assume that his work is the last word on the subject. The world *must* find a better way. For politics will not save humanity. It never has done so. Most political newspapers are bristling with hate, hate all the time. Too many are socialistic because they hate the rich instead of loving the poor.

How can we have happy homes with love in them when the home is a tiny corner of a homeland that shows hate socially in a hundred ways? You can see why I cannot look upon education as a matter of exams and classes and learning. The school evades the basic issue: All the Greek and math and history in the world will not help to make the home more loving, the child free from inhibitions, the parent free of neurosis.

The future of Summerhill itself may be of little import. But the future of the Summerhill idea is of the greatest importance to humanity. New generations must be given the chance to grow in freedom. The bestowal of freedom is the bestowal of love. And only love can save the world.

TWO

CHILD REARING

The Unfree Child

The molded, conditioned, disciplined, repressed child—the un-free child, whose name is Legion, lives in every corner of the world. He lives in our town just across the street. He sits at a dull desk in a dull school; and later, he sits at a duller desk in an office or on a factory bench. He is docile, prone to obey authority, fearful of criticism, and almost fanatical in his desire to be normal, conventional, and correct. He accepts what he has been taught almost without question; and he hands down all his complexes and fears and frustrations to his children.

Psychologists have contended that most of the psychic damage to a child is done in the first five years of life. It is possibly nearer the truth to say that in the first five months, or in the first five weeks or, perhaps even in the first five minutes, damage can be done to a child that will last a lifetime.

Unfreedom begins with birth. Nay, it begins long before birth. If a repressed woman with a rigid body bears a child, who can say what effect the maternal rigidity has on the newborn baby?

It may be no exaggeration to say that all children in our civilization are born in a life-disapproving atmosphere. The timetable feeding advocates are basically anti-pleasure. They want the child to be disciplined in feeding because non-timetable feeding suggests orgastic pleasure at the breast. The nutriment argument is usually a rationalization; the deep motive is to mold the child into a disciplined creature who will put duty before pleasure.

Let us consider the life of an average grammar school boy, John Smith. His parents go to church now and then, but nevertheless insist that John go to Sunday School every single week. The parents had married quite rightly because of mutual sex attraction; they *had* to marry, because in their milieu one could not live sexually together unless one was respectable—that is, married. As so often happens, the sex attraction was not enough; and differences of temperament made the home a strained place, with occasional loud-voiced arguments between the parents. There were many tender moments too, but little John took them for granted, whereas the loud quarrels between his parents hit him in the solar plexus, and he became frightened and cried and got spanked for crying for nothing.

From the very first, he was conditioned. Timetable feeding gave him much frustration. When he was hungry, the clock said his feeding time was still an hour away. He was wrapped up in too many clothes, and wrapped too tightly. He found that he could not kick out as freely as he wanted to do. Frustration in feeding made him suck his thumb. But the family doctor said that he must not be allowed to form bad habits, and Mamma was ordered to tie up his arms in his sleeves or to put some evil-smelling substance on his fingertips. His natural functions were left alone during the diaper period. But when he began to crawl and perform on the floor, words like *naughty* and *dirty* began to float about the house, and a grim beginning was made in teaching him to be clean.

Before this, his hand had been taken away every time it touched his genitals; and he soon came to associate the genital prohibition with the acquired disgust about feces. Thus, years later, when he became a traveling salesman, his story repertoire consisted of a balanced number of sex and toilet jokes.

Much of his training was conditioned by relatives and neighbors. Mother and father were most anxious to be correct—to do the proper thing—so that when relatives or next-door neighbors came, John had to show himself as a well-trained child. He had to say *Thank you* when Auntie gave him a piece of chocolate; and he had to be most careful about his table manners; and especially, he had to refrain from speaking when adults were speaking.

His abominable Sunday clothes were a concession to neighbors. With this training in respectability went an involved system of lying—a system he was usually consciously unaware of. The lying began early in his life. He was told that God does not love naughty boys who say *damn,* and that the conductor would spank him if he wandered along the train corridor.

All his curiosity about the origins of life were met with clumsy lies, lies so effective that his curiosity about life and birth disappeared. The lies about life became combined with fears when at the age of five his mother found him having genital play with his sister of four and the girl next door. The severe spanking that followed (Father added to it when he came home from work) forever conveyed to John the lesson that sex is filthy and sinful, something one must not even think of. Poor John had to bottle up his interest in sex until he came to puberty, and then he would guffaw in the movies when some woman said she was three months pregnant.

Intellectually, John's career was normal. He learned easily, and thus escaped the sneers and punishment a stupid teacher might have given him. He left school with a smattering of mostly useless knowledge and a culture that was easily satisfied with cheap tabloids, trite films, and the pulp library of crime.

To John, the name Colgate was associated only with a toothpaste; and Beethoven and Bach were intrusive guys who got in the way when you were tuning in to Elvis Presley or the Beiderbecke Band.

John Smith's rich cousin, Reginald Worthington, went to a private school; but his development, in essentials, was the same as that of poor John. He had the same acceptance of the second-

rate in life, the same enslavement to the *status quo,* the same negation of love and joy.

Are these pictures of John and Reginald one-sided caricatures? Not exactly caricatures, yet I have not given the complete
picture. I have left out the warm humanity of both, a humanity
that survives the most evil character conditioning. The Smiths
and the Worthingtons of life are in the main decent, friendly
folk, full of childish faith and superstitions, of childlike trust
and loyalties. They and their fellows make up the John Citizens
who make the laws and demand humaneness. They are the people who decree that animals must be killed humanely, that pets
must be properly cared for; but they break down when it comes
to man's inhumanity to man. They accept a cruel, un-Christian
criminal code without a thought; and they accept the killing of
other men in war as a natural phenomenon.

John and his rich cousin agree that love and marriage laws
should be stupid and unkind and hateful. They agree that there
must be one law for men, and another law for women, so far as
love is concerned. Both demand that the girls they marry should
be virgins. When asked if *they* are virgins, they frown and say,
"A man's different."

Both are staunch supporters of the patriarchal state, even if
neither ever heard of the term. They have been fashioned into a
product the patriarchal state finds necessary for its continued
existence. Their emotions tend to be *crowd* emotions rather
than *individual* feelings.

Long after leaving a school which they hated as schoolboys,
they will exclaim, "I was beaten at my school, and it did me a
lot of good," and then pack off their sons to the same or a similar school. In psychological terms, they accept the father without constructive rebellion against him; and so the father-author-
ity tradition is carried on for generation after generation.

To complete the portrait of John Smith I ought to give a short sketch of the life of his sister, Mary—short because, by and large, her repressive environment is the same as that which stifles her brother. She has, however, special handicaps that John does not have. In a patriarchal society she is a definite inferior, and she is trained to know it. She has to do house chores when her brother reads or plays. She soon learns that when she gets a job, she will get less pay than a man gets.

Mary does not as a rule rebel against her inferior status in a man-made society. Man sees that she has compensations, tawdry as they mostly are. She is the focus of good manners; she is treated with deference; a man will stand in her presence if she is not seated. A man will ask her if she will graciously marry him. Mary is subtly taught that one of her chief functions is to look as lovely as possible, the result being that many more millions are spent on dress and cosmetics than are spent on books and schools.

In the sex sphere, Mary is as ignorant and as repressed as her brother. In a patriarchal society, the menfolk have decreed that their women must be pure, virginal, innocent. It is not Mary's fault that she has grown up in the sincere belief that women have purer minds than men. In some almost mystical way, her menfolk have made her think and feel that her function in life is only reproduction, and that sexual pleasure is man's province.

Mary's grandmother, and probably her mother, too, were not supposed to have any sex until the right man came along and aroused the sleeping beauty. Mary has got away from that phase, but not so far as we would like to believe. Her love life is ruled by fear of pregnancy, for she realizes that an illegitimate child will very likely spoil her chance of getting a man.

One of the big tasks of today and tomorrow is the investigation of repressed sexual energy and its relation to human sickness. Our John Smith may die of kidney trouble and Mary Smith may die of cancer; and neither will wonder whether his nar-

row, repressed emotional life had any connection with his illness. One day humanity may trace all its miseries, its hates, and
its diseases to its particular form of civilization that is essentially
anti-life. If rigid character training makes rigid human bodies—
cramped and confined instead of being alive and pulsating—it
seems logical to conclude that the same rigid deadness will prohibit the pulsation in every human organ necessary to life.

To sum up, my contention is that unfree education results in
life that cannot be lived fully. Such an education almost entirely
ignores the *emotions* of life; and because these emotions are dynamic, their lack of opportunity for expression must and does
result in cheapness and ugliness and hatefulness. Only the head
is educated. If the emotions are permitted to be really free, the
intellect will look after itself.

The tragedy of man is that, like the dog, his character can be
molded. You cannot mold the character of a cat, an animal
superior to the dog. You can give a dog a bad conscience, but
you cannot give a conscience to a cat. Yet most people prefer
dogs because their obedience and their flattering tail-wagging
afford visible proof of the master's superiority and worth.

The nursery training is very like the kennel training; the
whipped child, like the whipped puppy, grows into an obedient,
inferior adult. And as we train our dogs to suit our own purposes, so we train our children. In that kennel, the nursery, the
human dogs must be clean; they must not bark too much; they
must obey the whistle; they must feed when we think it con-
venient for them to feed.

I saw a hundred thousand obedient, fawning dogs wag their
tails in the Templehof, Berlin, when in 1935, the great trainer
Hitler whistled his commands.

I should like to quote a few *Instructions for Expectant Mothers* issued some years ago by a hospital of a women's medical
college in Pennsylvania.

"The habit of thumb and finger sucking may be prevented by placing the infant's arms in a cardboard tube in order that it may not be able to bend the arm at the elbow."

"Private Parts. These should be kept scrupulously clean, to avoid discomfort, disease, *and the formation of bad habits.*" (My italics.)

I blame the medical profession for much of the wrong rearing of children. Doctors are not as a rule trained in child rearing; yet to many women, the doctor's word is the voice of God. If he says that a child must be spanked for masturbation, the poor mother does not know that he is talking through his own sex guilt and not through his scientific knowledge of child nature. I blame the doctors for prescribing the fatuous timetable feeding, the sucking deterrents, the stupid prohibition about playing with the baby, and about giving him his own way.

The problem child is the child who is pressured into cleanliness and sexual repression. Adults take it for granted that a child should be taught to behave in such a way that the adults will have as quiet a life as possible. Hence the importance attached to obedience, to manners, to docility.

The other day, I saw a boy of three put out in the garden by his mother. His suit was spotless. He began to play with earth and slightly soiled his clothes. Mamma rushed out, smacked him, took him indoors and later sent him out weeping in new clothes. In ten minutes, he had soiled his suit, and the process was repeated. I thought of telling the woman that her son would hate her for life; and worse, hate life itself. But I realized that nothing I could say would sink in.

Nearly every time I go to a town or city, I see a child of three stumble and fall, and then I shrink to see the mother spank the child for falling.

On almost every railway trip I hear a mother say, "If you go out to that corridor again, Willie, the conductor will arrest you."

Most children are reared on a tissue of lies and ignorant prohibitions.

Many a mother who treats her child fairly well at home will storm at him or spank him in public because she is fearful of the opinion of her neighbors. The child must from the start be forced to fit himself into our insane society.

Once, when I lectured in a seaside town in England I remarked, "Do you mothers realize that every time you spank your child, you show that you are hating your child?" The reaction was tremendous. The women shouted at me savagely. When later in the evening I gave my views on the question, "How can we improve the moral and religious atmosphere in the home?" the audience hissed me with great gusto. It was a shock to me, for when I go lecturing, I lecture mostly to those who believe what I believe. But here was a working-and-middle-class audience who had never heard of child psychology. It made me realize how entrenched is the compact majority that is against freedom for children—and freedom for themselves.

Civilization is sick and unhappy, and I claim that the root of it all is the unfree family. Children are deadened by all the forces of reaction and hate, deadened from their cradle days. They are trained to say *nay* to life because their young lives are one long nay. Don't make a noise; don't masturbate; don't lie; don't steal.

They are taught to say *yea* to all that is negative in life. Respect the old; respect religion; respect the schoolmaster; respect the law of the fathers. Don't question anything—just obey.

It is not virtuous to respect one who is not respectable; nor virtuous to live in legal sin with a man or woman you have ceased to love; nor virtuous to love a God you really fear.

The tragedy is that man, who holds his family in bondage, is, and must be, a slave himself—for in a prison the jailer also is confined. Man's slavery is his slavery to hate: he suppresses his family, and in doing so he suppresses his own life. He has to set up courts and prisons to punish the victims of his suppression.

Enslaved woman must give her son to the wars that man calls defensive wars, patriotic wars, wars to save democracy, wars to end wars.

There is never a problem child; there are only problem parents. Perhaps it would be better to say that *there is only a problem humanity*. That is why the atomic bomb is so sinister, for it is under the control of people who are anti-life—for what person whose arms were tied in the cradle is not anti-life?

There is a great amount of good fellowship and love in humanity, and it is my firm belief that new generations that have not been warped in babyhood will live at peace with each other —that is, if the haters of today do not destroy the world before these new generations have time to take control.

The fight is an unequal one, for the haters control education, religion, the law, the armies, and the vile prisons. Only a handful of educators strive to allow the good in all children to grow in freedom. The vast majority of children are being molded by anti-life supporters with their hateful system of punishments.

Girls in some convents still have to cover themselves when they take a bath, lest they see their own bodies. Boys are still told by parent and teacher that masturbation is a sin leading to madness and all sorts of fearful consequences. Recently, I saw a woman spank a baby of about ten months for crying when it was thirsty.

It is a race between the believers in deadness and the believers in life. And no man dare remain neutral: that will mean death. We must be on one side or the other. The death side gives us the problem child; the life side will give us the healthy child.

The Free Child

There are so few self-regulated babies in the world that any attempt to describe them must be tentative. The observed results so far suggest the beginnings of a new civilization, more profoundly changed in character than any new society promised by any kind of political party.

Self-regulation implies a belief in the goodness of human nature; a belief that there is not, and never was, original sin.

No one has ever seen a completely self-regulated child. Every child living has been molded by parents, teachers, and society. When my daughter Zoë was two, a magazine, *Picture Post,* published an article about her with photographs, saying that in their opinion, she of all the children of Britain had the best chance of being free. It was not entirely true, for she lived, and lives, in a school among many children who were not self-regulated. These other children had been more or less conditioned; and since character-molding must lead to fear and hate, Zoë found herself in contact with some children who were anti-life.

She was brought up with no fear of animals. Yet one day, when I stopped the car at a farm and said, "Come on, let's see the moo cows," she suddenly looked afraid and said, "No, no, moo cows eat you." A child of seven, who had not been brought up with self-regulation, had told her so. True, the fear lasted only for a week or two. A subsequent tale of tigers lurking in the bushes also had only a short life of influence.

It would seem that a self-regulated child is capable of overcoming the influences of conditioned children in a comparatively short time. Zoë's acquired fears and repressed interests never lasted long; but no one can say what permanent harm, if any, these acquired fears have already wrought on her character.

Scores of outsiders from all over the world have said of Zoë, "Here is something quite new, a child of grace and balance and happiness, at peace with her surroundings, not at war." It is true; she is, as near as can be in a neurotic society, the natural child who seems automatically to know the boundary between freedom and license.

One of the dangers of having a self-regulated child is that adults will show so much interest in her that she gets too much in the center of the picture. It is likely that in a community of self-regulated children, where all were natural and free, no single child would stand out. None would be encouraged to show off. And then, there would not be the jealousy that other children exhibit when faced with a free child who does not have their inhibitions.

Compared with her friend Ted, Zoë as a young child was supple and free of limb. You lifted her and her body was as relaxed as that of a kitten; but poor Ted lifted like a sack of potatoes. He could not relax; his reactions were all defensive and resisting; he was anti-life in every direction.

I prophesy that self-regulated children will not go through that unpleasant phase. I cannot see why they will ever need to. For if they have no feeling of being tied and restricted by parents when they are in the nursery, I cannot see any reason why rebellion against parents should arise later. Even in semifree homes, the equality between parents and children is often so good that the rebellious striving to get free from the parents does not arise.

Self-regulation means the right of a baby to live freely, without outside authority in things psychic and somatic. It means that the baby feeds when it is hungry; that it becomes clean in habits only when it wants to; that it is never stormed at nor spanked; that it is always loved and protected.

It all sounds easy and natural and fine, yet it is astounding how many young parents, keen on the idea, manage to misunderstand it. Tommy, aged four, bangs the notes of a neighbor's piano with a wooden mallet. His fond parents look on with a triumphant smile which means, "Isn't self-regulation wonderful?"

Other parents think that they ought never to put their baby of eighteen months to bed, because that would be interfering with nature. No, baby must be allowed to stay up; when he is tired out, mother will carry him to his cot. What actually happens is that baby gets increasingly tired and cross. He cannot say that he wants to go to sleep, because he cannot verbalize his need. Usually, the weary and disappointed mother lifts him and carries him screaming to bed. Another young couple came to me rather apologetically, and asked if it would be wrong for them to put up a fireguard in a baby's nursery. All these illustrations show that any idea, old or new, is dangerous, if not combined with common sense.

Only a fool in charge of young children would allow unbarred bedroom windows or an unprotected fire in the nursery. Yet, too often, young enthusiasts for self-regulation come to my school as visitors, and exclaim at our lack of freedom in locking poison in a lab closet, or our prohibition about playing on the fire escape. The whole freedom movement is marred and despised because so many advocates of freedom have not got their feet on the ground.

One such protested to me recently because I shouted sternly at a problem boy of seven who was kicking my office door. His idea was that I should smile and tolerate the noise until the child should live out his desire to bang doors. It is true that I spent a good few years of my life patiently tolerating the destructive behavior of problem children, but I did this as their psychological doctor and not as their fellow citizen.

If a young mother thinks that her child of three should be allowed to paint the front door with red ink on the ground that he is thereby expressing himself freely, she is incapable of grasping what self-regulation means.

I remember sitting with a friend in the Covent Garden theater. During the first ballet, a child in front of us talked loudly to her father. At the end of the ballet, I found other seats. My companion said to me, "What would you do if one of your kids from Summerhill did that?"

"Tell him to shut up," I said.

"You wouldn't need to," said my friend; "he just wouldn't act that way." And I don't think any of them would.

Once a woman brought her girl of seven to see me. "Mr. Neill," she said, "I have read every line you have written; and even before Daphne was born, I had decided to bring her up exactly along your lines."

I glanced at Daphne who was standing on my grand piano with her heavy shoes on. She made a leap for the sofa and nearly went through the springs. "You see how natural she is," said the mother. "The Neillian child!" I fear that I blushed.

It is this distinction between freedom and license that many parents cannot grasp. In the disciplined home, the children have *no* rights. In the spoiled home, they have *all* the rights. The proper home is one in which children and adults have equal rights. And the same applies to school.

It must be emphasized again and again that freedom does not involve spoiling the child. If a baby of three wants to walk over the dining table, you simply tell him he must not. He must obey, that's true. But on the other hand, you must obey him when necessary. I get out of small children's rooms if they tell me to get out.

There has to be a certain amount of sacrifice on the part of the adult if children are to live according to their inner nature.

Healthy parents come to some sort of a compromise agreement; unhealthy parents either become violent or they spoil their children by allowing them to have all the social rights.

In practice, the divergence of interests between parents and children can be mitigated, if not solved, by an honest give and take. Zoë respected my desk, and showed no compulsion to play with my typewriter and papers. In turn, I respected her nursery and playthings.

Children are very wise and soon accept social laws. They should not be exploited as they too often are. Too often a parent calls out, "Jimmy, get me a glass of water," when the child is intent on an engrossing game.

A great amount of naughtiness is due to the wrong method of handling. Zoë, when a little over a year old, went through a period of great interest in my glasses, snatching them off my nose to see what they were like. I made no protest, showed no annoyance by look or tone of voice. She soon lost interest in my glasses and never touched them. No doubt, if I had sternly told her not to—or worse, spanked her little hand—her interest in my glasses would have survived, mingled with fear of me and rebellion against me.

My wife let her play with breakable ornaments. The child handled them carefully and seldom broke anything. She found things out for herself. Of course, there is a limit to self-regulation. We cannot allow a baby of six months to discover that a lighted cigarette burns painfully. It is wrong to shout in alarm in such a case; the right thing to do is to remove the danger without any fuss.

Unless a child is mentally defective, he will soon discover what interests him. Left free from excited cries and angry voices, he will be unbelievably sensible in his dealing with material of all kinds. The harassed mother standing at the gas stove, frantic about what the children are doing, is she who has never trusted her children in their activities. "Go and see what baby is doing and tell him he mustn't" is still a phrase applying to many homes today.

When a mother writes asking me what she should do with children messing things up while she is busy cooking the dinner, I can only reply that perhaps she has brought them up that way.

One couple read some of my books and were conscience-stricken when they thought of the harm they had done in bringing up their children. They summoned the family to a conference and said, "We have brought you up all wrong. From now on, you are free to do what you like." I forget how much they said the breakage bill came to, but I can recall that they had to summon a second conference and rescind the previous motion.

The usual argument against freedom for children is this: *Life is hard, and we must train the children so that they will fit into life later on. We must therefore discipline them. If we allow them to do what they like, how will they ever be able to serve under a boss? How will they compete with others who have known discipline? How will they ever be able to exercise self discipline?*

People who protest the granting of freedom to children and use this argument do not realize that they start with an unfounded, unproved assumption—the assumption that a child will not grow or develop unless forced to do so. Yet the entire thirty-nine years of experience of Summerhill disproves this assumption. Take, among one hundred others, the case of Mervyn. He attended Summerhill for ten years, between the ages of seven to seventeen. During those ten years, Mervyn never attended a single class. At age seventeen, he hardly knew how to read. Yet when Mervyn left school and decided to become an instrument maker, he quickly taught himself how to read and absorbed in a short time through self-study all the technical knowledge he needed.

Through his own efforts, he made himself ready for his apprenticeship. Today, this same chap is thoroughly literate, commands a good salary, and is a leader in his community. As to self-discipline, Mervyn built a good part of his house with his own hands and he is bringing up a fine family of three boys from the fruits of his daily labors.

Similarly, each year boys and girls at Summerhill who up to then have rarely studied, decide to enter college; and of their own accord, they then begin the long and tiresome grind of preparing themselves for college entrance examinations. Why do they do it?

The common assumption that good habits that have not been forced into us during early childhood can never develop in us later on in life is an assumption we have been brought up on and which we unquestioningly accept merely because the idea has never been challenged. I deny this premise.

Freedom is necessary for the child because only under freedom can he grow in his natural way—the good way. I see the results of bondage in new pupils coming from prep schools and convents. They are bundles of insincerity, with an unreal politeness and phony manners.

Their reaction to freedom is rapid and tiresome. For the first week or two, they open doors for the teachers, call me "Sir," and wash carefully. They glance at me with "respect," which is easily recognized as fear. After a few weeks of freedom, they show what they really are. They become impudent, unmannerly, unwashed. They do all the things they have been forbidden to do in the past: they swear, they smoke, they break things. And all the time, they have a polite and insincere expression in their eyes and in their voices.

It takes at least six months for them to lose their insincerity. After that, they also lose their deference to what they regarded as authority. In just about six months, they are natural, healthy kids who say what they think without fluster or hate. When a child comes to freedom young enough, he does not have to go through this stage of insincerity and acting. The most striking thing about Summerhill is this absolute sincerity among the pupils.

This business of being sincere in life and to life is a vital one. It is really the most vital one in the world. If you have sincerity, all other things will be added to you. Everyone realizes the value of sincerity in, say, acting. We expect sincerity from our politicians (such is the optimism of mankind), from our judges and magistrates, teachers and doctors. Yet we educate our children in such a way that they dare not be sincere.

Possibly the greatest discovery we have made in Summerhill is that a child is born a sincere creature. We set out to let children alone so that we might discover what they were like. It is the only possible way of dealing with children. The pioneer school of the future must pursue this way if it is to contribute to child knowledge and, more important, to child happiness.

The aim of life is happiness. The evil of life is all that limits or destroys happiness. Happiness always means goodness; unhappiness at its extreme limits means Jew-baiting, minority torture, or war.

But I grant that sincerity has its awkward moments. As when recently a girl of three looked at a bearded visitor and said, "I don't think I like your face." The visitor rose to the occasion. "But I like yours," he said, and Mary smiled.

No, I won't argue for freedom for children. One half-hour spent with a free child is more convincing than a book of arguments. Seeing is believing.

To give a child freedom is not easy. It means that we refuse to teach him religion, or politics, or class consciousness. A child cannot have real freedom when he hears his father thunder against some political group, or hears his mother storm against the servant class. It is well-nigh impossible to keep children from adopting our attitude to life. The son of a butcher will not be likely to preach vegetarianism—that is, unless fear of his father's authority drives him into opposition.

The very nature of society is inimical to freedom. Society— the crowd—is conservative and hateful toward new thought.

Fashion typifies the crowd's dislike of freedom. The crowd demands uniformity. In town I am a crank because I wear sandals; in my village I would be a crank if I wore a tall hat. Few men dare to depart from *the correct thing*.

The law in England—the law of the crowd—forbids the buying of cigarettes after eight o'clock at night. I cannot think of one individual who approves of this law. As individuals, we calmly accept crowd rulings that are stupid.

Few individuals would care to take the responsibility of hanging a murderer, or of sending a criminal to the living death we call prison. The crowd can retain such barbarities as capital punishment and our prison system, for the crowd has no conscience. The crowd cannot think, it can only feel. To the crowd, the criminal is a danger; the easiest way of protection is to kill the danger or lock it up. Our obsolete criminal code is based fundamentally on fear; and our suppressive system of education is also fundamentally based on fear—fear of the new generation.

Sir Martin Conway in his delightful book, *The Crowd in Peace and War,* points out that the crowd likes old men. In war, it chooses old generals; in peace, it prefers old doctors. The crowd clings to the old because it fears the young.

The instinct of self-preservation in a crowd sees in the new generation a danger—the danger of having a new, rival crowd grow up—a crowd that may conceivably destroy the old crowd. In the smallest crowd of all—the family—freedom is denied to the young for the same reason. The adults cling to old values— old *emotional* values. There is no logical basis for a father's prohibiting his twenty-year-old daughter from smoking. The prohibition springs from emotional sources, from conservative sources. At the back of the prohibition is fear, *What may she do next?* The crowd is the guardian of morality. The adult fears to give freedom to the young because he fears that the young may do indeed all the things that he, the adult, has wanted to do. The eternal imposition on children of adult conceptions and values is a great sin against childhood.

To give freedom is to allow the child to live his own life. Thus expressed, it seems simple. Only our disastrous habit of teaching and molding and lecturing and coercing renders us incapable of realizing the simplicity of true freedom.

What is the child's reaction to freedom? Children clever and children not-so-clever gain something that they never had before —a something that is almost indefinable. Its chief outer sign is a great increase in sincerity and charity, plus a lessening of aggression. When children are not under fear and discipline, they are not patently aggressive. Only once in thirty-eight years at Summerhill have I seen a fight with bloody noses. We always have a small bully around—for no amount of freedom at school can completely counteract the influence of a bad home. Character acquired in the first months or years of life can be modified by freedom, but it can never be completely changed. The archenemy of freedom is fear. If we tell children about sex, will they not become licentious? If we do not censor plays, will the people not become immoral?

The adults who fear that youth will be corrupted are those who are themselves corrupt—just as it is the dirty-minded people who demand that we should all wear two-piece bathing suits. If a man is shocked by anything, it is by the thing that he is most interested in. The prude is the libertine without the courage to face his naked soul.

But freedom means the conquest of ignorance. A free people

would need no censor of plays or of costumes. For a free people would have no interest in shocking things, because a free people could not be shocked. Summerhill pupils are unshockable—not because they are advanced in sin—but because they have lived out their interests in shocking things and have no more use for them as subjects of conversation or wit.

People are always saying to me, "But how will your free children ever adapt themselves to the drudgery of life?" I hope that these free children will be pioneers in *abolishing* the drudgery of life.

We must allow the child to be selfish—ungiving—free to follow his own childish interests through his childhood. When the child's individual interests and his social interests clash, the individual interests should be allowed precedence. The whole idea of Summerhill is release: allowing a child to live out his natural interests.

A school should make a child's life a game. I do not mean that the child should have a path of roses. Making it all easy for the child is fatal to the child's character. But life itself presents so many difficulties that the artificially made difficulties which we present to children are unnecessary.

I believe that to impose anything by authority is wrong. The child should not do anything until he comes to the opinion—his own opinion—that it should be done. The curse of humanity is the external compulsion, whether it comes from the Pope or the state or the teacher or the parent. It is fascism in toto.

Most people demand a god; how can it be otherwise when the home is ruled by tin gods of both sexes, gods who demand perfect truth and moral behavior? Freedom means doing what you like, so long as you don't interfere with the freedom of others. The result is self-discipline.

In our educational policy as a nation, we refuse to let live. We persuade through fear. But there is a great difference between compelling a child to cease throwing stones and compelling him to learn Latin. Throwing stones involves others; but learning Latin involves only the boy. The community has the right to restrain the antisocial boy because he is interfering with the rights of others; but the community has no right to compel a boy to learn Latin—for learning Latin is a matter for the individual. Forcing a child to learn is on a par with forcing a man to adopt a religion by act of Parliament. And it is equally foolish.

I learned Latin as a boy—rather I was given Latin books to learn from. As a boy, I could never learn the stuff because my interests were elsewhere. At the age of twenty-one, I found that I could not enter the university without Latin. In less than a year, I learned enough Latin to pass the entrance exam. Self-interest made me learn Latin.

Every child has the right to wear clothes of such a kind that it does not matter a brass farthing if they get messy or not. Every child has the right to freedom of speech. I have had many years of hearing adolescent children let off all the *bloodies* and *hells* they had been forbidden to say in the nursery.

The surprising thing is that, with millions reared in sex hate and fear, the world is not more neurotic than it is. To me this means that natural humanity has the innate power of finally overcoming the evils that are imposed on it. There is a slow trend to freedom, sexual and otherwise. In my boyhood, a woman went bathing wearing stockings and a long dress. Today, women show legs and bodies. Children are getting more freedom with every generation. Today, only a few lunatics put cayenne pepper on a baby's thumb to stop sucking. Today, only a few countries beat their children in school.

Freedom works slowly; it may take several years for a child to understand what it means. Anyone who expects quick results is an incurable optimist. And freedom works best with clever children. I should like to be able to say that, since freedom primarily touches the emotions, all kinds of children—intelligent and dull—react equally to freedom. I cannot say it.

One sees the difference in the matter of lessons. Every child under freedom plays most of the time for years; but when the time comes, the bright ones will sit down and tackle the work necessary to master the subjects covered by government exams. In a little over two years, a boy or girl will cover the work that disciplined children take eight years to cover.

The orthodox teacher holds that exams will be passed only if discipline keeps the candidate's nose to the grindstone. Our results prove that with bright pupils that is a fallacy. Under freedom, it is only the bright ones who can concentrate on intensive study, a most difficult thing to do in a community in which so many counterattractions are going on.

I know that under discipline comparatively poor scholars pass exams, but I wonder what becomes of the passers later on in life. If all schools were free and all lessons were optional, I believe that children would find their own level.

I can hear some harassed mother, busy with her cooking—while her baby is crawling about and upsetting things—ask with irritation, "What's all this self-regulation anyway? All very well for rich women with nurses; but for the likes of me, just words and confusion."

Another might cry, "I'd like to, but how do I start? What books can I read on the subject?"

The answer is that there are no books, no oracles, no authorities. All there is, is a very small minority of parents and doctors and teachers who believe in the personality and the organism we call a child, and who are determined to do nothing to warp that personality and stiffen its body by wrong interference. We are all nonauthoritarian seekers after the truth about humanity. All we can offer is an account of our observations of young children brought up in freedom.

Love and Approval

The happiness and well-being of children depend on the degree of love and approval we give them. We must be on the child's side. Being on the side of the child is giving love to the child—not possessive love—not sentimental love—just behaving to the child in such a way that the child feels you love him and approve of him.

It can be done. I know scores of parents who are on the side of their children, demanding nothing in return, and therefore getting a lot. They realize that children are not little adults.

When a son of ten writes home, "Dear Mommy, please send me fifty cents. Hope you are well. Love to Daddy," the parents smile, knowing that that is what a child of ten writes if he is sincere and not afraid to express himself. The wrong type of parent sighs at such a letter, and thinks: *The selfish little beast, always asking for something.*

The right parents of my school never ask how their children are getting along; they see for themselves. The wrong type keep asking me impatient questions: *Can he read yet? When is he ever going to be tidy? Does she ever go to lessons?*

It is all a matter of faith in children. Some have it; most haven't it. And if you do not have this faith, the children feel it. They feel that your love cannot be very deep, or you would trust them more. When you approve of children you can talk to them about anything and everything, for approval makes many inhibitions fly away.

But the question arises, Is it possible to approve of children if you do not approve of yourself? If you are not aware of yourself, you cannot approve of yourself. In other words, the more conscious you are of yourself and your motives, the more likely you are to be an approver of yourself.

I express the earnest hope, then, that more knowledge of oneself and of child nature will help parents to keep their children free from neurosis. I repeat that parents are spoiling their children's lives by forcing on them outdated beliefs, outdated manners, outdated morals. They are sacrificing the child to the past. This is especially true of those parents who impose authoritative religion on their children just as it was once imposed on them.

I know well that the most difficult thing in the world is to renounce things we consider important, but it is only through renunciation that we find life, find progress, find happiness. Parents must renounce. They must renounce hate that is disguised as authority and criticism. They must renounce the intolerance that is the outcome of fear. They must renounce old morals and mob verdicts.

Or more simply, the parent must become an individual. He must know where he really stands. It is not easy. For a man is not just himself. He is a combination of everyone he has met, and he retains many of their values. Parents impose the authority of their own parents because every man has in him his own father, every woman her own mother. It is the imposing of this rigid authority that breeds hate, and with it, problem children. It is the opposite of giving the child approval.

Many a girl has said to me, "I can't do a thing to please Mommy. She can do everything better than I can, and she flies into a temper if I make a mistake in sewing or knitting."

Children do not need teaching as much as they need love and understanding. They need approval and freedom to be naturally good. It is the genuinely strong and loving parent who has the most power to give children freedom to be good.

The world is suffering from too much condemnation, which

is really a fancier way of saying that the world is suffering from too much hate. It is the parents' hate that makes a child a problem, just as it is society's hate that makes the criminal a problem. Salvation lies in love, but what makes it difficult is that no one can *compel* love.

The parent of the problem child must sit down and ask himself or herself these questions: *Have I shown real approval of my child? Have I shown trust in him? Have I shown understanding?* I am not theorizing. I know that a problem child can come to my school and become a happy, normal child. I know that the chief ingredients in the curing process are the showing of approval, of trust, of understanding.

Approval is just as necessary for normal children as for problem children. The one commandment that every parent and teacher must obey is this: *Thou shalt be on the child's side.* The obeying of this commandment is what makes Summerhill a successful school. For we are definitely on the child's side—and the child knows it unconsciously.

I do not say that we are a crowd of angels. There are times when we adults make a fuss. If I should be painting a door and Robert came along and threw mud on my fresh paint, I would swear at him heartily, because he has been one of us for a long time and what I say to him does not matter. But suppose Robert had just come from a hateful school and his mud slinging was his attempt to fight authority, I would join with him in his mud slinging because his salvation is more important than the door. I know that I must stay on his side while he lives out his hate in order for him to become social again. It isn't easy. I have stood by and seen a boy treat my precious lathe badly. I knew that if I protested he would at once identify me with his stern father who always threatened to beat him if he touched his tools.

The strange thing is that you can be on the child's side even though you sometimes swear at him. If you are on the side of the child, the child realizes it. Any minor disagreement you may have about potatoes or scratched tools does not disturb the fundamental relationship. When you treat a child without bringing in authority and morality, the child feels that you are on his side. In his previous life, authority and morality were like policemen who restricted his activities.

When a girl of eight passes me and says in passing, "Neill is a silly fool," I know that that is just her negative way of expressing her love, of telling me that she feels at ease. Children do not so much love as they want to be loved. To every child, adult approval means love; whereas disapproval means hate. The attitude of the children to the Summerhill staff is quite like the attitude of the children to me. The children feel that the staff is on their side all the time.

I have already mentioned the sincerity of free children. This sincerity is the result of their being approved of. They have no artificial standards of behavior to live up to, no taboos to restrain them. They have no necessity to live a life that is a lie.

New pupils, coming from schools where they had to respect authority, address me as *Mister*. Only when they discover that I am not an authority do they drop the *Mister* and call me Neill. They never seek to get my personal approval—only the approval of the whole school community. But in the days when I was a village schoolmaster in Scotland, any child would gladly stay behind to help me clean up the classroom or prune a hedge outdoors, seeking—insincerely—my approval because I was the boss.

No child in Summerhill ever does anything to gain my approval, although visitors may conclude otherwise when they see some boys and girls helping me clear weeds. The motive for the work has nothing to do with me personally. In this particular instance the children were weeding because a General-Meeting law made by the pupils themselves provided that everyone over twelve was obliged to do two hours of work each week in the garden. This law was later rescinded.

In any society, however, there is a natural desire for approval. The criminal is he who has lost the desire for approval by the large part of society, or rather the criminal is he who has been forced to change the desire for approval into its opposite, the contempt for society. The criminal is always Egoist No. 1: *Let me get rich quick and to hell with society.* Prison sentences merely armor his egoism. A prison term merely compels the criminal to become a lone bird, brooding on himself and the horrible society that punishes him. Punishment and prison sentences cannot reform the criminal, because to him they are only a proof of society's hate. Society eliminates the chance of his becoming social in order to gain the approval of others. This insane, inhuman prison system stands condemned because it does not touch anything of psychological value in the prisoner.

Hence I say that the first essential in any reform school is the chance of social approval. So long as boys have to salute overseers, stand in military lines, jump up if the superintendent enters the room, there is no real freedom, and therefore no chance of social approval. Homer Lane found that when a new boy came to the *Little Commonwealth,* he sought the approval of his fellows, generally using the technique he had used in his slum street: he boasted of his misdeeds, of his cleverness in lifting from shops, of his prowess in dodging policemen. When he found he was boasting to youths who had got over that form of seeking social approval, the newcomer was nonplused, and he often contemptuously dismissed his new companions as sissies. Gradually his natural love of approval forced him to seek the approval of the people in his new environment. And, without any individual analysis by Lane, he adapted himself to his new companions. In a few months he was a social being.

* * *

Let me now address the ordinary, decent, sympathetic husband who comes home on the 5:20 train every evening.

I know you, John Brown. I know you want to love your children and be loved by them in return. I know that when your son of five wakens at two in the morning and yells persistently without any apparent cause, you will not feel much love for him at the moment. Be assured he has some reason for crying, even if you cannot immediately discover what it is. If you are angry, try not to show it. A man's voice is more terrifying to a baby than is that of a woman, and you never know what life-time fears may be instilled into a baby by a loud angry voice at the wrong time.

"Don't lie in bed with the baby," says the pamphlet of instructions for parents. Forget it. Give the infant as much hugging and petting as you can.

Don't use your children as a means of showing off. In this be as careful of praising as of blaming. It is bad to rhapsodize about a child when he or she is present. *Oh, yes, Mary is getting on. First in her class last week. Clever girl.* Not that you should never praise your child. It is good to say to your son, *That's a very nice kite you have made,* but the praise in the service of impressing visitors is wrong. Young geese so easily stick out their necks like swans when admiration is floating around. It makes the child unrealistic about himself. You should never encourage your child in getting away from reality, in making a fantasy picture of himself. On the other hand, when the child fails, never rub it in. Even if the school report abounds with low marks, say nothing. And if Billy comes home weeping because he has been beaten in a fight, do not call him a sissy.

If you ever use the words *When I was your age* . . . you are making a dreadful mistake. The long and short of it is that you must approve your child as he is, and refrain from trying to make him in your own image.

My motto for the home, in education as in life, is this: *For heaven's sake, let people live their own lives.* It is an attitude that fits any situation.

This attitude is the only possible attitude that fosters toleration. It is strange that the word *toleration* has not occurred to me before. It is the proper word for a free school. We are leading the children along the way of being tolerant by showing *them* tolerance.

Fear

I have spent a good deal of my time patching up the children who have been wounded by people who gave them fear. Fear can be a terrible thing in a child's life. Fear must be entirely eliminated—fear of adults, fear of punishment, fear of disapproval, fear of God. Only hate can flourish in an atmosphere of fear.

We are afraid of so many things—afraid of poverty, afraid of ridicule, afraid of ghosts, afraid of burglars, afraid of accidents, afraid of public opinion, afraid of disease, afraid of death. A man's life is the story of his fears. Millions of adults fear to walk in the dark. Thousands have a vague feeling of uneasiness when a policeman rings the doorbell. Most travelers have fantasies of the ship's sinking or of the airplane's being wrecked. Railway travelers seek the middle coaches of a train. "Safety First" expresses man's leading concern.

There must have been a time in the history of man when the fear of being killed made him flee and hide. Today, life has become so safe that fear in the service of self-protection is no longer necessary. And yet today, humanity probably experiences more fear than did our Stone Age ancestors. Primitive man had only the large-bodied monsters to fear, but we have many monsters—trains, ships, airplanes, burglars, automobiles and, most potent of all, the fear of being found out. Fear is still necessary for us. Fear makes me cross the street carefully.

In nature, fear serves the purpose of race preservation. Rabbits and horses have survived because of the fear that forced them to run from danger. Fear is an important factor in the law of the wild.

Fear is always egoistic: we fear for our own skins, or for those we love. But mostly, we fear for our own skins. When I was a boy I used to fear the dark evening walk to the farm for the milk. Yet, when my sister went with me, I had no fear that she would be murdered on the way. Fear must be egoistic, for every fear is ultimately a fear of death.

A hero is a man who can change his fear into positive energy. The hero harnesses his fear. The fear of being afraid is the most distressing fear in a soldier. The coward is incapable of converting his fear into positive action. Cowardice is much more universal than bravery.

We are all cowards. Some of us manage to hide our cowardice; others betray it. Cowardice is always relative. You can be heroic about certain things and cowardly about others. I recall my first lesson in bomb-throwing as a recruit. One man failed to throw his bomb over into the pit. It exploded and knocked out a few men. Luckily none were killed. The bombing was ended for that day; but on the following day, we were marched back to the bombing ground. When I picked up my first bomb, my hand trembled. The sergeant looked at me with contempt and told me I was a damned coward. I admitted it.

This sergeant, a man who had done deeds deserving of the Victoria Cross, knew no physical fear. But not long afterwards he confided to me: "Neill, I hate to drill a squad when you are in it. I'm in a dead funk all the time." Surprised, I asked him why.

"Because you have an M.A. degree," he said—"and I murder the grammar."

We cannot tell from a study of psychology why one child is born with courage, but another is born with a shrinking soul. Prenatal conditions may have much to do with it. If a child is not wanted, it is quite possible that the mother transfers her own anxiety at the moment of birth to the unborn child. It may be that the unwanted child is born with a timid nature, with a character that fears life and desires to stay in the womb.

Although prenatal influences are beyond our power to deal with, it is certain that many children are made cowards by their early training. Cowardice of this kind is preventable.

A well-known psychoanalyst told me of the case of a young man. At the age of six, he was caught by his father expressing a mild sexual interest in a girl of seven. The father gave him a severe hiding. The hiding made the boy a coward for life. All through life he felt compelled to repeat that early experience—he kept looking for the beating, for punishment in one form or another. Thus, he could fall in love only with forbidden fruit, with women who were married or engaged; and he always experienced a great fear that the husband or lover would thrash him. The same fear was transferred to everything. The man was an unhappy, timid soul, always feeling inferior, always anticipating danger. He betrayed his timidity in little things. On a bright summer's day he would take a raincoat and an umbrella if he had to walk half a mile. He said *no* to life.

Punishing a child for an infantile sexual interest is a sure way to make that child a coward. Threatening hell fire is another sure way.

Freudians speak much about the *castration complex*. There certainly is a castration complex. At Summerhill we had a tiny chap who had been told that his penis would be cut off if he touched it. I find this to be a common fear in boys and girls. It is a fear that has terrible consequences, for a fear and a wish are never far apart. Often the fear of castration is a wish for castration—for castration as a punishment for masturbation, for castration as a means of getting rid of temptation.

To the frightened child sex *is* everything! Yes, the child uses sex as the chief peg on which to hang his fears. For he has been told that sex is wicked. The child with night terrors is often the child who is afraid of his sex thoughts. The devil may come and take him to hell, for is he not a sinful boy who deserves punishment? The bogeyman, the ghost, the goblin are only the devil in disguise. Fear comes from a guilty conscience. It is the ignorance of the parents that gives the child his guilty conscience.

A common form of fear in children originates from sleeping in their parents' room. A child of four will see and overhear what he cannot understand. Father becomes a bad man who abuses mother. Sadism in the child may result from this early misunderstanding and fears. The boy, identifying himself with father, later becomes a youth who associates sex with suffering. Out of fear he may do to his partner what he thought father did to mother.

Let me try to distinguish between anxiety and fear. Fear of a tiger is natural and healthy. Fear of being driven in a car by a bad driver is also natural and healthy. If we had no fear, we should all be run down by buses. But fear of a spider or a mouse or a ghost is unnatural and unhealthy. That kind of fear is merely anxiety. It is a phobia. A phobia is an irrational, exaggerated anxiety about something. In a phobia the object that excites terror is a comparatively harmless one. The object is only a symbol, although the anxiety it causes is real enough.

In Australia, fear of a spider is rational, for a spider can be death-dealing. In England and the United States, fear of a spider is irrational and therefore a phobia. The spider is a symbol for something else that one fears deep down. Thus, a child's fear of ghosts is a phobia. The ghosts symbolize something that the child is afraid of. It may be death, if he has had a God-fearing training. Or it might be his own sex impulses which his home has taught him to dread and repress as sinful.

I was once asked to see a schoolgirl who had a phobia of earthworms. I asked her to draw one and she drew a penis.

Then she told me of a soldier who used to exhibit himself to her on her way to school. This had frightened her. The fear was displaced to earthworms. But long before this phobia had developed, the girl had already been extremely interested in the origin of the phobia—*neurotically* interested. This neurotic interest had resulted from her education—or lack of it—in sex matters. The mystery and secrecy with which these matters were treated by her elders gave her an abnormal interest in them. Certainly she ought never to have been exposed to an exhibitionist, but a better education on sex matters would have enabled her to go through the ordeal without reacting neurotically to it, without a lasting anxiety about the male sexual organ.

Phobias often occur in quite young children. The son of a stern father may develop a phobia of horses or lions or policemen. The phobia becomes attached to these or any other obvious father symbols. Here again we see the awful danger of introducing fear of authority into a child's life.

The most potent influence for fear in a child's life is the idea of eternal damnation.

Often, in the street, I hear a mother say, "Stop that, Tommy! Here's the policeman coming!" A minor consequence of this kind of talk is that the child early discovers that his mother is a liar. The major evil consequence lies in the fact that to the child the policeman *is* the devil. He is the man who takes you away and locks you up in darkness. The child always attaches the fear to his worst transgressions. Thus the child who masturbates may show abnormal terror of a policeman when the latter catches him throwing stones. The fear is really a fear of a punishing god and a punishing devil.

Much fear is also due to thoughts of our past criminal acts. We have all killed people in fantasy. I believe that the child of five kills me in fantasy when I thwart his wishes.

Many a day, my pupils will joyfully cover me with water

pistols and cry, "Hands up! You're dead!", thus killing the authority symbol and relieving their fears. I have purposely acted in an authoritative manner on certain mornings in order to see the effect on the day's shooting. I have been killed many times on such occasions. After the fantasy, fear enters—*Suppose Neill were to die! I would be the guilty one, for I wished it.*

One of our girl pupils delighted in pulling other pupils under the water in swimming. Later, she developed a phobia about water. Although a good swimmer, she never went beyond her depth. What had happened was that in fantasy she had drowned so many rivals that she now feared poetic justice: *As a punishment for my thoughts, I'll be drowned.*

Little Albert used to get into a state of terror when he stood on the beach and watched his father swimming. He was afraid, because he had so often wished for his father's death. He was afraid of his guilty conscience. It is not so shocking to realize that a child kills people in fantasy when we realize that to a child death is simply getting the feared person out of the way.

I have seen adults who are unconsciously convinced that they were responsible for a father's death or a mother's death. This kind of fear is one that could be lessened if parents would refrain from rousing the child's hate, and consequent guilt, by storming and beating. And the hundreds of schools that still use physical punishment or other types of strict punishment are doing irreparable wrong to little children.

Many people believe down deep: *If children have nothing to fear, how can they be good?* Goodness that depends on fear of hell or fear of the policeman or fear of punishment is not goodness at all—it is simply cowardice. Goodness that depends on hope of reward or hope of praise or hope of heaven depends on bribery. Present-day morality makes children cowards, for it makes them *fear* life. And that is what the "goodness" of disciplined pupils really amounts to. Thousands of teachers do their work splendidly without having to introduce fear of punishment. The others are incompetent misfits who ought to be driven out of the profession.

Children may fear us and then accept our values. And what values we adults have! This week I bought a dog for seven dollars, tools for my turning lathe for ten dollars, and tobacco for eleven dollars. Although I reflect on and deplore our social evils, it did not occur to me to give all that money to the poor. Therefore, I don't preach to children that slums are an abomination unto the world. I used to—before I realized what a humbug I was about it.

The happiest homes I know are those in which the parents are frankly honest with their children without moralizing. Fear does not enter these homes. Father and son are pals. Love can thrive. In other homes, love is crushed by fear. Pretentious dignity and demanded respect hold love aloof. Compelled respect *always* implies fear.

Here, at Summerhill, children who fear their parents haunt the teacher's sitting room. The children of really free parents never come near us. The frightened children are always testing us out. One boy of eleven, whose father is a strict man, opens my door twenty times a day. He looks in, says nothing, and shuts the door again. I sometimes cry out to him, "No, I'm not dead yet." The boy has given me the love that his own father would not accept, and he has a fear that his ideal new father may disappear. Behind this fear is really hidden the wish that his unsatisfactory father would disappear.

It is much easier to live with children who fear you than with children who love you—that is, you have a quieter life. For when they fear you, children give you a wide berth. My wife and I and the Summerhill staff are loved by the children because we approve of them, and that is all they want. It is because they know that we will not give them disapproval that they enjoy being close to us.

I find hardly any fear of thunder among our small children. They will sleep out in small tents through the most violent storm. Nor do I find much fear of the dark. Sometimes a boy of eight will pitch his tent right at the far end of the field, and he will sleep there alone for nights. Freedom encourages fearlessness. I have often seen timid little chaps grow into sturdy, fearless youths. But to generalize would be wrong, for there are introverted children who never become brave. Some folks keep their ghosts for life.

If a child has been brought up without fear, and in spite of that still has fears, then it is possible that he has brought his fears with him into the world. And the chief difficulty in dealing with ghosts of this type is our ignorance of prenatal conditions. For no one knows whether or not a pregnant mother can convey her own fears to her unborn child.

On the other hand, a child most certainly acquires fears from the world around him. Today, even small children cannot help hearing about coming wars with their terrible atom bombs. It is only natural to associate fear with such things. But if there is no unconscious fear of sex and hell to compound the reality-fear of bombs, the fear of bombs will be a normal one—not a phobia, not a pervasive anxiety. Healthy, free children do not fear the future. They anticipate it gladly. Their children in their turn will face life without the sick fear of tomorrow.

It was Wilhelm Reich who pointed out that, in sudden fear, we all catch our breath for the moment, and that the child who lives in fear has a life of catching its breath . . . and holding it. The sign of a well-reared child is his free, uninhibited breathing. It shows that he is not afraid of life.

I have some important things to say to the father who is concerned about raising his child free from the crippling fear born of hate or distrust:

Never try to be the boss, the censor, the ogre in your home that your wife implies you to be when she says, "Wait till Daddy comes home!" Don't stand for that! It means that you will get the hate that should have gone to your wife at the moment.

And do not put yourself on a pedestal. If your boys ask you if you ever wet the bed or ever masturbated, tell them the truth —courageously and sincerely. If you are a boss, you will get their respect, but respect of the wrong kind—the kind mixed with fear. If you come down to their level and tell them how cowardly you were as a boy at school, you will get their true respect—the respect that contains love and understanding and a complete absence of fear.

It is comparatively easy for parents to rear a child without giving him complexes. The child must never be made afraid, must never be made to feel guilty. One cannot eliminate all reactions of fear: one may start suddenly if a door bangs. But you can eliminate the unhealthy fear that is superimposed on a child: fear of punishment, fear of an angry God, fear of an angry parent.

Inferiority and Fantasy

What gives a child a sense of inferiority? He sees grownups do things that he cannot do or that he is not permitted to do.

The phallus has much to do with inferiority. Small boys are often ashamed of the size of their phallus, girls often feel inferior because they lack a phallus. I am inclined to think that the importance of the phallus as a power symbol is mainly due to the mystery and taboo associated with it by moral education. Repressed thoughts about the phallus come out as fantasies. The mysterious thing that is guarded so carefully by mother and nurse takes on an exaggerated importance. We see this in stories of the wonderful power of the phallus. Aladdin rubs his lamp — masturbation — and all the pleasures of the world come to him. Similarly, children have fantasies which make excrement a matter of great importance.

A fantasy is always egoistic. It is a dream with the dreamer as hero or heroine. It is a story of the world as it ought to be. The world we adults enter through a whisky glass or through the pages of a novel or through the doors of a movie is the world that the child enters through the door of fantasy. Fantasy is always an escape from reality—a world of wish-fulfillment, a world with no boundaries. The lunatic goes there on a jaunt. But fantasies are also quite usual in the normal child. The world of fantasy is a more attractive world than the dream world. In dreams we have nightmares; but in fantasy, we have a certain control; and we fantasy only that which pleases the ego.

When I taught school in Germany, I had a ten-year-old Jewish girl as a pupil. The child had many fears. She was afraid of being late for class. On her first day she brought a huge bag of books to school, sat down at a table and began to work out dull sums of the old type: divide *4,563,207,867* by *4,379.* For three solid days, she worked at these sums. I asked her if she enjoyed doing sums like that, and got a timid *Ja* for answer.

On the fourth day, I looked at her as she continued her miserable counting. "Do you really like doing these sums?" I asked.

She burst into tears, and I quietly took the book and threw it to the other end of the room. "This is a free school," I said. "You can do exactly what you like." She began to look happier and whistled the whole day. She did no work; she just whistled.

Months later, I was out skiing, and walked through a wood. I heard a voice, and then I saw Slovia. She had taken off her skis, and was walking through the snow, laughing and talking. She was obviously taking the part of various actors. She did not see me as she passed by.

Next morning, I told her I had heard her talking in the wood. She got confused and rushed out of the room. In the afternoon, she hung near my door. At last she came in and said, "It is very difficult to tell you what I was doing, but I think I can tell you now."

It was a wonderful story. For years, she had lived in a dream village which she called Grunwald. She showed me maps of the village which she had made, and she even showed me plans of its houses. She had peopled the village with different characters; and, of course, she knew every one of them intimately. What I had heard had been a conversation between two boys, Hans and Helmuth.

It took me a few weeks to discover what was at the back of her fantasy. Slovia was an only child and had few playmates, so she had created a village of playmates. The key to the fantasy was given when she told me that Helmuth had been beaten severely by the gamekeeper for trespassing in the plantation. Later she mentioned that the plantation looked like her newly arrived pubic hairs. Then she revealed a true story of a man who had touched her sexually. I then understood that Helmuth represented the man who had trespassed in the plantation; and Helmuth also represented her hand in masturbation.

I decided to break the fantasy by telling her what lay behind it. For two days, she went about looking wretched. "I tried to go back to Grunwald last night," she said to me, weeping bitterly, "and I couldn't. You have spoiled the thing I liked best in life."

Ten days later, one of the teachers said to me, "What's happened to Slovia? She sings all day, and she is becoming pretty." It was true, she had become pretty. And she had suddenly begun to take an interest in everything. She even asked for lessons and learned them well. She took up painting and turned out some good sketches. In short, she got in touch with reality. Her horrible sex experience and her loneliness had forced her to seek in fantasy a new world where there was no temptation and were no bad men. Yet even in pleasant daydreams, Helmuth kept trespassing into her heaven.

Another girl used to daydream of herself as a fine actress. Crowds recalled her sixteen times.

Jim, a boy who flies into fits of temper, tells me fantasies of urinating and defecating. He is using sex in terms of power.

Another little boy of nine spins long fantasies about trains. He is always the driver, and usually the King and Queen (father and mother) are passengers.

Little Charlie imagines he has squadrons of airplanes and fleets of automobiles.

Jim talks about his rich uncle who has presented him with a Rolls Royce — boy's size — but gasoline-driven. Jim says he doesn't need a license to drive his new car. Once, I discovered that a few youngsters, prodded by Jim, were walking to a railway station four miles away. Jim's uncle, they were told, had sent the car to this station and they were to drive back. I thought of the bitter disappointment of walking four miles through mud to find a motorcar that existed only in Jim's imagination, and I decided to try to prevent the expedition. I pointed out that they would miss lunch. Jim, who appeared ill at ease, cried, "We don't want to miss our lunch." Their house mother suddenly thought of a compensation, and offered to take the boys to the movies. They hastily took off their raincoats. Jim was very much relieved, for of course he knew that the uncle who had presented him with the car was an uncle of fantasy.

Jim's fantasy had nothing to do with sex. Since his arrival at Summerhill, Jim had been impressing the other boys in this way. For days, a group of youngsters stood and watched the approaches to Lyme harbor. Jim had told them of another uncle of his who owned two ocean liners. The boys had persuaded Jim to write to this uncle and ask him to present them with a motorboat. They expected to see an ocean liner towing their boat into the harbor. Thus Jim found his superiority. He was a poor wee chap who was boarded out, and he compensated for his inferiority by fantasying.

To destroy all fantasies would be to make life a dull thing. Every act of creation must be preceded by a fantasy. Wren's fantasy must have built St. Paul's before a single stone was laid.

The dream worth keeping is the one that can be carried out in reality. The other kind—the flight fantasy—should be broken if possible. Such fantasies, if long pursued, keep the child back. In any school, the so-called dunces are usually those children who live most in fantasy. How can a boy have an interest in mathematics when he is expecting an uncle to send him a Rolls Royce?

I have sometimes had acrimonious discussions with mothers and fathers about reading and writing. A mother writes, "My boy must be able to fit into society. You must force him to learn to read." My reply is generally this: "Your child lives in a world of fantasy. It will take me possibly a year to break that world in two. To ask him to read now is to commit a crime against the child. Until he has lived out his interest in his fantasy world, he cannot possibly have a scrap of interest to give to reading."

Oh, yes, I could take the boy into my room and say sternly: "Put all this nonsense about uncles and motorcars out of your head. It is all a made-up story, and you know it. Tomorrow morning, you take a reading lesson or you'll know the reason why." That would be a crime. To break a child's fantasy before the child has something to put in its place is wrong. The best way is to encourage the child to talk about the fantasy. In nine cases out of ten, he will slowly lose interest in it. Only in some special case where a fantasy has persisted for years does one dare to rudely break the dream.

I have said that there must be something to put in place of the fantasy. To be at all healthy, every child and every adult should have at least one province in which he can be superior. In the classroom the methods of gaining superiority are two: (1) To be at the top of the class, and (2) to be able to lord it over the boy at the bottom of the class. The latter is the more enticing way of being superior; and thus an extraverted type of child easily finds superiority.

It is the introverted child who flees into fantasy to find his superiority. In the world of reality he has no superiority. He cannot fight; he does not excel at games; he cannot act, or sing, or dance. But in his own world of fantasy, he may be the heavyweight champion of the world. To find ego satisfaction is a vital necessity for every human being.

Destructiveness

Adults find it very hard to realize that young children have no regard for property. They do not destroy it deliberately—*they destroy it unconsciously.*

I once saw a normal, happy girl burning holes with a red-hot poker into the walnut mantelpiece in our staff room. When challenged, she started and seemed quite surprised. "I did it without thinking," she said, and she spoke truthfully. Her action was a symbolic one beyond the control of the conscious mind.

The fact is that adults are possessive about things of value and children are not. Any living together between children and adults must therefore result in conflict over material things. At Summerhill, the children will turn up the furnace five minutes before going up to bed. They will generously heap it with coals—for coals to them are only black rocks while to me they mean a bill of one thousand dollars a year. The children will leave electric lights on because they do not associate light with electricity bills.

Furniture to a child is practically nonexistent. So at Summerhill we buy old car seats and old bus seats. And in a month or two they look like wrecks. Every now and again at mealtime, some youngster waiting for his second helping will while away the time by twisting his fork almost into knots. This is usually done unconsciously or, at best, semiconsciously. And it isn't only school property that a child neglects or destroys: he leaves his new bicycle out in the rain after the newness has had a three weeks' vogue.

Children's destructiveness at the age of nine or ten is not

meant to be evil or antisocial. Things as personal property are simply not real to them as yet. When the flight into fantasy is on them, they take their sheets and blankets and make pirate ships in their rooms, and the sheets get black and the blankets get torn in the process. And what does a dirty sheet matter when you have hoisted the black flag and fired a broadside?

Really, any man or woman who tries to give children freedom should be a millionaire, for it is not fair that the natural carelessness of children should always be in conflict with the economic factor.

The argument of the disciplinarian who says that children must be *compelled* to respect property does not appeal to me, for it always means some sacrifice of childhood's play life. My view is that a child should arrive at a sense of value out of his own free choice. As children leave the stage of preadolescent indifference to property, they become respecters of property. When children have freedom to live out their indifference to property, they have little chance of ever becoming profiteers and exploiters.

Girls do not wreak as much destruction as boys. That is because their fantasy life does not demand pirate ships and gangster holdups. Yet to be fair to the boys, the state of the girls' sitting room is pretty bad. I am not convinced by the girls' explanation that the wreckage is all the result of scraps with the visiting boys.

Some years ago, we lined the children's bedrooms with beaverboard in order to keep the bedrooms warmer. Beaverboard is a kind of thick pasteboard; and a small child has only to see it to start picking holes in it. The beaverboard wall of the ping-pong room looked like Berlin after the bombardment. The boring of beaverboard is similar to nose boring: it is usually quite unconscious, and like other forms of destructiveness, it often has a hidden motive—often a creative meaning. If a boy needs a piece of metal for a boat keel, he will use a nail if he can find one. But if he cannot find a nail, he will use my expensive small tools if one of them happens to be about the right size. A chisel, like a nail, is only a chunk of metal to a child. A bright lad once used a very expensive whitewash brush for tarring a roof.

We have learned that children have entirely different values from adult values. If a school tries to uplift a child by hanging beautiful classical paintings on the walls and placing beautiful furniture in the rooms, it is beginning at the wrong end. Children are primitives; and until they ask for culture, they should live in as primitive and informal an environment as we can give them.

A number of years ago when we moved to our present house, we had the agony of seeing lads throwing knives at beautiful oak doors. We hastily bought two railway carriages and made them into a bungalow. There our primitives could chuck their knives as much as they wanted to. Yet, today, thirty-three years later the carriages are not in a bad state. They are inhabited by boys of from twelve to sixteen years of age. The majority of those boys have reached the stage of caring for comfort and decorations. Most of them keep their compartments beautifully tidy and clean. Others live in untidiness; these are mostly boys who have recently arrived from private schools.

You can always tell the ex-private school boys in Summerhill: they are the dirtiest, the most unwashed, and wear the greasiest clothes. It always takes time for them to live out their primitive drives, which had been merely suppressed at the private schools. It takes time for these boys to become genuinely social under freedom.

A workshop is the most troublesome department of a free school. In the very early days, the workshop was always open to the children, and as a result, every tool got lost or damaged.

A child of nine would use a fine chisel as a screwdriver. Or he would take a pair of pliers to mend his bike, and leave them lying on the path.

I then decided to have my own private workshop separated from the main workshop by a partition and locked door. But my conscience kept pricking me; I felt that I was being selfish and antisocial. At last, I knocked down the partition. In six months, there wasn't a good tool left in what had been my private section. One boy used up all the wire staples in making cotter pins for his motorcycle. Another tried to put my lathe in screw-cutting gear when it was running. Polished planishing hammers for brass and silver work were used for breaking bricks. Tools disappeared and were never found. Worst of all, the interest in crafts died out completely, for the older pupils said, "What's the good of going into the workshop? All the tools are rotten now." And rotten they were. Planes had teeth in their blades, while saws had none.

I proposed at a General School Meeting that my workshop be locked again. The motion was carried. But in showing visitors around, I had a feeling of shame when I had to unlock my workshop door each time. *What? Freedom and locked doors?* It looked bad indeed, and I decided to give the school an extra workshop which would remain open all the time. I had one fitted out with everything necessary—bench, vise, saws, chisels, planes, hammers, pliers, set squares, and so on.

One day, about four months later, I was showing a group of visitors around the school. When I unlocked my workshop, one of them said, "This doesn't look like freedom, does it?"

"Well, you see," I said hurriedly, "the children have *another* workshop which is open all day long. Come along, I'll show it to you." There was nothing left in it except the bench. Even the vise had gone. In what sundry corners of our twelve acres the chisels and hammers lay, I never knew.

The workshop situation continued to worry the staff. I was the most worried of all, because tools mean a great deal to me. I concluded that what was wrong was that the tools were used communally. "Now," I said to myself, "if we introduce the possessive element—if each child who really wants tools has his own kit of tools—things will be different."

I brought it up at a meeting, and the idea was well received. Next term, some of the older pupils brought their own kits of tools from home. They kept them in excellent condition and used them far more carefully than before.

Possibly it is the wide range of ages in Summerhill that causes most of the trouble. For certainly tools mean almost nothing to the very young boys and girls. Nowadays, our handiwork teacher keeps the workshop locked. I graciously allow a few senior pupils to use my shop when they want to. They do not abuse it, for they have arrived at the stage where giving tools the proper care is a conscious necessity for good work. They now also understand the difference between freedom and license.

Still, the locking of doors has increased recently at Summerhill. I brought the matter up one Saturday night at the meeting. "I don't like it," I said. "I took visitors round this morning and had to unlock the workshop, the laboratory, the pottery, and the theater. I propose that all public rooms be left open all day."

There was a storm of dissent. "The laboratory must be kept locked because of the poisons in there," said some of the children, "and since the pottery adjoins the laboratory, that has to be kept locked, too."

"We won't have the workshop left open. Look what happened to the tools last time!" said others.

"Well, then," I pleaded, "we can at least leave the theater open. Nobody will run away with the stage."

The playwrights, actors, actresses, stage manager, lighting man all rose at once. Said the lighting man, "You left it open this morning, and in the afternoon some idiot switched on all the lights and left them on—3,000 watts at 9 cents per watt!"

Another said, "The small kids take out the costumes and dress up in them."

The upshot was that my proposal to leave doors unlocked was supported by two hands—my own and that of a girl of seven. And I discovered later that she thought we were still voting on the previous motion, that children of seven be allowed to go to the movies. The children were learning out of their own experience that private property should be respected.

The sad truth is that we adults are more often concerned for the safety of materials than for the safety of children. A man's piano, his carpenter's tools, his clothes—a hundred things—have become part of himself. To see a plane being misused is to feel a personal hurt. This love for possessions is frequently greater than the love for children. Every *Let that alone!* is a preferring of the object to the child. The child is a nuisance because his wishes conflict with the egoistic wishes of the adult.

Three little boys once borrowed my expensive electric torch. They began to explore to see what was in it and ruined it. To say that I enjoyed their exploration would be to lie. I was annoyed in spite of the fact that I suspected the psychological meaning of that act of destruction: symbolically, father's torch represented father's phallus.

One of my daydreams is that I get a millionaire's son as a pupil. In my fantasy, I allow him to try all sorts of elaborate experiments—*at his father's expense!*—for to give a neurotic child freedom is an expensive business. As a steady diet, no healthy child wants to hammer nails into the television console.

This brings to mind a question that crops up everywhere I lecture. *What would you do if a boy started to hammer nails into the grand piano?* Nowadays I am so expert that I can often spot the person who is going to ask the question. She generally sits in the front seat and shakes her head disapprovingly at times during the lecture.

The best answer to the question is: *It doesn't matter what you do to a child if your attitude toward that child is right.* It doesn't matter if you take the child away from the piano, so long as you don't give the child a bad conscience about hammering nails. No harm is done by insisting on your individual rights, unless you introduce the moral judgment of right and wrong. It is the use of words like *naughty* or *bad* or *dirty* that does harm.

To return to the young hammerer. Of course, he ought to have wood to hammer nails into, instead of the piano. Every child has a right to the tools with which he can express himself. And the tools should be his very own. But bear in mind that he will not attach a dollar-and-cents value to them.

The constant destructiveness of the problem child is something quite different from the normal child's acts of destruction. The latter usually are not aroused by hate or anxiety: they are creative fantasy-acts not meant in a spiteful way.

Real destructiveness means hate in action. Symbolically, it means murder. It is not confined to problem children. People whose houses were occupied by the military during the war learned that soldiers are much more destructive than children. This is natural, for their job is destruction.

Creation equals life: destruction equals death. The destructive problem child is anti-life.

Destructiveness in anxious children has many components. One of them can be jealousy of a brother or sister, better loved than the destroyer feels himself to be. Another can be rebellion against all limiting authority. And still another component can be simple curiosity to see what's inside an object.

The main factor that should concern us is not the actual destruction of the object but the repressed hate expressed by the destruction—the hate that, given the circumstances, will make a sadist out of the child.

This is a very vital question. It deals with the sickness of a world where hate flourishes from the nursery to the grave. There is, of course, much love in the world. If there were not, we could only despair for humanity. Every parent and every educator should seriously try to discover that love in himself.

Lying

If your child lies, either he is afraid of you or he is copying you. Lying parents will have lying children. If you want the truth from your child, do not lie to him. This statement is not a moral one, for we all lie at times. Sometimes we lie to keep from hurting someone else's feelings, and of course we lie about ourselves when we are accused of egoism or bumptiousness. Instead of saying, "Mommy has a headache; be quiet," it is much better and more honest to shout "Stop that damned row!" But you can only say that with impunity if your children do not fear you.

Parents lie sometimes in order to preserve their dignity. "Daddy, you could fight six men, couldn't you?" It takes some courage to reply, "No, my son, with my big stomach and my flabby muscles, I couldn't fight a midget."

How many fathers will confess to their children that they fear thunder or fear policemen? Hardly a man is big enough not to flinch from letting his children know that he was called "Snuffles" at school.

The family lie has two motives: to keep the child well-behaved, and to impress the child with parental perfection. How many fathers and teachers would answer truthfully a child's questions: *Were you ever drunk? Did you ever swear?* It is this fear of children that makes adults hypocrites.

As a small boy, I could not forgive my father for jumping over a wall to escape a wild bull. The children in their fantasies make us heroes and knights, and we try to live up to it. But one day, we are found out. One day, a child sees clearly that his parents and teachers have been liars and deceivers.

Possibly in every young life comes a period when the parents are criticized and despised as out-of-date. This period follows the finding out of the parents by the child. The contempt is simply a contempt for the wished-for parents of the child's fantasies. The contrast between the wonderful dream parents and the real weak parents is too great. Later, the child returns to his parents with sympathy and understanding, but without illusions. And yet all this misunderstanding would be unnecessary if parents told the truth about themselves in the first place.

The main difficulty in telling children the truth is this: we all fail to tell ourselves the truth. We lie to ourselves, and we lie to our neighbors. Every autobiography ever written is a lie. We lie because we have been taught to live up to an unreachable standard of morality. It was our early training that gave us the skeleton that we ever after try to hide.

The adult who lies to children—lies even by indirect means —is he or she who has no real understanding of the child. Hence our whole educational system is full of lies. Our schools hand on the lie that obedience and industry are virtues, that history and French are education.

There is not a confirmed or habitual liar among my pupils. When they first come to Summerhill, they lie because they fear to tell the truth. When they find that the school is a school without a policeman, they find no use for lies. Most lying on the part of children is prompted by fear; and when fear is absent, lying diminishes. I cannot say it disappears entirely. A boy will tell you he has broken a window, but he will not tell you he has raided the icebox or stolen a tool. The complete absence of lying would be too much to hope for.

Freedom will not do away with fantasy lies in children. Too often parents make a mountain out of this agreeable molehill. When little Jimmy came to me saying that his Daddy had sent him a real Rolls Bentley I said to him, "I know. I saw it at the front door. Terrific car."

"Go on," he said, "You know I was really only kidding."

Now it may seem paradoxical and illogical, but I make a distinction between lying and being dishonest. You can be honest and yet a liar—that is, you can be honest about the big things in life although sometimes dishonest about the lesser things. Thus many of our lies are meant to save others pain. Truthtelling would become an evil if it impelled me to write, "Dear Sir, your letter was so long and dull that I could not be bothered reading it all." Or if it forced you to say to a would-be musician: "Thank you for playing, but you murdered that Etude." Adults' lying is generally altruistic, but children's lying is always local and personal. The best way to make a child a liar for life is to insist that he speak the truth and nothing but the truth.

I grant it is very hard to be always truthful, but when one makes a decision not to lie to a child or in front of a child, one finds it easier than one expected. The only good permissible lie is the kind of lie one has to tell when life is in danger— for example, when a seriously ill child is not told of his mother's death.

Most of our mechanical etiquette is a living lie. We say "Thank you" when we do not mean it; we doff our hats to women we do not respect.

Speaking a lie is a minor frailty; living a lie is a major calamity. It is the parent who lives a lie who is really dangerous. "I have asked from my son only one thing—absolute truth at all times," said the father of a thieving son of sixteen. That man hated his wife and was hated by her in return, although the fact was disguised under a mask of *darlings* and *dearests*. The son dimly sensed that something was very wrong with his home. What possible chance has the son of such a man to grow up being anything but conventionally dishonest when the home itself is a glaring lie? The boy's stealing was his pathetic way of finding the love that was lacking in the home.

Indeed, a child may lie in imitation of parental falsehood. It is impossible for a child to be truthful in a home where the father and mother no longer love each other. The wretched pretense that the poor couple have to keep up cannot deceive the child. He is then driven into an unreal fantasy world of make-believe. Remember that children *feel* when they do not know.

The churches perpetuate the lie that man is born in sin and that he requires redemption. The law furthers the lie that humanity can be bettered by hate in the form of punishment. The doctors and drug firms keep up the lie that health depends on loading oneself with inorganic drugs.

In a society full of lies, the parent finds it most difficult to be honest. He tells his child, "If you masturbate, you'll go mad." In all parental lying, there is incredible ignorance of the damage done to the child.

I hold that the parent does not need to lie; moreover, he *dare* not lie. Many homes exist without lying, and it is from such homes that come clear-eyed, sincere children. A parent can answer any and every question with truth, from where babies come from to telling mother's age.

I have never consciously told a lie to my pupils in thirty-eight years, and indeed never had any desire to. But that is not quite correct, for I told a big lie one term. A girl, whose unhappy history I knew, stole a pound. The theft committee—three boys—saw her spend money on ice cream and cigarettes, and they cross-examined her. "I got the pound from Neill," she told them, and they brought her to me, asking, "Did you give Liz a quid?" Hastily sensing the situation, I replied blandly, "Why, yes, I did." Had I given her away, I knew that forever afterward she would have no trust in me. Her symbolic stealing of love in the form of money would have received another hostile setback. I had to prove that I was on her side all the way. I know that if her home had been honest and free, such a situation would never have arisen. I lied with a purpose—a *curative* purpose—but in all other circumstances, I dare not lie.

Children, when free, do not lie very much. Our village policeman, calling one day, was much astonished when a boy came into my office saying, "Hi, Neill, I've broken a lounge window." Children lie mostly to protect themselves. Lying flourishes in homes where fear flourishes. Abolish fear and the lying will decay.

There is, however, a type of lie that has no fear basis—the lie due to fantasy. "Mommy, I saw a dog as big as a cow" is on the same level as the angler's lie about the one that got away. In these cases, the lie enhances the personality of the liar. The obvious way to react to such lies is to enter into the spirit of the game. So that when Billy tells me his daddy has a Rolls Royce, I say, "I know. Beauty, isn't it. Can you drive it?" I question if this romantic lying would exist among children who had been self-regulated from birth. I don't think they would need to overcompensate for their inferiority by making up tall stories.

An illegitimate child does not know he is born out of wedlock, yet he feels that he is different from other children. Not, of course, if he knows the truth, and is among people who don't care whether or not he was born in wedlock. It is because feeling is so much more important than knowing that ignorant parents do so much harm with their lies and prohibitions. It is the heart of the child that is damaged, rather than the head. *But heads never cause neurosis; only hearts do.*

Parents must tell adopted children the truth about their adoption. A stepmother who lets a child of the first marriage believe that he is her own son is looking for trouble, and in most cases will get it. I have seen some bad traumas in later life when adolescents discovered hidden truths. There are always a few hateful people around who will gladly tell youth spiteful truths.

Armor your children against all spiteful busybodies by making up your mind never to lie to any child—your own or the children of anyone else. There is no other way but the way of absolute truth for a child. If daddy is an ex-convict, sonny should know it. If mommy was a barmaid, daughter should be told.

The truth becomes awkward when the question is, "Mommy, which of us kids do you love best?" The universal and often untrue answer is the sweet "I love all of you the same, darling." What the answer should be, I do not know. Perhaps the lie is justified here, for the shattering "I love Tommy best" would have disastrous results.

The parent who is honest about sex will not be dishonest about other things. Lies about the policeman coming to punish naughty children, lies that smoking stops growth, lies about Mommy having a headache instead of Mommy having a period, are rife in a million homes.

Recently, a woman teacher left Summerhill to teach in a London kindergarten. Her little pupils asked her where babies came from. Next morning, half a dozen furious mothers came to the school, calling her a "dirty-minded bitch" and demanding that she be fired.

A child brought up in freedom will not consciously lie because there is no need to. He will not lie to protect himself because of fear of retribution. But he will engage in fantasy lying—telling tall stories of things that never happened.

As to lying through fear, I see a new generation that will have no skeletons to hide. It will be frank and honest about everything. It will not require the word "lie" in its vocabulary. Lying is always cowardice, and cowardice is the result of ignorance.

Responsibility

In many homes, the child's ego is suppressed because the parents treat the child as a perpetual infant. I have known girls of fourteen who were not trusted by their parents to light a fire. Parents, with the best of intention, keep back responsibility from the child.

"You must take your sweater, dear; I am sure it is going to rain."

"Now don't go near the railway tracks."

"Have you washed your face?"

Once, when a new pupil came to Summerhill, her mother told me that the girl was very dirty in her habits; that she had to tell her ten times a day to wash. From the day following her arrival, that child took a cold bath every morning, and at least two hot ones a week. She was always clean in face and hands. Her lack of cleanliness at home—which may have existed only in the mother's imagination—was due to her being treated as a baby.

Children should be allowed almost infinite responsibility. Montessori-trained infants carry tureens full of hot soup. One of our youngest pupils, aged seven, uses all sorts of tools: chisels, axes, saws, knives. I cut my fingers oftener than he does.

Duty should not be confused with responsibility. A sense of duty should be acquired later in life, if at all. The word *duty* has so many sinister associations. I think of women who have missed life and love because they felt compelled by a sense of duty to stay and look after elderly parents. I think of the married couples who have long since ceased to love each other but go on living together miserably because of their sense of duty. Many a child away at boarding school or at summer camp feels the duty to write home is irksome, especially when he must write the letter on Sunday afternoon.

It is a fallacy that responsibility should be reckoned by age, a fallacy that puts the lives of youth in the hands of the feeble old men whom we call statesmen, who might better be described as staticmen. It is this fallacy that assumes that every member of a family is the protector and guide of the ones immediately younger than himself. It is hard for parents to realize that their son of six is not a reasonable, logical being who will understand such a sentence as, "You are older than Tommy, and at your age you should know that he isn't allowed to run out on the road."

A child should not be asked to face responsibilities for which he is not ready, nor be saddled with decisions he is not yet old enough to make. The watchword must be common sense.

At Summerhill we do not ask our five-year-olds whether or not they want fireguards. We do not ask a six-year-old to decide whether or not he should go outdoors when he is running a temperature. Nor do we ask a rundown child whether or not he should go to bed when he is overtired. One does not seek a child's permission to give him prescribed remedies when he is sick.

But the imposition of authority—necessary authority—on a child does not in any way conflict with the idea that a child should be given just about as much responsibility as he can accept at his particular age. In determining the amount of responsibility that a parent should give his child, the parent must always consult his inner soul. He must first examine himself.

Parents who refuse to let children select their own clothes, for example, are generally motivated by the idea that the child might choose clothes which would not do credit to the parents' social standing.

Parents who censor their child's reading, movie-going, or friends are, generally speaking, trying to impose their own ideas on the child by pressure. Such parents merely rationalize that they know what is best, whereas their deep motivation is likely to be one of exercising authoritarian power.

By and large, parents should bestow as much responsibility as they can upon a child, with due regard for his physical safety. Only in this way will a parent develop the child's self-assurance.

Obedience and Discipline

An impious question comes up: Why should a child obey? My answer is: He must obey to satisfy the adult's desire for power. Otherwise, why should a child obey?

"Well," you say, "he may get his feet wet if he disobeys the command to put on shoes; he may even fall over the cliff if he disobeys his father's shout." Yes, of course, the child should obey when it is a matter of life and death. But how often is a child punished for disobeying in matters of life and death? Seldom, if ever! He is generally hugged with a "My precious! Thank God, you're safe!" It is for *small things* that a child is usually punished.

Now it is possible to run a house where obedience is not required. If I say to a child, "Get your books and take a lesson in English," he may refuse if he is not interested in English. His disobedience merely expresses his own desires, which obviously do not intrude on or hurt anyone else. But if I say, "The center part of the garden is planted; no one is to run over it!" all the children accept what I say in much the same way that they accept Derrick's command, "Nobody is to use my ball unless they ask me first." For obedience should be a matter of give and take. Occasionally, at Summerhill, there is disobedience of a law passed in the General School Meeting. Then the children may themselves take action. However, in the main, Summerhill runs along without any authority or any obedience. Each individual is free to do what he likes *as long as he is not trespassing on the freedom of others.* And this is a realizable aim in any community.

Under self-regulation, there is no authority in the home. This means that there is no loud voice that declaims, "I say it! You must obey." In actual practice there is, of course, authority. Such authority might be called protection, care, adult responsibility. Such authority sometimes demands obedience but at other times gives obedience. Thus I can say to my daughter, "You can't bring that mud and water into our parlor." That's no more than her saying to me, "Get out of my room, Daddy. I don't want you here now," a wish that I, of course, obey without a word.

Akin to punishment is the parental demand that a child should not bite off more than it can chew. Literally—for often a child's eye is bigger than his stomach and he will demand a plateful that he cannot consume. To force a child to finish what is on his plate is wrong. Good parenthood is the power of identifying oneself with a child, understanding his motives, realizing his limitations, without harboring ulterior motives or resentment.

One mother wrote me that she wanted her daughter to obey her. I was teaching her daughter to obey *herself*. The mother finds her disobedient, but I find her *always* obedient. Five minutes ago, she came into my room to argue about dogs and their training. "Buzz off," I said, "I'm busy writing." And she went out—without a word.

Obedience should be social courtesy. Adults should have no right to the obedience of children. It must come from within—not be imposed from without.

Discipline is a means to an end. The discipline of an army is aimed at making for efficiency in fighting. All such discipline subordinates the individual to the cause. In disciplined countries life is cheap.

There is, however, another discipline. In an orchestra, the first violinist obeys the conductor because he is as keen on a good performance as the conductor is. The private who jumps to attention does not, as a rule, care about the efficiency of the army.

Every army is ruled mostly by fear, and the soldier knows that if he disobeys he will be punished. School discipline can be of the orchestra type when teachers are good. Too often it is of the army type. The same applies to the home. A happy home is like an orchestra and enjoys the same kind of team spirit. A miserable home is like a barracks that is ruled by hate and discipline.

The odd thing is that homes with team-spirit discipline often tolerate a school with army discipline. Boys are beaten by teachers—boys who are never beaten at home. A visitor from an older and wiser planet would consider the parents of this country morons if he were told that in some elementary schools, even today, small children are punished for mistakes in addition or in spelling. When humane parents protest against the beating discipline of the school and go to court about it, in most cases the law takes the side of the punishing teacher.

Parents could abolish corporal punishment tomorrow—if they wanted to. Apparently the majority do not want to. The system suits them. It disciplines their boys and girls. The hate of the child is cleverly directed to the punishing teacher and not to the parents who hire him to do the dirty work. The system suits these parents because they themselves were never allowed to live and love. They, too, were made slaves to group discipline, and the poor souls cannot visualize freedom.

It is true that there must be some discipline in the home. Generally, it is the type of discipline that safeguards the individual rights of each member of the family. For example, I do not allow my daughter, Zoë, to play with my typewriter. But in a happy family this kind of discipline usually looks after itself. Life is a pleasant give and take. Parents and children are chums, co-workers.

In the unhappy home, discipline is used as a weapon of hate, and obedience becomes a virtue. Children are chattels, things owned, and they must be a credit to their owners. I find that the parent who worries most about Billy's learning to read and write is one who feels a failure in life because of lack of educational attainment.

It is the self-disapproving parent who believes in strict discipline. The jovial man-about-town with a stock of obscene stories will sternly reprove his son for talking about excrement. The untruthful mother will spank her child for lying. I have seen a man, with pipe in mouth, whipping his son for smoking. I have heard a man say as he hit his son of twelve, "I'll teach you to swear, you little bastard." When I remonstrated, he said glibly, "It's different when I curse. He's just a kid."

Strict discipline in the home is always a projection of self-hate. The adult has striven for perfection in his own life, has failed miserably to reach it, and now attempts to find it in his children. And all because he cannot love. All because he fears pleasure as the very devil. That, of course, is why man *invented* the Devil—the fellow who has all the best tunes, who loves life and joy and sex. The aim of perfection is to conquer the Devil. And from this aim derive mysticism and irrationalism, religion and asceticism. From this derives, too, the crucifixion of the flesh in the form of beating and sexual abstinence and impotency.

It might justly be said that strict home discipline aims at castration in its widest sense, castration of life itself. No obedient child can ever become a free man or woman. No child punished for masturbation can ever be fully orgastically potent.

I have said that the parent wants the child to become what he or she has failed to become. There is more to it than that: every repressed parent is at the same time determined that his child shall not get more out of life than he, the parent, got. Unalive parents won't allow children to be alive. And such a parent always has an exaggerated fear of the future. Discipline, he thinks, will save his children. This same lack of confidence in his inner self makes him postulate an outside God who will *compel* goodness and truth. Discipline is thus a branch of religion.

The main difference between Summerhill and the typical school is that at Summerhill we have faith in the child's personality. We know that if Tommy wants to be a doctor, he will voluntarily study to pass the entrance examinations. The disciplined school is sure that Tommy will never be a doctor unless he is beaten or pressured or forced to study at prescribed hours.

I grant that in most cases it is easier to eliminate discipline from the school than from the home. In Summerhill, when a child of seven makes himself a social nuisance, the whole community expresses its disapproval. Since social approval is something that everyone desires, the child learns to behave well. No discipline is necessary.

In the home, where so many emotional factors and other circumstances enter, things are not so easy. The harassed housewife, cooking the dinner, cannot treat her fractious child with social disapproval. Nor can the tired father when he finds his new seedbed trampled upon. What I wish to emphasize is that *in a home where the child has had self-regulation from the start, ordinary demands for discipline do not arise!*

Some years ago, I visited my friend Wilhelm Reich in Maine. His son, Peter, was three years old. The lake at the doorstep was deep. Reich and his wife simply told Peter that he should not go near the water. Having had no hateful training and therefore having trust in his parents, Peter did not go near the water. The parents *knew* that they need not worry. Parents who discipline with fear and authority would have lived on that lakeshore with their nerves on edge. Children are so accustomed to being lied to that when mother says that water is dangerous, they simply don't believe her. They have a defiant wish to go to the water.

The disciplined child will express his hate of authority by annoying his parents. Indeed, much childish misbehavior is a visible proof of wrong treatment. The average child accepts the parental voice of knowledge—if there is love in the home. If there is hate in the home, he accepts nothing. Or he accepts things negatively· he is destructive and insolent and dishonest.

Children are wise. They will react to love with love, and will react to hate with hate. They will respond easily to discipline of the team type. I aver that badness is not basic in human nature any more than it is basic in rabbit nature or lion nature. Chain a dog and a good dog becomes a bad dog. Discipline a child and a good social child becomes a bad, insincere hater. Sad to say, most people are sure that a bad boy wants to be bad; they believe that with the help of God or a big stick, the child has the power of choosing to be good. And if he refuses to exercise this power, then they'll damn well see to it that he suffers for his contumaciousness.

In a way, the old school spirit symbolizes all that discipline stands for. The principal of a large boys' school said to me not long ago when I asked him what sort of boys he had, "The sort that goes out with neither ideas nor ideals. They would join up as cannon fodder in any war, never stopping to consider what the war was about and why they were fighting."

I haven't hit a child for nearly forty years. Yet as a young teacher, I used the strap vigorously without ever stopping to think about it. I never beat a child now because I have become aware of the dangers in beating and I am quite aware of the hate behind the beating.

At Summerhill we treat children as equals. By and large, we respect the individuality and personality of a child just as we would respect the individuality and personality of an adult, knowing that the child is different from an adult. We adults do not demand that adult Uncle Bill must clear his plate when he dislikes carrots, or that father must wash his hands before he sits down to a meal. By continually correcting children, we make them feel inferior. We injure their natural dignity. It is all a question of relative values. In heaven's name, what does it really matter if Tommy sits down to a meal with unwashed hands?

Children brought up under the wrong type of discipline live one lifelong lie. They never dare be themselves. They become slaves to established futile customs and manners. They accept their silly Sunday clothes without question. For the mainspring of discipline is fear of censure. Punishment from their playfellows does not involve fear. But when an adult punishes, fear comes automatically. For the adult is big and strong and awe-inspiring. Most important of all, he is a symbol of the feared father or feared mother.

For thirty-eight years, I have seen nasty, cheeky, hateful children come to the freedom of Summerhill. In every case, a gradual change took place. In time, these spoiled children have become happy, social, sincere, and friendly children.

The future of humanity rests with the new parents. If they ruin the life force in their children by arbitrary authority, crime and war and misery will go on flourishing. If they carry on in the footsteps of their disciplinary parents, they will lose the love of their children. Fo no one can love what he fears.

Neurosis begins with parental discipline—which is the very opposite of parental love. You cannot have a good humanity by treating it with hate and punishment and suppression. The only way is the way of love.

A loving environment, without parental discipline, will take care of most of the troubles of childhood. This is what I want parents to realize. If their children are given an environment of love and approval in the home, nastiness, hate, and destructiveness will never arise.

Rewards and Punishment

The danger in rewarding a child is not as extreme as that of punishing him, but the undermining of the child's morale through the giving of rewards is more subtle. Rewards are superfluous and negative. To offer a prize for doing a deed is tantamount to declaring that the deed is not worth doing for its own sake.

No artist ever works for a monetary reward only. One of his rewards is the joy of creating. Moreover, rewards support the worst feature of the competitive system. To get the better of the other man is a damnable objective.

Giving rewards has a bad psychological effect on children because it arouses jealousies. A boy's dislike of a younger brother often dates from mother's remark, "Your little brother can do it better than you can." To the child, mother's remark is a reward given to brother for being better than he is.

When we consider a child's natural interest in things, we begin to realize the dangers of both rewards and punishment. Rewards and punishment tend to pressure a child into interest. But true interest is the life force of the whole personality, and such interest is completely spontaneous. It is possible to compel attention, for attention is an act of consciousness. It is possible to be attentive to an outline on the blackboard and at the same time to be interested in pirates. Though one can compel attention, one cannot compel interest. No man can force me to be interested in, say, collecting stamps; nor can I compel myself to be interested in stamps. Yet both rewards and punishment attempt to compel interest.

I have a large garden. A group of little boys and girls would be of great assistance during weeding time. To order them to help me with my work is quite possible. But these children of eight, nine, and ten years of age have formed no opinion of their own on the necessity of weeding. They are not interested in weeding.

I once approached a group of small boys. "Anyone want to help me do some weeding?" I asked. They all refused.

I asked why. The answers came: "Too dull!" "Let them grow." "Too busy with this crossword puzzle." "Hate gardening."

I, too, find weeding dull. I, too, like to tackle a crossword puzzle. To be quite fair to those youngsters, of what concern is the weeding to them? It is *my* garden. *I* get the pride in seeing the peas come through the soil. *I* save money on vegetable bills. In short, the garden touches my self-interest. I cannot compel an interest in the children, when the interest does not originate in them. The only possible way would be for me to hire the children at so much an hour. Then, they and I would be on the same basis: I would be interested in my garden, and they would be interested in making some extra money.

Interest is, at root, always egoistic. Maud, aged fourteen, often helps me in the garden, although she declares that she hates gardening. But she does not hate *me*. She weeds because she wants to be with me. This serves her self-interest for the moment.

When Derrick, who also dislikes weeding, volunteers to help me, I know he is going to renew his request for a pocket knife of mine that he covets. That is his only interest in the matter.

A reward should, for the most part, be subjective: self-satisfaction in the work accomplished. One thinks of the ungratifying jobs of the world: digging coal, fitting nut No. 50 to bolt No. 51, digging drains, adding figures. The world is full of jobs that hold no intrinsic interest or pleasure. We seem to be adapting our schools to this dullness in life. By compelling our students' attention to subjects which hold no interest for them, we, in effect, condition them for jobs they will not enjoy.

If Mary learns to read or count, it should be because of her interest in these subjects—not because of the new bicycle she will get for excellence in study or because Mother will be pleased.

One mother told her son that if he stopped sucking his thumb, she would give him a radio set. What an unfair conflict to give any child! Thumb-sucking is an unconscious act, beyond the control of will. The child may make a brave, conscious effort to stop the habit. But like the compulsive masturbator, he will fail again and again, and thereby acquire a mounting load of guilt and misery.

Parental fear of the future is dangerous when such fear expresses itself in suggestions that approach bribery: "When you learn to read, darling, Daddy will buy you a scooter." That way leads to a ready acceptance of our greedy, profit-seeking civilization. I am glad to say that I have seen more than one child prefer illiteracy to a shiny, new bicycle.

A variant of this form of bribery is the declaration that seeks to touch off the child's emotions: "Mommy will be very unhappy if you are always at the bottom of the class." Both methods of bribery bypass the child's genuine interests.

I have equally strong feelings about getting children to do our jobs. If we want a child to work for us, we ought to pay him according to his ability. No child wants to collect bricks for me just because I've decided to rebuild a broken wall. But if I offer a few cents a barrow load, a boy may help willingly, for then I've enlisted his self-interest. But I do not like the idea of making a child's weekly pocket money depend on his doing certain chores. Parents should give without seeking anything in return.

Punishment can never be dealt out with justice, for no man can be just. Justice implies complete understanding. Judges are no more moral than garbage collectors, nor are they less free of prejudice. A judge who is a strong conservative and a militarist could find it difficult to be just to an antimilitarist arrested for crying "Down with the Army."

Consciously or unconsciously, the teacher who is cruel to a child who has committed a sexual offense is almost certain to have deep feelings of guilt toward sex. In a law court, a judge with unconscious homosexual leanings would likely be very severe in sentencing a prisoner charged with homosexual practices.

We cannot be just because we do not know ourselves, and do not recognize our own repressed strivings. This is tragically unfair to the children. An adult can never educate beyond his own complexes. If we ourselves are bound by repressed fears, we cannot make our children free. All we do is to bestow upon our children our own complexes.

If we try to understand ourselves, we find it difficult to punish a child on whom we are venting the anger that belongs to something else. Years ago, in the old days, I whacked boys again and again because I was worried—the inspector was coming, or I had had a quarrel with a friend. Or any other old excuse would serve me in place of self-understanding, of knowing what I was really angry about. Today, I know from experience that punishment is unnecessary. I never punish a child, never have any temptation to punish a child.

Recently I said to a new pupil, a boy who was being antisocial, "You are pulling all these silly tricks merely to get me to whack you, for your life has been one long whacking. But you are wasting your time. I won't punish you, whatever you do." He gave up being destructive. He no longer needed to feel hateful.

Punishment is always an act of hate. In the act of punishing, the teacher or parent is hating the child—and the child realizes it. The apparent remorse or tender love that a spanked child shows toward his parent is not real love. What the spanked child really feels is hatred which he must disguise in order not to feel guilty. For the spanking has driven the child into fantasy! *I wish my father would drop dead.* The fantasy immediately brings guilt—*I wanted my father to die! What a sinner I am.* And the remorse drives the child to father's knee in seeming tenderness. But underneath, the hatred is already there—and to stay.

What is worse, punishment always forms a vicious circle. Spanking is vented hatred, and each spanking is bound to arouse more and more hatred in the child. Then as his increased hatred is expressed in still worse behavior, more spankings are applied. And these second-round spankings reap added dividends of hatred in the child. The result is a bad-mannered, sulky, destructive little hater, so inured to punishment that he sins in order to trigger some sort of emotional response from his parents. For even a hateful emotional response will do when there is no love emotion. And so the child is beaten—and he repents. But the next morning he begins the same old cycle again.

So far as I have observed, the self-regulated child does not need any punishment and he does not go through this hate cycle. He is never punished and he does not need to behave badly. He has no use for lying and for breaking things. His body has never been called filthy or wicked. He has not needed to rebel against authority or to fear his parents. Tantrums he will usually have, but they will be short-lived and not tend toward neurosis.

True, there is difficulty in deciding what is and what is not punishment. One day, a boy borrowed my best saw. The next day I found it lying in the rain. I told him that I should not lend him that saw again. That was not punishment, for punishment always involves the idea of morality. Leaving the saw out in the rain was bad for the saw, but the act was not an immoral one. It is important for a child to learn that one cannot borrow someone else's tools and spoil them, or damage someone else's property or someone else's person. For to let a child have his own way, or do what he wants to *at another's expense,* is bad for the child. It creates a spoiled child, and the spoiled child is a bad citizen.

Some time ago, a little boy came to us from a school where he had terrorized everyone by throwing things about and even threatening murder. He tried the same game with me. I soon concluded that he was using his temper for the purpose of alarming people and thus getting attention.

One day, on entering the playroom I found the children all clustered together at one end of the room. At the other end stood the little terror with a hammer in his hand. He was threatening to hit anyone who approached him.

"Cut it out, my boy," I said sharply. "We aren't afraid of you."

He dropped the hammer and rushed at me. He bit and kicked me.

"Every time you hit or bite me," I said quietly, "I'll hit you back." And I did. Very soon he gave up the contest and rushed from the room.

This was not punishment. It was a necessary lesson: learning that one cannot go about hurting others for his own gratification.

Punishment in most homes is punishment for disobedience. In schools, too, disobedience and insolence are looked upon as bad crimes. When I was a young teacher and in the habit of spanking children, as most teachers in Britain were allowed to do, I always was most angry at the boy who had disobeyed me. My little dignity was wounded. I was the tin god of the classroom, just as Daddy is the tin god of the home. To punish for disobedience is to identify oneself with the omnipotent Almighty: *Thou shalt have no other Gods.*

Later on, when I taught in Germany and Austria, I was always ashamed when teachers asked me if corporal punishment was used in Britain. In Germany, a teacher who strikes a pupil is tried for assault, and generally punished. The flogging and strapping in British schools is one of our greatest disgraces.

A doctor in one of our large cities said to me once, "There is a brute of a teacher at the head of one of our schools here, who beats the children cruelly. I often have nervous children brought to me because of him, but I can do nothing. He has public opinion and the law on his side."

Not too long ago, the papers carried the story of a case in which a judge told two erring brothers that if they had only had a few good hidings, they would never have appeared in court. As the evidence unfolded, it developed that the two boys had been beaten almost nightly by their father.

Solomon with his rod theory has done more harm than his proverbs have done good. No man with any power of introspection could beat a child, or could even have the wish to beat a child.

To repeat: hitting a child gives him fear *only when it is associated with a moral idea, with the idea of wrong*. If a street urchin knocked off my hat with a lump of clay and I caught him and gave him a swat on the ear, my reaction would be considered by the boy to be a natural one. No harm would have been done to the boy's soul. But if I went to the principal of his school and demanded punishment for the culprit, the fear introduced by the punishment would be a bad thing for the child. The affair would at once become an affair of morals and of punishment. The child would feel that he had committed a crime.

The ensuing scene can easily be imagined! I stand there with my muddy hat. The principal sits and fixes the boy with a baleful eye. The boy stands with lowered head. He is overawed by the dignity of his accusers. Running him down on the street, I had been his equal. I had no dignity after my hat had been

knocked off. I was just another guy. The boy had learned a nec‑
essary lesson of life—the lesson that if you hit a guy he'll get an‑
gry and sock you back.

Punishment has nothing to do with hot temper. Punishment
is cold and judicial. Punishment is highly moral. Punishment
avows that it is wholly for the culprit's good. (In the case of
capital punishment, it is for society's good.) Punishment is an
act in which man identifies himself with God and sits in moral
judgment.

Many parents live up to the idea that since God rewards and
punishes, they too should reward and punish their children.
These parents honestly try to be just, and they often convince
themselves that they are punishing the child for his own good.
This hurts me more than it hurts you is not so much a lie as it is
a pious self-deception.

One must remember that religion and morality make *punish‑
ment* a quasi-attractive institution. For punishment salves the
conscience. "I have paid the price!" says the sinner.

At question time in my lectures, an old-timer often stands up
and says, "My father used his slipper on me, and I don't regret it,
sir! I would not have been what I am today if I had not been
beaten." I never have the temerity to ask, "By the way, what
exactly *are* you today?"

To say that punishment does not *always* cause psychic dam‑
age is to evade the issue, for we do not know what reaction the
punishment will cause in the individual in later years. Many an
exhibitionist, arrested for indecent exposure, is the victim of
early punishment for childish sexual habits.

If punishment were ever successful, there might be some ar‑
gument in its favor. True, it can inhibit through fear, as any ex‑
soldier can tell you. If a parent is content with a child who has
had his spirit completely broken by fear, then, for such a parent,
punishment succeeds.

What proportion of chastised children remain broken in spirit and castrated for life, and what proportion rebel and become even more antisocial, no one can say. In fifty years of teaching in schools, I have never heard a parent say, "I have beaten my child and now he is a good boy." On the contrary, scores of times, I have heard the mournful story, "I have beaten him, reasoned with him, helped him in every way, and he has grown worse and worse."

The punished child *does* grow worse and worse. What's more, he grows into a punishing father or a punishing mother, and the cycle of hate goes on through the years.

I have often asked myself, "Why is it that parents, who are otherwise kind, tolerate cruel schools for their children?" These parents seem, primarily, to be concerned about a good education for their children. What they overlook is that a punishing teacher will compel interest, but the interest he compels is in the punishment and not in the sums on the blackboard. As a matter of fact, the majority of our top students in schools and colleges sink into mediocrity later on. Their interest in making good was born, for the most part, of the parental pushing, and they had little real interest in the subject.

Fear of teachers and fear of the punishments they deal out is bound to affect the relationship between the parent and the child. For symbolically, every adult is a father or a mother to the child. And every time a teacher punishes, the child acquires a fear and a hate of the adult behind the symbol—a hate of his father or a hate of his mother. This is a disturbing thought. Though children are not conscious of the feeling, I have heard a boy of thirteen say, "My last principal used to flog me a lot, and I can't understand why my father and mother kept me at that school. They knew he was a cruel brute, but they didn't do anything about it."

The punishment that takes the form of a lecture is even more dangerous than a whipping. How awful those lectures can be! "But didn't you *know* you were doing wrong?" A sobbing nod. "Say you are sorry for doing it."

As a training for humbugs and hypocrites, the lecture form of punishment has no rival. Worse still is praying for the erring soul of the child in his presence. That is unpardonable, for such an act is bound to arouse a deep feeling of guilt in the child.

Another type of punishment—noncorporal but just as injurious to a child's development—is nagging. How many times have I heard a mother nag her ten-year-old daughter all day long: *Don't go in the sun, darling . . . Dearest, please keep away from that railing . . . No, love, you can't go into the swimming pool today; you will catch your death of cold!* The nagging is certainly not a love token: it is a token of the mother's fear that covers an unconscious hate.

I wish that the advocates of punishment could all see and digest the delightful French film telling the life story of a crook. When the crook was a boy, he was punished for some misdeed by being forbidden to partake of the Sunday evening meal of poisoned mushrooms. Afterward, as he watched all the family coffins being carried out, he decided that it didn't pay to be good. An immoral story with a moral, which many a punishing parent cannot see.

Defecation and Toilet Training

Visitors to Summerhill must often get an odd impression about us, for sometimes we all talk about toilets. I think it is absolutely necessary to do so. I find that *every* child is interested in feces.

So much has been written about a child's interest in his feces and urine that I expected to learn a lot by observing my infant daughter. However, she showed no interest at all nor any disgust. She had no desire to play with her body products. But when she was three, a friend of hers—a girl a year older who had been trained to be clean—introduced her to a hole-and-corner excrement game marked by much whispering and shame and guilty giggling. It was a tiresome game and we could do nothing about it, knowing that to interfere would be to risk inhibition. Luckily, Zoë soon tired of the other little girl's one-track activities, and the feces game came to a end.

Adults seldom realize that there is nothing shocking to a child in feces and smells. It is the shocked attitude of the adult that makes the child conscience-stricken. I recall a girl of eleven who came to Summerhill. Her only interest in life was toilets. Her delight was to peep through the keyhole. I promptly changed her lessons from geography to toilets, making her very happy. After ten days, I made a remark about toilets. "Don't want to hear about them," she said wearily. "I'm fed up talking about toilets."

Another pupil, a boy, could not take an interest in any lesson because he was so preoccupied with excrement and its likenesses. I knew that only when he had exhausted this interest would he be able to go on to mathematics. And so it was.

A teacher's work is simple: find out where a child's interest lies and help him to live it out. It is *always* so. Suppression and silence simply drive the interest underground.

"But won't this method of yours make the children filthy-minded?" asks Mrs. Morality.

"No, it is *your* method that permanently fixes an interest in what you call filth. Only when one has lived out an interest is one free to go on to something new."

"Do you actually encourage children to talk about toilets?"

"Yes, when I find them interested in toilets. It is only in the more neurotic cases that the talking out takes more than a week."

One such neurotic case occurred some years ago. We had a small boy sent to us because he messed his trousers all day long. His mother had thrashed him for it and, in desperation, she had finally made him eat his feces. You can imagine the problem we had to cope with. It turned out that this boy had a younger brother, and the trouble began with the birth of the younger child. The reason was obvious enough. The boy reasoned: *He has taken Mommy's love from me. If I am like him and mess my trousers the way he dirties his diapers, Mommy will love me again.*

I gave him "private lessons" designed to reveal to him his true motive, but cures are seldom sudden and dramatic. For over a year, that boy messed himself three times daily. No one said a bitter word to him. Mrs. Corkhill, our nurse, performed the cleaning chores without a word of reproach. But she did protest when I began to reward him every time he made a really big mess. The reward meant that I was giving approval of his behavior.

During the entire period, the boy was a hateful little devil. No wonder! He had problems and conflicts. But after his cure he became absolutely clean and stayed with us three years. Eventually, he became a very lovable lad. His mother took him away from Summerhill on the grounds that she wanted a school where he would *learn* something. When he came back to see us after a year at the new school, he was a changed boy—insincere, afraid, unhappy. He said he would never forgive his mother for taking him away from Summerhill, and he never will. Strangely enough, he is the only example of trouser messing we have had in all these years. It may be that many such a case is one of hate against the mother for withholding her love.

It is possible to make a child clean without giving him a fixed and repressed interest in his bodily functions. The kitten and the calf seem to have no complex about excrement. The complex in the child comes from the manner of his instruction. When the mother says *naughty* or *dirty* or even *tut tut,* the element of right and wrong arises. The question becomes a *moral* one— when it should remain a *physical* one.

Thus, the wrong way to deal with a coprophilic child is to tell him he is being dirty. The right way is to allow him to live out his interest in excrement by providing him with mud or clay. In this way, he will sublimate his interest without repression. He will live through his interest; and in doing so, kill it.

Once, in a newspaper article, I mentioned a child's right to make mud pies. A well-known Montessorian educator replied in a letter that his experience showed that a child did not want to make mud pies *when given something better to do* (the italics are mine). But there is nothing better to do when one's interest is fixed in mud. However, the problem child *must be told* what he is doing, for it is possible to make mud pies for years without living out the original interest in excrement.

I recall Jim, an eight-year-old, who had fantasies about feces. I encouraged Jim to make mud pies. But all the time, I told him what he was really interested in. In this way, the process of curing was hurried along. I did not directly say, "You are doing this because it is a substitute for that." I only reminded him of the similarity between the two elements. This worked. A younger child, say, about five, need not be told, as he would easily live out his fantasies merely in the making of mud pies.

To a child, excrement is a most important subject for study. Any suppression of this interest is dangerous and stupid. On the other hand, one should not attach too much importance to excrement, unless the child is proud of his production—in which case, admiration is in order. If a child makes a mess accidentally, it should be treated casually as something normal.

Defecation is not only a work of creation to a child, but is so to many adults as well. Adults often take pleasure and pride in the fact that they had a big movement. Symbolically, it is something of great value. A burglar who defecates on the carpet after robbing the safe does not intend to add insult to injury. He is symbolically showing his guilty conscience by leaving something of value to replace what he has stolen.

Animals are unconscious of natural functions. Dogs and cats that automatically cover their dung with earth are performing an instinctive act which, far back, must have been necessary when food had to be kept clean. Man's moral attitude toward his dung may have much to do with his unnatural diet. The dung of horses and sheep and rabbits is clean stuff and not at all disgusting. On the other hand, the excrement of man is disgusting because his food is such a nasty hash of artificial products. I have sometimes thought that if human excrement were as easy to touch as that of animals, children would stand a better chance of growing up with emotional freedom.

The disgust that adults have for human feces cannot help but play a great part in developing the negative, hate-forming part of the child's psyche. Because nature has placed the excretory and the sexual organs close to each other, the child concludes that both are filthy. Therefore, parental disapproval of excrement will most certainly make the child regard sex in the same light. Thus, disapproval of sex and excrement forms one repression.

A mother may have no feeling of disgust when washing out her baby's diapers. Three years later, however, she may show considerable annoyance when she has to wipe up a small pile from the carpet. Any mother should be very careful in dealing with the excrement situation, remembering that no emotional anger is ever lost on a baby. It sinks in and stays, and is registered in the character.

Food

Totalitarianism began, and totalitarianism still begins in the nursery. The first interfering with child nature is despotism. That first interference is always in the matter of food. It starts with forcing the newborn child to fast and to feed according to a timetable.

The surface explanation for this is that timetable feeding interferes less with the daily routine and the comfort of adults. But deep down, the real motive is hatred of newborn life and its natural needs. This is seen in the indifference and ease with which certain families sometimes listen to the screams of the hungry baby.

Self-regulation should begin with birth, with the very first feedings. Every baby has the birthright of being fed when it wants to be fed. It is easy for the mother to give the infant its way if the mother has the baby at home. But in most hospital maternity wards, the baby is taken away from the mother at birth and placed in a nursery ward. The mother is not allowed to nurse it or give it a bottle for the first twenty-four hours. Who can say what permanent damage is done to that baby?

In some hospitals today, rooming-in care is provided so that the infant is with the mother and under her personal care during her entire stay. Registering in a maternity ward without first making sure of this means that one must accept the system as it is. Any mother who means to use self-regulation for her baby should beware of going into a hospital that does not provide rooming-in care—in other words, that does not approve of self-regulation for the infant. It is far better to have your baby at home than to subject it to such cruelty.

Timetable feeding, so long the system of doctors and nurses, has been attacked so effectively that many practitioners have given it up. It is obviously wrong and dangerous. If a child is crying from hunger at four o'clock but is not fed until the time indicated by a chart, he is being subjected to a stupid, cruel, anti-life discipline of infinite harm to his bodily and spiritual growth. *Baby must feed when he wants to feed.* In the beginning, his wants will be frequent, for he cannot absorb large quantities at a time.

The practice of giving baby a bottle of water at night is a bad one. During the night, if it is hungry, the baby should be fed as usual. After two or three months, the baby will regulate itself to larger quantities of food, and there will be longer intervals between each feeding. At the age of about three or four months, the baby will want to be fed, say, between ten and eleven at night and between five and six the next morning. There is, of course, no hard and fast rule about this.

One fundamental truth should be written out in every nursery: *Baby must not be allowed to cry himself out.* His needs must be attended to every time.

With timetable training, the mother is always a few steps ahead of the baby. Like an efficiency expert, she will know exactly what to do next. But she will be rearing a mechanical baby, a molded baby. Such a baby will, of course, give minimum trouble to adults—at the cost of its own natural development. But with self-regulation for the baby, every day—every minute—means a new discovery for the mother. For then, mother is always a step *behind* the baby, and learning by intimate observation all the time. Thus if a baby cries a half-hour after a good feeding, the young mother will have to think the problem out for herself, regardless of what the timetable mechanists say about it. Is he uncomfortable? Is he suffering from gas in the stomach? Or does he want more food? Does he just want attention because he feels lonely? The mother should react with her spontaneous love, not with any wretched rule out of some book.

Every baby will, if left to itself, evolve its own timetable. This means that a baby has the capacity for self-regulation, not only in milk feeding, but later on in solid feeding.

Thumb-sucking in later childhood, often continuing into adolescence, is the most obvious result of timetable feeding. Sucking has two components: the hunger for food, and the sensual joy in sucking. When feeding time comes, there is a rush of oral pleasure, which is satisfied before the hunger. If the baby has to scream and wait because the clock says he isn't hungry, both components become dammed up.

I have seen a mother in a maternity ward, acting upon the instruction of a doctor, snatch the baby from the breast because the clock said that the baby had had its allotted minutes to feed. I can think of no more effective way to produce a problem child.

It is almost incredible that ignorant doctors and parents should dare to interfere with a baby's natural impulses and behavior, destroying joy and spontaneity with their absurd ideas of guiding and molding. It is people like these who begin the universal sickness of mankind, both psychic and somatic. Later, school and church continue the process of disciplinary education that is anti-pleasure and anti-freedom.

One mother wrote about her small boy who was self-regulated: When he started eating solid foods, he was, for instance, offered his choice of foods and the amounts he would take. If he refused a certain kind of vegetable, he would either be given another vegetable or he might even be given his dessert. Very often, he would eat the refused vegetable *after* he had eaten his dessert. Sometimes he would refuse to eat anything—a sure sign that he was not hungry. Then at his next meal, he would eat particularly well.

All too often, a mother thinks that she knows what her child needs better than the child knows. This just isn't so. This fact about child feeding is easily tested. Any mother can set out on a table ice cream, candy, whole-wheat bread, tomatoes, lettuce, and other foods, and then allow the child complete freedom to choose what he wants. The average child, if not interfered with, will select a balanced diet in just about a week. I understand that this fact has also been borne out in controlled experiments conducted in the United States.

In Summerhill, we always give even the smallest child complete freedom to choose from the daily menu. There is always a choice of three main-course dishes at dinner. One result is, of course, that there is less waste at Summerhill than at most schools. But that is not our motive, for we want to save the child rather than the food.

When children are fed a balanced diet, the candy they buy with their pocket money does no harm. Children like candy because their bodies crave sugar, and sugar they should have.

To compel a child to eat bacon and eggs when he hates bacon and eggs is absurd and cruel. Zoë has always been allowed to choose what she wanted to eat. Whenever she had a cold, she ate only fruit and drank only fruit juices without any suggestion on our part. I never before had seen a child who had so little interest in eating as Zoë. A bag of chocolates could sit on her table for days without being touched, and the most delectable dish at lunch or supper would often leave her indifferent. If she sat down to breakfast and another child shouted from outside to come and play, she always left her food and never came back to eat it. But as her physique was always excellent, we had nothing to worry about.

Naturally, most parents will plan a menu according to their own pet ideas about diet. If parents are vegetarians, they will give their children vegetarian meals. I often notice, however, that children from vegetarian homes wolf meat portions with great gusto.

As a layman unskilled in dietetics, I am of the opinion that it does not matter whether a child is a meat eater or not. As long as his diet is balanced, his health is likely to be good. I never hear of diarrhea in Summerhill, and seldom of constipation. We always have lots of raw greens, but sometimes new children refuse to eat them. Usually, in the course of time, pupils accept them and get to like them. At any rate, Summerhill children are mostly unconscious of the cuisine, which is as it should be.

Because eating provides a great deal of pleasure in childhood, it is too fundamental, too vital, to be marred by table manners. The sad truth is that the children in Summerhill who have the worst table manners are those who have been brought up very genteelly. The more demanding and rigid the home, the worse the table manners and all other manners—once the child is given the freedom to be himself. There is nothing to do but to let the child live out the repressed tendency until he develops his own natural good manners later on in adolescence.

Food is the most important thing in a child's life, much more important than sex. The stomach is egocentric and selfish. Egoism belongs to childhood. The boy of ten is far more possessive about his plate of mutton than the old tribal chief was about his women. When the child is allowed freedom to live out his egoism as he does at Summerhill, this egoism gradually becomes altruism and natural concern for others.

Health and Sleep

In thirty-eight years at Summerhill, we have had very little sickness. I think the reason is that we are on the side of the living process—for we approve of the flesh. We put happiness before diet. Visitors to Summerhill generally remark on how well the children look. I think it is happiness that makes our girls look attractive and our boys handsome.

Eating raw greens may play an important part in curing kidney disease. But all the greens in the world won't affect the sickness of the soul if that sickness is due to repression. A man who eats a balanced diet can warp his children by moralizing, whereas a nonneurotic man will not harm his offspring. My experience leads me to conclude that warped children are less healthy physically than free children.

Incidentally, I note that many of our boys at Summerhill grow to be six footers, even when their parents are comparatively short. There may be nothing in it; then again, it may be that freedom to grow in grace also means freedom to grow in inches. Certainly, I have seen boys grow more rapidly after the masturbation prohibition has been removed.

Then there is the question of sleep. I wonder how much truth there is in the dictum of doctors that so and so much sleep is necessary for a child. With small children, yes. Allow a child of seven to sit up late at night, and he suffers in health because he often cannot go on sleeping late in the morning. Some children resent being sent to bed because they feel they will be missing something.

In a free school, bedtime is the very devil—not with the juniors so much as with the seniors. Youth likes to burn the midnight oil, and I can sympathize, for I hate to go to bed myself.

Work settles the problem for most adults. If you have to be in your job at 8 A.M., you renounce the temptation to stay up until the small hours.

Other factors, such as happiness and good food, may balance any loss of sleep. Summerhill pupils make up their loss of sleep on Sunday mornings, preferring to miss lunch if need be.

As for work in relation to health, much of the work I do has a dual motive. I dig for potatoes, realizing that I could use the time more profitably if I wrote newspaper articles and paid a laborer to dig in the garden. However, I dig because I want to keep healthy—a motive that is more important to me than newspaper dollars. A friend, who is a car dealer, tells me what a fool I am to dig in an age of mechanics, and I tell him that motors are ruining the health of the nation because no one walks or digs nowadays. He and I are old enough to be conscious of health problems.

A child, however, is completely unconscious of health. No boy digs in order to keep fit. In any work, he has only a single motive—his interest at the time.

The good health that we enjoy at Summerhill is due to freedom, good food, and fresh air—in that order.

Cleanliness and Clothing

In the matter of personal cleanliness, girls on the whole are tidier than boys. At Summerhill our boys and girls from about fifteen onward are concerned about their appearance. On the other hand, girls are no tidier about their rooms than boys are—that is, girls up to fourteen. They dress dolls, make theater costumes, and leave their floors littered with rubbish, but it is all creative rubbish.

Seldom do we have a girl at Summerhill who won't wash. We did have one, aged nine, from a home where her granny had a complex about cleanliness and apparently washed Mildred ten times a day. Her housemother came to me one day, saying: "Mildred hasn't washed for a week. She won't have a bath and she is beginning to smell. What shall I do?"

"Send her in to me," I said.

Mildred came in presently, her hands and face very dirty.

"Look here," I said sternly, "this won't do."

"But I don't want to wash," she protested.

"Shut up," I said. "Who's talking about washing? Look in the glass." (*She did so.*) "What do you think of your face?"

"It isn't very clean, is it?" she asked, grinning.

"It's *too* clean," I said. "I won't have girls with clean faces in this school. Now get out!"

She went straight to the coal cellar and rubbed her face black. She came back to me triumphantly. "Will that do?" she asked.

I examined her face with due gravity. "No," I said. "There is a patch of white on that cheek."

Mildred took a bath that night. But I can't fathom just why she did.

I recall the case of a boy of seventeen who came to us from a private school. A week after his arrival, he became chummy with the men who filled coal carts at the station, and he began to help them with their loading. His face and hands were black when he came to meals, but no one said a word. No one cared.

It took him several weeks to live down his private school and home idea of cleanliness. When he gave up his coal-heaving, he once more became clean in person and dress, but with a difference. Cleanliness was something no longer forced on him; he had lived out his dirt complex.

When Willie makes mud pies, his mother is alarmed lest the neighbors criticize his dirty clothes. In this case, the social claim —what society thinks—must give way to the individual claim— the joy of playing and making.

Too often parents attach far too much importance to tidiness. It is one of the seven deadly virtues. The man who prides himself on his tidiness is usually a second-rate fellow who values the second best in life. The tidiest person often has the most untidy mind. I say this with all the detachment of a man whose desk always looks like a heap of papers under a *No Litter* notice in a public park.

In my own family, the biggest difficulty with self-regulation centered around the matter of clothing. Zoë would have liked to run about naked all day long if she had been permitted to do so. Another parent of a self-regulated child reported that when the day turned cold, her daughter of two automatically came into the house and asked for warm clothes. We did not have this experience. Zoë shivered until her nose and cheeks turned blue, and then resisted all our efforts to get her to put on more clothes.

Courageous parents might say, "Her own organism will guide her. Let her shiver, she'll be all right!" But we were not courageous enough to risk pneumonia, so we bullied her into wearing what we thought she ought to wear.

Parents must decide what clothes small children should wear. When children grow to adolescence, however, they should be allowed to choose their own clothes. A million daughters suffer because their mothers insist upon selecting their clothes for them. As a rule, boys are easier to dress. If a parent can afford it, a good way is to give a boy or girl a clothes allowance. If he wants to spend the money on movies and candy, that's up to him.

What is unpardonable is to dress your child in a way that will set him apart from his friends. To put an overgrown boy into short pants when all his classmates are wearing long ones is cruel.

Daughters should be free to do as they like with their hair: to have it long, short, or braided. If they want to use lipstick, why not? Personally, I hate the sight of the stuff, but if my daughter feels otherwise, I shall not try to dissuade her.

Young children have no innate interest in clothes, but the child whose parents are neurotic on the subject of clothes soon acquires a complex himself. He fears to climb a tree lest he rip his pants.

Normal children shed their clothes anywhere and everywhere, discarding a sweater and forgetting where it was left. If I walk over our school grounds on a summer evening, I can always pick up an assortment of shoes and jerseys.

Children who do not go to boarding schools have to contend with the opinions of neighbors. Think of the thousands of children who are sacrificed to that abomination called Sunday clothes. You see them solemnly walking out in stiff collars and white dresses, fearful to kick a ball or climb a gate. Fortunately, that idiocy is dying out.

At Summerhill on a hot day, boys and teachers will sit at lunch, shirtless. No one minds. Summerhill relegates minor things to their proper place, treating them with indifference.

It is chiefly in the matter of clothes that a parent shows his money complex. We once had a very bad young thief in Summerhill who was cured after four years of hard work and infinite patience on the part of his teachers. This boy left at seventeen. His mother wrote, "Bill has arrived home. Two pairs of his socks are missing. Can you please see that they are returned to us."

At times, parents exhibit jealousy of the housemother who looks after their children in Summerhill. I have had visiting mothers go straight to their children's clothes closets with many a frown and a *tut tut,* suggesting that the housemother was inadequate. Such a mother usually experiences great anxiety about her child, for an anxiety about clothes always means an anxiety about learning and everything else.

Toys

If I had any business sense, I would open a toy shop. Every nursery is filled with toys that are broken and neglected. Every middle-class child gets far too many toys. In fact, most toys that cost more than a few cents are wasted.

Once Zoë received a gift from an old pupil of a wonderful walking and talking doll. It was obviously an expensive toy. About the same time, a new pupil gave Zoë a small cheap rabbit. She played with the big expensive doll for half an hour, but she played with the cheap little rabbit for weeks. In fact, she took the rabbit to bed with her each night.

Of all her toys, the only one that Zoë retained a liking for was Betsy Wetsy, a self-wetting doll I bought for her when she was eighteen months old. The wetting arrangement did not interest her one bit; perhaps because it was a puritanical fake, its "wee-wee hole" having been placed in the small of the back. Only when she reached four and a half did Zoë say one morning, "I'm tired of Betsy Wetsy and want to give her away."

Some years ago, I tried out a questionnaire on older children. "When do you get most annoyed with your little brother or sister?" In practically every case, the answer was the same, "When he breaks my toys."

One should never show a child how a toy works. Indeed, one should never help a child in any way until or unless he is not capable of solving a problem for himself.

Self-regulated children seem content to amuse themselves for long periods with their toys and games. They do not smash them about as molded children so often do.

There is no reason why a baby in a private home or a fairly

soundproof home should not be allowed to play with kitchen things when they are not in use, such as noisy lids with wooden spoons for drumsticks. He is likely to prefer these to the usual toys sold in toy shops. Indeed, the average toy can be a soporific, lulling baby into a dull somnolence.

All parents have a tendency to overbuy toys. Baby eagerly holds out his hands toward some gadget—a tractor, a giraffe that nods—and parents buy it on the spot. Thus, most nurseries are full of toys in which the child never shows real interest.

There are far too few creative toys on the market. There are many construction toys in metal and wood, but few creative toys. Construction toys are like crossword puzzles or mathematical riddles. Since someone else has made them, their solutions can never be wholly original. I confess that I could not invent a creative toy of any kind, and have no suggestions to offer in that department. But I am certain that the toy world is awaiting some wizard who will get nearer the heart of a child than toy makers do today.

Noise

Children are naturally noisy, and parents must accept this fact and learn to live with it. A child, if he is to grow in health, must be allowed a fair amount of noisy play.

For nearly forty years now, I have lived with children's noise. As a rule I do not consciously hear that noise. An analogy would be living in a brass factory; one becomes accustomed to the perpetual clang of hammers. And those who live on busy streets come to be unaware of the roar of traffic. One difference is that hammering and traffic are more or less constant sounds, whereas the noise of children is ever varied and strident. The noise can get on one's nerves. I must confess that when I moved out of the main building to live in the cottage some years ago, the peace of the evening was most pleasant after years of the noise of some fifty children.

The Summerhill dining room is a noisy place. Children, like animals, are loud at meal times. We only allow visitors without noise complexes to dine with us. My wife and I dine alone, but then we spend about two hours a day serving out the children's dinners, and we need the respite from noise. The teachers do not like too much noise, but the adolescents do not seem to mind the noise of the juniors. And when a senior does bring up the question of the juniors' noise in the dining room, the juniors quite truthfully roar their protests that the seniors make just as much noise.

The suppression of noise never gives the child so strong a repression as does the suppression of interest in bodily functions. Noise is never called *dirty*. The tone of voice that father adopts in shouting "Stop that row!" is an open, heartfelt expression of impatience. The tone of mother when she says "Pfui! Dirty!" is a shocked, moral tone.

At Summerhill, some children play all day, especially when the sun is shining. Their play is generally noisy. In most schools noise, like play, is suppressed. One of our former pupils who went to a Scottish university said, "The students make a hell of a row in classes, and it gets rather tiresome; for we at Summerhill lived out that stage when we were ten."

I recall an incident in that great novel, *The House with the Green Shutters,* where the students of Edinburgh University played *John Brown's Body* with their feet in order to heckle and tease a weak lecturer. Noise and play go together, but it is best when they go together at the age of seven to fourteen.

Manners

To have good manners means to think of others, no—to feel for others. One must be group-conscious, have the gift of putting oneself in the other man's shoes. Manners prohibit the wounding of anyone. To be mannerly is to have genuine good taste. Manners cannot be taught, for they belong to the unconscious.

Etiquette, on the other hand, can be taught, for it belongs to the conscious. It is the veneer of manners. Etiquette allows one to talk during a concert; etiquette permits gossip and scandal. Etiquette requires us to dress for dinner, to rise when a lady approaches our table, to say "Excuse me" when we leave the table. This is all conscious, outer, meaningless behavior.

Bad manners always spring from a disordered psyche. Slander and scandal and gossip and backbiting are all subjective faults; they show hatred of self. They prove that the scandal-monger is unhappy. If we can take children into a world where they will be happy, we shall automatically rid them of all desire to hate. In other words, these children will have good manners in the deepest sense; that is, they will show forth loving-kindness.

If children eat peas with knives, these same children will not necessarily offend by talking through a Beethoven symphony. If they pass Mrs. Brown without doffing their caps, these same children will not necessarily pass on the report that Mrs. Brown drinks brandy.

Once when I was lecturing, an old man got up and complained about the manners of children today. "Why," he said with warmth, "last Saturday I was walking in the park, and two small children came by. 'Hello, man,' said one of them."

I answered him, "What is wrong with 'Hello, man?' Would it have pleased you better if they had said, 'Hello, gentleman?' The truth is that you were injured. Your sense of dignity was offended. You want subservience from children, not manners."

This is true of many adults. It is pure conceit. It is the treating of children as if they were vassals under feudalism. It is selfishness—a type of selfishness that has far less justification than has the selfishness of children. Children *must* be selfish, but an adult ought to confine his selfishness to things, and not to people.

I find that children correct each other. One of my pupils made eating a very loud affair until the others jeered at him. On the other hand, when one little fellow used his knife for eating mince, the others were inclined to think it a good plan. They asked each other why you shouldn't eat with a knife. The reply that you might cut your mouth was dismissed on the grounds that most knives are blunt enough for anything.

Children should be free to question the rules of etiquette, for eating peas with a knife is a personal thing. They should not be free to question what might be called *social manners*. If a child enters our drawing room with muddy boots, we shout at him, for the drawing room belongs to the adults, and the adults have the right to decree what and who shall enter and what and who shall not.

When a boy was impudent to our butcher, I told the pupils at a General School Meeting that the butcher had complained to me. But I think it would have been better if the butcher had boxed the boy's ears. What people generally call manners are not worth teaching. They are at best survivals of customs. The doffing of the hat in the presence of ladies is a meaningless custom. As a boy, I doffed my hat to the minister's wife, but not to my mother or sisters. I suppose I dimly realized that I did not have to pretend in their presence. Still, customs like doffing the hat are, at worst, harmless. The boy will conform to custom later on. At the age of ten, however, anything savoring of sham should be kept away from him.

Manners should never be taught. If a child of seven wants to eat with his fingers, he should be free to do so. No child should ever be asked to behave in a certain way, so that Aunt Mary will approve. Sacrifice all the relations and neighbors in the world rather than stunt a child for life by making him behave insincerely. Manners come of themselves. Old Summerhillians have excellent manners—even if some of them licked their plates at the age of twelve. No child should be forced to say "Thank you"—not even encouraged to say "Thank you."

Most people, parents or otherwise, would be startled at the lack of depth in manners among the usual, character-molded boys and girls who come to Summerhill. Boys come with beautiful manners and soon drop them completely, realizing no doubt that their insincerity is out of place in Summerhill. The gradual dropping of insincerity in voice, in manner, and in action is the norm. Pupils from private schools generally take longest to drop their insincerity and cheek. Free children are never insolent.

To me, respect for a schoolteacher is an artificial lie, demanding insincerity; when a person really gives respect, he does so unawares. My pupils can call me a silly ass any time they like to; they respect me because I respect their young lives, not because I am the principal of the school, not because I am on a pedestal as a dignified tin god. My pupils and I have mutual respect for each other because we approve of each other.

An inquiring mother once asked me, "But if I send my son here, won't he behave like a barbarian when he comes home for holidays?"

My answer was, "Yes, if you have already made him a barbarian.

It is true that the spoiled child coming to Summerhill goes home as a barbarian for at least the first year. If he has been brought up with manners, he will regress to barbarism every time. Which only shows how little artificial manners sink into a child.

Artificial manners are the first layer of hypocritical veneer to be dropped under freedom. New children generally show marvelous manners—that is, they behave insincerely. In Summerhill, in time, they come to have good manners—real manners, for in Summerhill we ask for no manners at all, not even a "Thank you" or a "Please." Yet again and again, visitors say, "But their manners are delightful!"

Peter, who was with us from the age of eight to nineteen, went to South Africa. His hostess wrote, "Everyone here is charmed with his good manners." Yet I was quite unconscious of whether he had any manners or not when he was at Summerhill.

Summerhill is a classless society; the wealth and position of one's father does not count. What counts is one's personality. And what counts for most is one's sociability, that is, being a good member of the community. Our good manners spring from our self-government; each one is constantly being compelled to see the other person's point of view. It is unthinkable that any Summerhill child would mock a stutterer or jeer at one who is lame; yet prep school boys sometimes do both. Boys who say "Please," and "Thank you," and "Excuse me, sir" may have very little real concern for others.

Manners are a matter of sincerity. When Jack, after leaving Summerhill, went to a factory, he found that the man who gave out nuts and bolts was always in a vile temper. Jack thought it over and came to the conclusion that the trouble was this: The men would go up to Bill and shout, "Hey, Bill, chuck over some Whitworth half-inch nuts." But Bill wore a coat and collar, and

Jack concluded that he must have felt himself a cut above the ordinary mechanics in overalls, and that his bad temper was due to his not getting the respect he thought he deserved. So when Jack needed bolts or nuts, he went up to Bill and said, "Excuse me, Mr. Brown, I need nuts and bolts."

Said Jack to me, "It wasn't boot-licking on my part. It was just using psychology. I was sorry for the guy."

"What was the result?" I asked.

"Oh," said Jack, "I'm the only chap in the factory he's civil to."

I call that an excellent example of the manners that a community life gives to boys—thinking of and feeling for others.

I never notice bad manners among the small children, no doubt, because I do not look for them. Yet I have never seen a child rush in between two visitors who were talking together. The children never knock at my sitting-room door, but if I have visitors they simply retire quietly, often saying, "Sorry."

A good compliment to their manners was recently given by a salesman. He said to me, "I've come here with cars for the last three years, and never once has a kid scratched a fender or attempted to enter a car. And this is the school where the kids are alleged to break windows all day long."

I have already mentioned the friendliness of Summerhill children to visitors. This friendliness might be classed as good manners, for I have never heard the most antagonistic visitor complain of being molested in any way by any pupil who has been six months in the school.

Our theater performances are always marked by excellent audience manners. Even a bad turn or a poor play is applauded more or less—naturally less—but the general feeling is that the actor or dramatist has done his best, and he should not be censured or despised.

The question of manners is an absolute bugbear with some parents. A ten-year-old boy from a good home came to Summerhill. He knocked at the drawing-room door when he entered, always closed the door when he went out. Said I, "It will last a week." I was wrong. It only lasted two days.

Of course, I shout at a child, "Shut the door," not because I try to train his manners, but because I do not want to rise and shut it myself. Manners are an adult concept. Children, be they the children of a professor or a porter, have no interest in manners.

The progress of civilization consists in ridding the world of sham and shoddy. We must leave the children free to go a step farther than our veneered civilization has gone. By ridding the children of fears and hates, we are helping forward the new civilization of good manners.

Money

To most children money has a love symbolism: Uncle Bill gives me a quarter; Aunt Margaret gives me a dollar; therefore, Auntie loves me more than Uncle Bill does. Parents unconsciously know this; and too often, they spoil the child by giving him too much. As a compensation, the unloved child very often gets the biggest allowance.

None of us can escape the money valuation in life. It is forced upon us everywhere. We sit in the orchestra or we sit in the balcony. Our children go to private camps or spend the summer in the city parks. Money values are a danger to every one of us.

A mother will cry, half in jest, "I wouldn't sell my child for all the gold in the world," and five minutes later, she will spank her child for breaking a ten-cent cup. It is the money value that is at the root of so much discipline in the home. Don't touch *that—that* having cost money.

Too often children are balanced against money—but only children, not adults. My mother used to spank us if we broke a plate; but when father broke a plate, it was just an accident.

Parents give their children much anxiety about money. Far too often have I heard a child cry in dismay, "I've dropped my watch and broken it. What will Mommy say? I'll be scared to tell her."

Occasionally, one sees the opposite mechanism. I have seen a boy or a girl break things deliberately as a hate reaction against home: "I'll make my parents, who don't love me, pay for it. Won't they be wild when Neill sends in the bill?"

Some Summerhill parents send their children too much, some too little. This has always been a problem to me, one that

I cannot solve. Summerhill pupils get their age in tuppence (two-cent pieces) as pocket money each Monday; but some get extra money sent by post, while others get little or nothing.

At our General School Meeting, I have more than once advocated the pooling of all pocket money, saying that it is unfair that one boy should get five dollars a week while another should get only a quarter. In spite of the fact that the pupils with the big incomes are always in a very small minority, I have never had my proposals carried by general vote. Children with a dime a week will hotly defend any proposal to limit the income of their richer schoolmates.

It is better to give a child too little than too much. The parent who slips a boy of eleven a five-dollar bill is being unwise, unless the gift has a special purpose, like buying a lamp for a bicycle. Too much money spoils a child's values. A child will get a beautiful, expensive bicycle which he does not take care of or a radio set, or an expensive toy that is uncreative.

Too much money handicaps a child's fantasy life. To give a child a twenty-dollar boat robs him of all the creative joy of fashioning a boat out of a chunk of wood. A little girl often prizes the rag doll she made herself, and scorns the elaborate, expensive, well-dressed, commercial doll that sleeps or quacks.

I notice that small children do not value money. Our five-year-olds drop their pennies or sometimes throw them away. This suggests that it is wrong to teach children to save. The home savings bank asks too much from the child; it says to him, "Think of the morrow," at a time when only today matters to him. To a child of seven, it means nothing that he has twenty-seven dollars in the bank, especially if he suspects that his parents will one day draw it out to buy him something he does not want.

Humor

There is far too little humor in our schools and certainly in our educational journals. I know that humor can have its dangers; and that some men use humor to cover up more serious matters in life, for it is so easy to laugh something off instead of facing it. Children do not use humor for that purpose. To them humor and fun mean friendliness and comradeship. Stern teachers, realizing this, banish humor from their classrooms.

The question arises, *Can a stern teacher have a sense of humor at all?* I doubt it. I find in my own daily work that I use humor all day long. I joke with each child, but they all know that I am deadly serious when the occasion presents itself.

Whether you are a parent or a teacher, in order to successfully deal with children you must be able to understand their thoughts and feelings. And you must have a sense of humor— *childish* humor. To be humorous with a child gives him the feeling that you love him. However, the humor must never be cutting or critical.

It is delightful to watch how a child's sense of humor grows. Call it fun rather than humor, for a child has a sense of fun before humor develops. David Barton was practically born in Summerhill. When he was three, I would say to him, "I'm a visitor and I want to find Neill. Where is he?"

David would look at me scornfully, "Silly ass, you're him."

When David was seven, I stopped him in the garden one day. "Tell David Barton I want to see him," I said solemnly. "He's over at the cottage, I think."

David grinned broadly. "Righto," he replied, and went over to the cottage. He came back in two minutes.

"He says he won't come," he said, with a sly smile.

"Did he give a reason?"

"Yes, he said he was feeding his tiger."

David rose to this foolery at the age of seven. But when I told Raymond, who was nine, that he was fined half his pocket money for stealing the front door, he wept, and I knew that I had blundered. Two years later, he saw through my jokes.

Sally, aged three, chuckles when I meet her on the road to town and ask her the way to Summerhill; but the girls of seven and eight react by directing me the wrong way.

When I take visitors around, I usually introduce the cottage kids as "the pigs," and they grunt appropriately. One time, it was disconcerting when I introduced them as "the pigs" and a girl of eight said haughtily, "Isn't that joke rather stale now?" I had to admit that it was.

Girls have as much sense of humor as boys, but they seldom use humor to protect themselves as boys do. Some boys successfully defend themselves in this way. I have seen Dave being tried for some antisocial act. By giving his evidence in a hilarious way, he wins the gang's appreciation and succeeds in getting only a minor punishment. A girl, ever too ready to see herself in the wrong, never does this. Even in the most enlightened homes, the girls suffer from the general inferiority that our society forces on womanhood.

Never treat a child with humor at the wrong time nor attack his dignity. If he has a genuine grievance, it must be taken seriously. To joke with a child who has a temperature of 102 is a mistake. But when he is convalescing, you can pretend to be the doctor or even the undertaker, and he will appreciate the joke. Perhaps children like to be treated with humor because humor involves friendliness and laughter. Even the seniors who practice witticisms do not use wit that bites. Much of the success of Summerhill is due to its sense of fun.

THREE

SEX

Sex Attitudes

I have never had a pupil who did not bring to Summerhill a diseased attitude toward sexuality and bodily functions. The children of modern parents who were told the truth about where babies come from have much the same hidden attitude toward sex that the children of religious fanatics have. To find a new orientation to sex is the most difficult task of the parent and teacher.

We know so little of the causes of the sex taboo that we can only hazard guesses as to its origin. Why there is a sex taboo is of no immediate concern to me. That there *is* a sex taboo is of great concern to a man entrusted to cure repressed children.

We adults were corrupted in infancy; we can never be free about sex matters. *Consciously,* we may be free; we may even be members of a society for the sex education of children. But I fear that *unconsciously* we remain to a large extent what conditioning in infancy made of us: haters of sex and fearers of sex.

I am quite willing to believe that my unconscious attitude toward sex is the Calvinistic attitude a Scottish village imposed on me in my first years of life. Possibly there is no salvation for adults; but there is every chance of salvation for children, if we do not force on them the awful ideas of sex that were forced on us.

Early in life, the child learns that the sexual sin is the great sin. Parents invariably punish most severely for an offense against sex morality. The very people who rail against Freud because he "sees sex in everything" are the ones who have told sex stories, have listened to sex stories, have laughed at sex stories. Every man who has been in the army knows that the language of the army is a sex language. Nearly everyone likes to read the spicy accounts of divorce cases and of sex crimes in the Sunday papers, and most men tell their wives the stories they bring home from their clubs and bars.

Now our delight in a sex story is due entirely to our own unhealthy education in sex matters. The savory sex interest is due to repressions. The story, as Freud says, lets the cat out of the bag. The adult condemnation of sex interest in the child is hypocritical and is humbug; the condemnation is a projection, a throwing of the guilt onto others. Parents punish severely for sex offenses because they are vitally, if unhealthily, interested in sex offenses.

Why is the crucifixion of the flesh so popular? Religious people believe that the flesh drags one downward. The body is called vile: it tempts one to evil. It is this hatred of the body that makes talk of childbirth a subject for dark corners of the schoolroom, and that makes polite conversation a cover up for everyday plain facts of life.

Freud saw sex as the greatest force in human behavior. Every honest observer must agree. But moral instruction has over-emphasized sex. The first correction that a mother makes, when the child touches his sexual organ, makes sex the most fascinating and mysterious thing in the world. To make fruit forbidden is to make it delectable and enticing.

The sex taboo is the root evil in the suppression of children. I do not narrow the word *sex* down to genital sex. It is likely that the child at the breast feels unhappy if his mother disapproves of any part of her own body, or impedes his pleasure in his own body.

Sex is the basis of all negative attitudes toward life. Children who have no sex guilt never ask for religion or mysticism of any kind. Since sex is considered the great sin, children who are fairly free from sex fear and sex shame do not seek any God from whom they can ask pardon or mercy, because they do not feel guilty.

When I was six my sister and I discovered each other's genitals, and naturally played with each other. Discovered by our mother, we were severely thrashed; and I was locked in a dark room for hours, and then made to kneel down and ask forgiveness from God.

It took me decades to get over that early shock; and, indeed, I sometimes wonder if I ever fully got over it.

How many of today's adults have had a similar experience? How many of today's children are having their whole natural love of life changed into hate and aggression because of such treatment? They are being told that touching the genitals is bad or sinful and that natural bowel movements are disgusting.

Every child who is suffering from sex suppression has a stomach like a board. Watch a repressed child breathe and then look at the beautiful grace with which a kitten breathes. No animal has a stiff stomach, nor is self-conscious about sex or defecation.

In his well-known work, *Character Analysis,* Wilhelm Reich pointed out that a moralistic training not only warps the thinking process, but enters structurally into the body itself, armoring it literally with stiffness in posture and contraction of pelvis. I agree with Reich. I have observed, during many years of dealing with a variety of children at Summerhill, that when fear has not stiffened the musculature, the young walk, run, jump and play with a wonderful grace.

What then can we do to prevent sex suppression in children? Well, for one thing, from the earliest moment the child must be completely free to touch any and every part of his body.

A psychologist friend of mine had to say to his son of four, "Bob, you must not play with your wee-wee when you are out among strange people, for they think it bad. You must do it only at home and in the garden."

My friend and I talked about it and agreed that it is impossible to guard the child against the anti-life haters of sex. The only comfort is that when the parents are sincere believers in life, the child will generally accept the parental standards and is likely to reject the outside prudery. But all the same, the mere fact that a child of five learns that he cannot bathe in the sea without pants is enough to form some kind—if only a minor kind—of sex distrust.

Today many parents put no ban on masturbation. They feel that it is natural, and they know the dangers of suppressing it. Excellent. Fine.

But some of these enlightened parents balk at the next step. Some do not mind if their little boys have sex play with other little boys, but they stiffen with alarm if a small boy and a small girl have sex play.

If my good, well-meaning mother had ignored the sex play of my year younger sister and me, our chances of growing up with some sanity toward sex would have been good.

I wonder how much impotence and frigidity in adults date from the first interference in a heterosexual relationship of early childhood. I wonder how much homosexuality dates from the tolerance of homosexual play and the forbidding of heterosexual play.

Heterosexual play in childhood is the royal road, I believe, to a healthy, balanced adult sex life. When children have no moralistic training in sex, they reach a healthy adolescence— not an adolescence of promiscuity.

I know of no argument against youth's love life that holds water. Nearly every argument is based on repressed emotion or hate of life—the religious, the moral, the expedient, the arbitrary, the pornographic. None answer the question why nature gave man a strong sex instinct, if youth is to be forbidden to use it unless sanctioned by the elders of society. Those elders, some of them, have shares in companies that run films full of sex appeal, or in companies that sell all sorts of cosmetics to make girls more delectable to boys, or companies that publish magazines which make sadistic pictures and stories a magnet to their readers.

I know that adolescent sex life is not practical today. But my opinion is that it is the right way to tomorrow's health. I can *write* this, but if in Summerhill I approved of my adolescent pupils sleeping together, my school would be suppressed by the authorities. I am thinking of the long tomorrow when society will have realized how dangerous sex repression is.

I do not expect every Summerhill pupil to be unneurotic, for who can be complex-free in society today? What I hope for is that in generations to come this beginning of freedom from artificial sex taboos will ultimately fashion a life-loving world.

The invention of contraceptives must in the long run lead to a new sex morality, seeing that fear of consequences is perhaps the strongest factor in sex morality. To be free, love must feel itself safe.

Youth today has little opportunity for loving in the true sense. Parents will not allow sons or daughters to live in sin, as they call it, so that young lovers have to seek damp woods or parks or automobiles. Thus everything is loaded heavily against our young people. Circumstances compel them to convert what should be lovely and joyful into something sinister and sinful, into smut and leers, and shameful laughter.

The taboos and fears that fashioned sex behavior are those same taboos and fears that produce the perverts who rape and strangle small girls in parks, the perverts who torture Jews and Negroes.

Sex prohibition anchors sex to the family. The masturbation prohibition forces a child to interest himself in the parents. Every time a mother smacks a child's hands for touching his genitals, the sex drive of the child gets constellated with his mother, and the hidden attitude toward the mother becomes one of desire and repulsion, love and hate. Repression flourishes in an unfree home. Repression helps to retain adult authority, but at the price of a plethora of neurosis.

If sex were allowed to go over the garden wall to the boy or girl next door, the authority of the home would be in danger; the tie to father and mother would loosen and the child would automatically leave the family emotionally. It sounds absurd but those ties are a very necessary pillar of support to the authoritative state—just as prostitution was a necessary safeguard for the morality of nice girls from nice homes. Abolish sex repression and youth will be lost to authority.

Fathers and mothers are doing what their parents did to them: bringing up respectable, chaste children, conveniently forgetting all the hidden sex play and pornographic stories of their own childhood, forgetting the bitter rebellion against their parents that they had to repress with infinite guilt. They do not realize that they are giving their own children the same guilt feelings that gave them miserable nights many long years ago.

Man's serious neurosis starts with the earliest genital prohibitions: Touch not. The impotence, frigidity, and anxiety of later life date from the tying up of the hands or the snatching away of the hands, usually with a spank. A child left to touch its genitals has every chance of growing up with a sincere, happy attitude toward sex. Sex play among small children is a natural, healthy act that ought not to be frowned on. On the contrary, it should be encouraged as a prelude to a healthy adolescence and adulthood. Parents are ostriches hiding their heads in the sand if they are ignorant that their children have sex play in dark corners. This kind of clandestine and furtive play breeds a guilt that lives on in later life, a guilt that usually betrays itself in disapproval of sex play when these same children become parents. Bringing sex play out into the light is the only sane thing to do. There would be infinitely less sex crime in the world if sex play were accepted as normal. That is what moral parents cannot see or dare not see, that sex crime and sex abnormality of any kind are a direct result of disapproval of sex in early childhood.

The famous anthropologist, Malinowski, tells us that there was no homosexuality among the Trobrianders until the shocked missionaries segregated boys and girls in separate hostels. There was no rape among the Trobrianders, no sex crimes. Why? Because small children were given no repressions about sex.

The question for parents today is this: Do we want our children to be like us? If so, will society continue as it is, with rape and sex murder and unhappy marriages and neurotic children? If the answer to the first question is yes, then the same answer must be given to the second question. And both answers are the prelude to atomic destruction, because they postulate the continuance of hate and the expression of this hate in wars.

I ask moralist parents: Will you worry much about your children's sex play when the atomic bombs begin to drop? Will the virginity of your daughters assume great importance when clouds of atomic energy make life impossible? When your sons are conscripted for the Great Death, will you still hold on to your little chapel faith in the suppression of all that is good in childhood? Will the God you blasphemously pray to then save your life and those of your children?

Some of you may answer that this life is only the beginning, that in the next world there will be no hate, no war, no sex. In that case, shut this book—for we have no contact.

To me, eternal life is a dream—an understandable dream indeed—for man has failed in practically everything except mechanistic invention. But the dream is not good enough. I want to see heaven on earth, not in the clouds. And the pathetic thing is that most people want the same thing. They *want,* but haven't the will to reach it, the will that was perverted by the first slap, the first sex taboo.

For a parent there is no sitting on the fence, no neutrality. The choice is between guilty-secret sex or open-healthy-happy sex. If parents choose the common standard of morality, they must not complain of the misery of sex-perverted society, for it is the result of this moral code. Parents then must not hate war, for the hate of self that they give their children will express itself in war. Humanity is sick, emotionally sick, and it is sick because of this guilt and the anxiety acquired in childhood. The emotional pest is everywhere in our society.

When Zoë was six she came to me and said, "Willie has the biggest cock among the small kids, but Mrs. X [a visitor] says it is rude to say *cock.*" I at once told her that it was not rude. Inwardly, I cursed that woman for her ignorant and narrow understanding of children. I might tolerate propaganda about politics or manners, but when anyone attacks a child by making that child guilty about sex, I fight back vigorously.

All our leering attitude toward sex, our guffaws in music halls, our scribbling of obscenities on urinal walls spring from the guilty feeling arising from suppression of masturbation in infancy and from driving mutual sex play into holes and corners. There is secret sex play in every family; and because of the secrecy and guilt, there are many fixations on brothers and sisters that last throughout life and make happy marriages impossible. If sex play between brother and sister at the age of five were accepted as natural, each of them would advance freely to a sex object outside the family.

The extreme forms of sex hate are seen in sadism. No man with a good sex life could possibly torture an animal, or torture a human, or support prisons. No sex-satisfied woman would condemn the mother of a bastard.

Of course, I lay myself open to the accusation: "This man has sex on the brain. Sex isn't everything in life. There is friendship, work, joy, and sorrow. Why sex?"

I answer: Sex affords the highest pleasure in life. Sex with love is the supreme form of ecstasy because it is the supreme form of both giving and receiving. Yet sex is obviously hated; otherwise no mother would forbid masturbation—no father forbid a sex life outside conventional marriage. Otherwise, there would be no obscene jokes in vaudeville halls, nor would the public waste its time seeing love films and reading love stories; it would be practicing love.

The fact that nearly every motion picture deals with love proves that sex is the most important factor in life. The interest in these films is, in the main, neurotic. It is the interest of sex-guilty, sex-frustrated people. Unable to love naturally because of sex guilt, they flock to film stories that make love romantic, even beautiful. The sex-repressed live out their interest in sex by proxy. No man, no woman with a full love life could be bothered sitting twice a week in a movie house seeing trashy pictures which are only imitations of real life.

So it is also with popular novels. They either deal with sex or with crime, usually a combination of the two. A very popular novel, *Gone with the Wind,* was a favorite, not because of the background of the tragedy of the Civil War and the slaves, but because it centered around a tiresome, egocentric girl and her love affairs.

Fashion journals, cosmetics, leg shows, highbrow sophisticated reviews, sex stories—all show clearly that sex is the most important thing in life. At the same time, they prove that only the trappings of sex are approved of—in other words, fiction, films, leg shows.

It was D. H. Lawrence who pointed out the iniquity of sex films, where the sex-repressed youth, fearful of actual girls in his own circle, showers all his sex emotion on a Hollywood star—and then goes home to masturbate. Lawrence, of course, did not mean that masturbation is wrong; he meant that it is unhealthy sex that seeks masturbation with the fantasy of a film star. Healthy sex would most surely seek a partner in the neighborhood.

Think of the enormous vested interests that thrive on repressed sex: the fashion people, the lipstick merchants, the church, the theaters and movies, the best-seller novelists, and the stocking manufacturers.

It would be foolish to say that a society sexually free would abolish beautiful clothes. Of course not. Every woman would want to look her best before the man she loved. Every man would like to appear elegant when he dated his girl. What would disappear would be fetishism—the valuing of the shadow because the reality is forbidden. Sex-repressed men would no longer stare at women's lingerie in shop windows. What a horrible pity that sex interest is so repressed. The highest pleasure in the world is enjoyed with guilt. This repression enters into every aspect of human life, making life narrow, unhappy, hateful.

Hate sex and you hate life. Hate sex and you cannot love your neighbor. If you hate sex, your sexual life will be, at the worst, impotent or frigid; at best, incomplete. Hence the common remark by women who have had children, "Sex is an overrated pastime." If sex is unsatisfactory, it must go somewhere, for it is too strong an urge to be annihilated. It goes into anxiety and hate.

Not many adults look upon the sex act as a giving; otherwise the percentage of people afflicted with impotency and frigidity would not be about seventy per cent, as quite a few experts have claimed it is. To many men, intercourse is polite rape; to many women, a tiresome rite that has to be endured.

Thousands of married women have never experienced an orgasm in their lives; and even some educated men do not know that a woman is capable of an orgasm. In such a system, giving must be minimal; and sex relations are bound to be more or less brutalized and obscene. The perverts who require to be scourged with whips or to beat women with rods are merely extreme cases of people who, owing to sex miseducation, are unable to give love except in the disguised form of hate.

Every older pupil at Summerhill knows from my conversation and my books that I approve of a full sex life for all who wish one, whatever their age. I have often been asked in my lectures if I provide contraceptives at Summerhill, and if not, why not? This is an old and a vexed question that touches deep emotions in all of us. That I do not provide contraceptives is a matter of bad conscience with me, for to compromise in any way is to me difficult and alarming. On the other hand, to provide contraceptives to children either over or under the age of consent would be a sure way of closing down my school. One cannot advance in practice too much ahead of the law.

A familiar question asked by critics of child freedom is, "Why don't you let a small child see sexual intercourse?" The answer that it would give him a trauma, a severe nervous shock, is false. Among the Trobrianders, according to Malinowski, children see not only parental sexual intercourse but birth and death as matters of course, and are not affected adversely. I do not think that seeing sexual intercourse would have any bad emotional effect on a self-regulated child. The only honest answer to the question is to say that love in our culture is not a public matter.

I do not forget that many parents have religious or other negative views on the sinfulness of sex. Nothing can be done about them. They cannot be converted to our views. On the other hand, we must fight them when they infringe on our own children's right to freedom, genital or otherwise.

To other parents, I say: Your big headache will come when your daughter of sixteen wants to live her own life. She will come in at midnight. On no account ask her where she has been. If she has not been self-regulated, she will lie to you just as you lied, and I lied, to our parents.

When my daughter is sixteen, should I find her in love with some insensitive man, I shall have more than one worry. I know that I shall be powerless to do anything. I hope I will have sense not to try. Since she has been self-regulated, I do not anticipate that she will fall for an undesirable type of young man; but one can never tell.

I am sure that many a bad companionship is fundamentally a protest against parental authority. *My parents don't trust me, and I don't care. I'll do what I like, and if they don't like it, they can lump it.*

Your fear will be that your daughter will be seduced. But girls are not as a rule seduced; they are partners in a seduction. This sixteen stage should not be difficult if your daughter has been your friend and not your subordinate. You will have to face the truth that no one can live another's life, that one cannot hand on experience in such essential things as emotional matters.

The basic question, after all, is the home attitude toward sex. If it has been healthy, you can safely give your daughter her own private room and a key to it. If it has been unhealthy, she will seek sex in the wrong way—possibly with the wrong men —and you are powerless.

So with your son. You will not be so worried about him— because he cannot become pregnant. Yet with the wrong sex attitudes, he can easily mess up his life.

Few marriages are happy. Considering the infant training

that the majority of people have had, it is a matter for astonishment that there should be any happy marriages at all. If sex is dirty in the nursery, it cannot be very clean in the wedding bed.

Where the sex relationship is a failure, everything else in the marriage is a failure. The unhappy couple, reared to hate sex, hate each other. The children are a failure, for they miss the warmth of the home that is necessary to their own warm life. The sex repressions of their parents unconsciously give them the same repressions. The worst problem children come from such parents.

Sex Instruction

If the child's questions are answered truthfully and without inhibition on the part of the parents, sex instruction becomes part of natural childhood. The pseudoscientific method is bad. I know a youth who was taught sex in this way, and he claims that he blushes when someone uses the word *pollen*. The factual truth about sex is, of course, important, but what's more important is the emotional content. Doctors know all about the anatomy of sex, but they are not better lovers than the South Sea Islanders—most likely they are not nearly as good.

The child is not so much interested in daddy's statement that he puts his wee-wee into mother's wee-wee as he is in *why daddy does it*. The child who has been allowed his own sex play will not need to ask why.

Sex instruction should not be necessary for a self-regulated child, for the term instruction implies previous neglect of the subject. If the child's natural curiosity has been satisfied all the way by open and unemotional answers to all his questions, sex will not stand out as something that has to be specially taught. After all, we do not give a child lessons on his digestive apparatus or his excretory functions. The term *sex instruction* springs from the fact that sex activity is inhibited and made a mystery.

Inclusion of sex instruction in the public school curriculum provides dangerous opportunities for encouraging sex repression by moralizing. The mere term *sex instruction* suggests a formal, awkward lesson on anatomy and physiology by a timid teacher who fears that the subject may slip over the border into forbidden territory.

In most public schools, to tell the whole truth about love and

birth would be to risk getting fired. Public opinion, as represented by the mothers, would not stand it. I have known more
than one case of an irate mother who threatened dire consequences to a woman teacher who allegedly corrupted her child
by her "filthy, godless, obscene teachings."

On the other hand, the only difficulty about giving a free
child all the knowledge about sex that he asks for is that of
knowing how to make things clear. A child wants to know why
every male horse is not a stallion or every male sheep is not a
ram. The answer involves concepts beyond the range of a four-
year-old, for castration is a process that cannot be explained in
simple terms. Here each parent must do the best he can, remembering that nothing must be done in the way of lying or evasion.

A boy of five found a condom in his father's pocket and naturally asked what it was. He accepted easily his father's clear
and simple explanation without any evident emotion.

In certain cases, however, I cannot see any objection in saying
to the child that the subject is too difficult and should wait.
After all, one often does this about other subjects. For example,
when a child asks how an engine works, or who made God, a
parent may say that the answer is too complex for him to understand at his age.

It is far better and safer to postpone an answer than to do
what some foolish parents do—tell a child far too much. I recall a pupil, a Swiss girl of fifteen, saying, "Irmgart (aged ten)
thinks that the doctor brings the babies. I knew where babies
came from long ago. Mother told me. She told me more."

I asked her what more she knew and she told me all about
homosexuality and perversions. Here was a case of unwise truthtelling. The mother should have answered only the question
that the child asked. Her ignorance of child nature made her
tell the child much that the child could not possibly assimilate.

The result was a neurotic daughter. Yet, in the main, I think that this unwise mother was wiser than the mother who deliberately lies to her child when he asks the secret of birth. For the child soon finds out that his mother lied. When the child does find out the truth—usually half told by companions in a dirty way—he thinks he knows why his mother told him a lie. *How could Mother tell me anything as dirty as that!*

And that is the attitude of society today toward birth. It is a dirty business, a shameful business. The fact that a pregnant mother tries to dress in a way to disguise her condition is enough to damn what we call our morality.

There are mothers who tell their children the truth about babies. Yet even among these there are many who tell the truth about birth but who lie about sex. They dodge telling their children that sexual intercourse is highly pleasurable.

My wife and I have never had to think twice about Zoë and her sex education. It has all seemed so simple, so obvious, and so charming—even if it has had its awkward moments, as when Zoë informed a spinster visitor that she, Zoë, had come into the world because Daddy fertilized Mommy, adding with interest, "And who fertilizes you?"

By the way, we have found that a self-regulated child learns tact very early in life. Zoë could speak thus at three and a half; but at five our daughter began to realize that some things must not be said to some people. I have seen a similar sophistication in others who, unlike Zoë, had not had self-regulation from the beginning.

Since Freud discovered the positive sexuality of small children, not enough has been done to study its manifestations. Books have been written about sexuality in babies; but as far as I know, no one has written a book about self-regulated children. Our daughter showed no marked interest in her own sex or that of her parents and playmates. She always saw us naked in the bathroom and in the lavatory. She disproved to my satisfaction the theory held by some psychologists that there is an instinctive, unconscious, innate modesty that makes a child embarrassed on seeing adult genitals or natural functions. That theory, like the similar one that there is an innate guilt about masturbation, is nonsense.

Parents of a self-regulated child will be likely to avoid all the dangerous and stupid mistakes about sex education, the mistakes that connect sex with wrongness and sin; but I am not so sure that there is not a danger from another quarter—the idealistic quarter. Long before there was any talk of self-regulation, some parents taught their children that sex was sacred and spiritual, something to be treated with awe and wonder and a kind of mystical, religious reverence. The modern parent may have no temptation to follow that kind of teaching, yet may succumb to something similar: the worship of the sexual function as a new-found god. It is difficult to define—perhaps it is too vague to define—all I can sense is a sort of holiness attached to sex, a subtle change in the voice when it is mentioned. This attitude suggests a fear of pornography: *God, if I don't speak about sex with awe, they'll think I am one of those who think sex something to make jokes about.* I have been somewhat perturbed to see earnest young parents use words and tones not much different from those of the old brigade that talked reverently about the parts of the body that are holy. Sex has been so long a vulgar joke that the tendency is to jump to the opposite extreme and make it unmentionable—not because it is too evil, but because it is too good. That attitude must surely lead to a new sex fear and repression. If the child is to have a healthy attitude toward sex and a subsequent healthy love life, sex must remain on the earth. It has in itself everything, and all attempts to enhance it by raising it to a higher power are futile attempts to paint the lily.

Telling children that sex is sacred is simply a variant of the old story that sinners will go to hell. If you agree to call eating and drinking and laughing sacred, then I am with you when you call sex sacred. We can call *everything* sacred; but if we only select sex, then we are cheating ourselves and misguiding our children. It is the child who is sacred—sacred in the sense of being that which is not to be spoiled by ignorant teaching.

As the religious hatred of sex slowly dies, other enemies arise. We have the sex-instruction enthusiasts who show children diagrams and tell about the bees and the pollen, saying in effect, "Look, sex is just science. Nothing exciting about it, is there?" We have all been so conditioned about sex that it is almost impossible for us to see the middle, natural way; we are either too pro-sex or too anti-sex. To be pro-sex is good, but to be pro-sex as a protest against an anti-sex training in childhood is likely to be neurotic. Hence the necessity of finding a sane attitude toward sex, an attitude we can find only by noninterference with and approval of the natural child's acceptance of sex.

If that sounds vague or impossible, I suggest that the young parent avoid any show of shame or disgust or moral feeling, refrain from teaching and from placating the neighbors when talking about sexual matters. Then, and only then, will the sex attitudes of a baby grow without inhibition or hatred of his flesh. For such a child sex will never have to be a subject of instruction or warning or anything else.

If we could prevent a child from seeing evil in sex, he would grow up a moral man—not a moralist, not a teacher of others. A Don Juan seemingly fulfills the pleasure component of sex while rejecting the love component. Masturbation, Don Juanism, homosexuality are all unproductive because they are asocial. The new moral man will find that he must fulfill *both* functions of sex: he will find that unless he loves, he will not find the greatest pleasure in the sexual act.

Masturbation

Most children are masturbators. Yet youth has been told that masturbation is evil, that it prevents growth, that it leads to disease or what not. If a wise mother paid no attention to her child's first exploration of his lower body, masturbation would be less compulsive. It is the prohibition that fixes the interest of the child.

To a tiny child, the mouth is much more of an erogenous zone than are the genitals. If mothers took the virtuous attitude toward mouth activities that they take to genital activities, thumb-sucking and kissing would become a matter of conscience.

Masturbation satisfies the desire for happiness, for it is the climax of tension. But immediately the act is over, the conscience of the morally instructed takes hold and shouts, "You are a sinner!" It has been my experience that when the feeling of guilt is abolished, the child has less interest in masturbation.

It almost seems as though some parents would rather their children were criminals than masturbators. I find that suppressed masturbation is at the root of many delinquencies.

A boy of eleven who came to Summerhill had the habit of incendiarism, among other habits. He had been thrashed by his father and by his teachers. Worse still, he had been taught the narrow religion of hell fire and an angry God. Soon after coming to Summerhill, he took a bottle of gasoline and poured it into a vat of paint and turpentine. Then he set fire to the mixture. The house was saved only by the energy of two servants.

I took him to my room. "What is fire?" I asked.

"It burns," he said.

"What sort of a fire do you think of now?" I continued.

"Hell," he said.

"And the bottle?"

"A long thing with a hole at the end," he answered. (*Long pause.*)

"Tell me more about this long thing with a hole in the end," I said.

"My peter," he said awkwardly, "has a hole at the end."

"Tell me about your peter," I said kindly. "Do you ever touch it?"

"Not now. I used to, but I don't now."

"Why not?"

"Because Mr. X [his last schoolmaster] told me that it was the greatest sin in the world."

I concluded that his fire-making was a substituted act for masturbation. I told him that Mr. X was quite wrong, that his peter was no better and no worse than his nose or his ear. From that day on, his interest in fire went away.

When there is no problem during early masturbation, the child naturally goes on at the proper time to heterosexuality. Many unhappy marriages are due to the fact that both the husband and the wife are suffering from an unconscious hate of sexuality—a hate arising from the buried self-hate due to the prohibition of masturbation imposed on them when they were children.

The question of masturbation is supreme in education. Subjects, discipline, games are all vain and futile if the problem of masturbation remains unsolved. Freedom in masturbation means glad, happy, eager children who are really not much interested in masturbation. The prohibition of masturbation means miserable, unhappy children, prone to colds and epidemics, hating themselves and consequently hating others. I say that one of the root reasons for the happiness of Summerhill children is the removal of the fear and self-hate that sex prohibitions induce.

Freud has made us all familiar with the idea that sex exists from the beginning of life, that the baby has sexual pleasure in sucking, and that gradually the erotic zone of the mouth gives place to the erotic zone of the genitals. Thus, masturbation in a child is a natural discovery; not a very important discovery at first, because the genitals are not as pleasurable to the infant as the mouth is or even the skin. It is solely the parental prohibition that makes masturbation so great a complex. The sterner the prohibition, the deeper the sense of guilt; and the greater the compulsion to indulge.

The well-brought-up infant should come to school with no guilty feeling at all about masturbation. There are few, if any, kindergarten children in Summerhill who have any special interest in masturbation. Sex to them has not the attraction of something mysterious. From their earliest time with us (if they have not already been told at home), they know the facts of birth—not only where babies come from, but how they are made. At that early age, such information is received without emotion, partly because it is given without emotion. So it comes about that at the age of fifteen or seventeen, boys and girls in Summerhill can discuss sex openly without any feeling of wrongdoing and without a pornographic attitude.

The parent speaks to the young child with the voice of Almighty God. What mother says about sex is holy writ. The child wholly accepts her suggestion. One mother told her son that masturbation would make him stupid. He accepted the suggestion, and became incapable of learning anything. When his mother was persuaded to tell him that she had told him nonsense, he automatically became a brighter boy.

Another mother told her boy that everyone would hate him if he masturbated. The boy became what mother's suggestion indicated: he was the most unlikable lad in the school. He stole and he spat at people, and he broke things in his pathetic attempts to live up to mother's suggestion. In this case, the mother could not be persuaded to confess her previous error, and the boy remained, more or less, a hater of society.

We have had boys who had been told they would go mad if they masturbated—and they were making a brave attempt to become mad.

I doubt if any subsequent influence has the power fully to counteract an early suggestion from a child's parents. In my work, I always try to get the parent to undo the mischief, for I know that I mean little or nothing to the child. I generally come into his life too late. Hence it is that when a boy hears me say that masturbation cannot make people mad, he finds it difficult to believe me. Father's voice heard when the boy was five was the voice of Holy Authority.

When baby includes his genitals in the play scheme, parents meet the great test. Genital play must be accepted as good and normal and healthy; and any attempt to suppress it will be dangerous. And I include the underhand, dishonest attempt at drawing the child's attention to something else.

I recall the case of a self-regulated little girl who was sent to a nice day school. She seemed unhappy. She had christened her genital play *snuggling in.* When her mother asked her why she didn't like school, she said, "When I try to snuggle in, they don't tell me not to—but they say *Look at this* or *Come and do this,* so I can't ever snuggle in at the kindergarten."

Infantile genital play is a problem because nearly all parents were conditioned in an anti-sex way in their cradles, and they cannot overcome a sense of shame and sin and disgust. It is possible for a parent to have a strong intellectual opinion that genital play is good and healthy, and at the same time—by tone of voice or by look of the eyes—convey to the child that emotionally, he has not accepted the child's right to his own genital satisfaction.

A parent may seem to approve wholly when baby touches its genitals; yet when stiff-stomached Aunt Mary comes to visit, the parent may experience great anxiety lest baby perform in front of the life-disapprover. It is easy to say to such a parent, "Aunt Mary represents the anti-sex element in your repressed self," but saying this does not in itself help parent or child.

The parental fear that infantile genital play will lead to sexual precocity is a deep fear and is widespread. It is a rationalization, of course. Genital play does not lead to precocity. And if it does, what about it? The best way to make sure a child will take an abnormal interest in sex when he reaches adolescence is to prohibit his genital play when he is in the cradle.

It may be a grim necessity to tell a child who has reached the age of understanding not to play with his genitals in public. This advice may sound cowardly and unfair to the child; but the alternative has its own particular danger, too. For if the child comes up against stern disapproval expressed in hateful and shocked terms by hostile adults, more harm might be done to him than that which derives from his loved parents reasoning with him.

When a small child is free to live his life fully without punishment and instruction and taboos, he finds life far too full of interest to confine his activity to the sexual apparatus.

I have no personal knowledge of how self-regulated children would react to each other in genital play. Boys who have been taught that sex is wrong generally link up genital play with sadism. Girls who have had a similar anti-sex training seem to accept sadistic genital play as the norm. Because of the comparative absence of aggressive hate in the self-regulated child, genital play between two free children would probably be gentle and loving.

Our self-disapproval stems mainly from infancy. A large part of it originates from the guilt about masturbation. I find that the unhappy child is so often one who has a heavy conscience about masturbation. The removal of this guilt is the greatest step we can take toward changing a problem child into a happy child.

Nudity

Many couples, especially among the working class, never see each other's bodies until one of them dresses the other's corpse. A peasant woman I knew was a witness in a court case of exhibitionism. She was genuinely shocked. "Come, come, Jean," I chided her. "Why, you've had seven children."

"Mr. Neill," she said solemnly, "I never saw John's . . . I never saw my man naked all my married life."

Nakedness should never be discouraged. The baby should see its parents naked from the beginning. However, the child should be told when he is ready to understand that some people don't like to see children naked and that, in the presence of such people, he should wear clothes.

There was the woman who complained because our daughter bathed in the sea *au naturel*. At the time, Zoë was one year old. This matter of bathing tersely sums up the whole anti-life attitude of society. We all know the irritation arising from trying to undress on the beach without exposing our so-called private parts. Parents of self-regulated, free children know the difficulty of explaining to a child of three or four why he must wear a bathing suit in a public place.

The very fact that the law does not permit exposure of the sex organs is bound to give children a warped attitude toward the human body. I have gone nude myself, or encouraged one of the women on the staff to do so, in order to satisfy the curiosity of a small child who had a sense of sin about nakedness. On the other hand, any attempt to force nudism on children is wrong. They live in a clothed civilization, and nudism remains something that the law does not permit.

Many years ago, when we came to Leiston, we had a duck pond. In the morning, I would take a dip. Some of the faculty and the older girls and boys used to join me. Then we got a batch of boys from private schools. When the girls took to wearing bathing suits, I asked one, a pretty Swede, why.

"It's these new boys," she explained. "The old boys treated nudity as a natural thing. But these new ones leer and gape and —well, I don't like it." Since then, the only communal nude bathing has been done during the evening trips to the sea.

One would think that being brought up free, the children at Summerhill would run about naked in summer. They don't. Girls up to the age of nine will remain nude on a hot day, but small boys seldom do. This is puzzling when one takes into consideration the Freudian statement that boys are proud of having a penis while girls are ashamed of not having one.

Our small boys at Summerhill show no desire to exhibit themselves, and the senior boys and girls hardly ever strip. During the summer, the boys and men wear only shorts without shirts. The girls wear bathing suits. There is no sense of privacy about taking baths, and only new pupils lock bathroom doors. Although some of the girls take sun baths in the field, no boys ever think of spying on them.

I once saw our English teacher digging a ditch in the hockey field, assisted by a group of helpers of both sexes ranging in age from nine to fifteen. It was a hot day and he had stripped. Another time, one of the men on the staff played tennis in the nude. At the School Meeting he was told to put on his pants in case tradesmen and visitors should happen by. This illustrates Summerhill's down-to-earth attitude toward nudity.

Pornography

All children are pornographic, sometimes openly, other times secretly. The least pornographic are those who have had no moral taboos about sex in their infancy and early childhood. I am sure that later on our pupils from Summerhill will be less inclined toward pornography than children brought up under hush-hush methods. As one boy said to me when he came back for a visit during his vacation from the university, "Summerhill spoils you in one way. You find chaps of your own age too dull. They talk about things I grew out of years ago."

"Sex stories?" I asked.

"Yes, more or less. I like a good sex story myself, but the ones they tell are crude and pointless. But it isn't only sex. It's other things, too—psychology, politics. Funny, I find myself tending to chum with fellows who are ten years older than I am."

One new boy at Summerhill, who had not outlived the smutty phase of his prep school, tried to be pornographic. The others shut him up not because he was being pornographic but merely because he was sidetracking an interesting conversation.

Some years ago, we had three girl pupils who had passed through the usual stage of talking out forbidden topics. Later, a new girl came to Summerhill and was assigned to a room with these three girls. One day, this new girl complained to me that the three other girls were dreadfully dull companions. "When I talk about sex things in the bedroom at night, they tell me to shut up. They say they are not interested."

It was true. Naturally, they had an interest in sex but not in its hidden aspect. These girls had had their conscience about sex as a dirty subject destroyed. To a new girl, fresh from the sex talk of a girls' school, they appeared to be highly moral. And they really *were* highly moral, for their morality was founded on knowledge—not on a false standard of good and bad.

Children who are freely brought up about sex matters have an open mind about so-called vulgarity. Some time back, I heard a vaudevillian in the London Palladium who sailed very near the wind in a breezy Elizabethan manner. It struck me then that he got laughs from his audience that he couldn't have got from the Summerhill crowd. Women shrieked when he mentioned ladies' undergarments, but Summerhill children would not consider such remarks at all funny.

Once, I wrote a play for the kindergarten children. It was quite a vulgar play about a woodcutter's son who found a hundred-pound note and ecstatically showed it around to his family, including the cow. The dumb beast swallowed it, and all the family's efforts to get the cow to drop the note proved futile. Then the boy conceived a brilliant idea. They would open a booth at a fair, and charge a shilling for two minutes of attendance. If the cow dropped the money during someone's attendance, that person would win the money.

The play would have brought down the house in a West End music hall. Our children, however, took it in their stride. Indeed, the actors (six to nine years old) saw nothing funny in it at all. One of them, a girl of eight, told me that I was silly not to use the proper word in the play; of course, she meant what other people would call an *improper* word.

The free child is not likely to suffer from voyeurism at Summerhill. Our pupils do not snigger or feel guilty when a film shows a toilet or mentions birth. Every now and then we have an epidemic of writing on toilet walls. To a child, the toilet is the most interesting room in any house. The toilet seems to inspire many writers and artists, which is natural when one considers that the bathroom is a place for creation.

It is a fallacy that women are more pure-minded than men. A man's club or bar, however, is much more likely to be pornographic than a woman's club. The vogue of the risqué story is entirely due to its unmentionableness. In a society without sex repressions, the unmentionable would disappear. At Summerhill, nothing is unmentionable and no one is shockable. *Being shocked implies having an obscene interest in what shocks you.*

Those people who cry in horror, "What a crime to rob little children of their innocence!" are ostriches hiding their heads in the sand. Children are never innocent, though they are often ignorant. And the ostriches fly into hysterics over depriving the child of ignorance.

The most suppressed child is really not ignorant about much. His contact with other children gives him that dreadful "knowledge" that miserable little kids give to each other in dark corners. For those who have been at Summerhill since an early age, there are no dark corners. These children do have an interest in sex matters, but it is not an unhealthy interest. Such children have a really clean attitude toward life.

Homosexuality

Recently, a homosexual wrote me, imploring me to tell him of any land that would allow him to be a homosexual legally. I replied that I knew of no such place. (Since then, I've heard that in Holland and Denmark homosexuality is legally permissible.) Indeed, I cannot think of any country where people can be heterosexual without treading on the corns of the killjoys.

There is no homosexuality in Summerhill. However, as in every group of children who come to Summerhill, there is unconscious homosexuality during a certain stage of development.

Our boys of nine and ten have no use for girls at all. They despise them. They gang up in groups that are not interested in members of the opposite sex. Rather, their interest is in making someone "stick 'em up!" Girls of this same age are likewise only interested in youngsters of their own sex, and form their own groups. Even when they first come into puberty, they do not run after the boys. It appears that the unconscious homosexuality of girls lasts longer than it does with boys. Although they may challenge and rally the boys in a friendly way, they keep to their gangs. But at this age, girls are jealous of their rights. The superiority of the boys in strength and the roughness of the boys annoys them. This is their age of protest against masculinity.

Generally speaking, boys and girls are not much interested in each other until they are about fifteen or sixteen. They show no natural inclination to pair off with each other. In fact, their interest in the opposite sex takes an aggressive form.

It is because Summerhill children do not suffer from a guilt complex about masturbation that they do not respond in an unhealthy way to the latent homosexual phase. Some years ago, a new boy fresh from a private school tried to introduce sodomy. He was unsuccessful. Incidentally, he was surprised and alarmed when he discovered that the whole school knew about his efforts.

Homosexuality is linked in some way to masturbation. You masturbate with the other guy, and he shares the guilt with you, thus lightening your own burden. However, when masturbation is not considered a sin, the necessity to share guilt does not arise.

I do not know what early repressions lead to homosexuality, but it seems quite certain that they must have originated in very early childhood. Summerhill nowadays does not take children under five, and therefore we have often had to deal with children who were wrongly handled in the nursery. Nevertheless, over a period of thirty-eight years, the school has not turned out a single homosexual. The reason is that freedom breeds healthy children.

Promiscuity, Illegitimacy, and Abortion

Promiscuity is neurotic; it is a constant change of partner in the hope of finding the right partner at last. But the right partner never is found, for the fault lies in the impotent, neurotic attitude of the Don Juan or his female counterpart.

If the term *free love* has a sinister meaning, it is because it describes sex that is neurotic. Promiscuous sex—the direct result of repression—is always unhappy and shameful. Among a free people, free love would not exist.

Repressed sex will attach itself to any likely object: a glove, a handkerchief, anything connected with the body. Thus, free love is promiscuous because it is lust without tenderness or warmth or real affection.

A young woman, after a period of promiscuity, said to me, "With Bill I have an orgastic life for the first time." I asked why this was the first time. "Because I *love* him and I didn't love the others."

There is a tendency among those children who come late to Summerhill (thirteen or over) to be promiscuous in desire if not always in practice. The roots of promiscuity go far back in a child's life. The chief thing we know is that they are unhealthy roots. Such behavior leads to variety, but seldom to fulfillment and almost never to happiness.

Real freedom in love does not lead to promiscuity. Love may not last forever. However, with healthy people while love *does* last, it is true and loyal and happy.

The illegitimate child often has a hard road to travel. To tell him, as some mothers do, that his father was killed in the war or died of disease is definitely wrong. He develops a sense of injury because he sees other boys with fathers. On the other hand, the social condemnation of bastardy cannot fail to reach him in some way. At Summerhill, we have had a few children of unmarried mothers, but no one cared a brass button. Under freedom, such children grow up as happily as children born in wedlock.

In the world outside, the bastard child sometimes blames his mother and behaves badly toward her. Again, he may adore his mother and fear that one day she will marry a man who is not his father.

What an odd world it is! Abortion is illegal, and bastardy too often means ostracism. It is gratifying that today many women do not accept the social disapproval of bastardy. They openly have their love children, are proud of them, work for them, rear them well and happily. As far as I have seen, their children are well-balanced and sincere human beings.

No woman teacher in a public school could have an illegitimate child and keep her job. More than once have I heard of a parson's wife who threw her maid out when she became pregnant.

The abortion question is one of the most sickening, hypocritical symptoms of the illness of humanity. There is hardly a judge, parson, doctor, teacher, or any so-called pillar of society who would not prefer an abortion for his daughter rather than have his family face the disgrace of bastardy.

The rich often avoid unpleasant complications by sending their daughters to swanky nursing homes. There they are supposedly treated for irregularity of their menstrual periods, or what not. It is the lower middle class and the poor who are left, literally, holding the baby. There is no other alternative for them. If a middle-class girl tries hard enough, she can find a doctor who will perform an abortion for a goodly sum. Her poorer sister either runs the danger of an abortion by an unskilled, perhaps unscrupulous, abortionist or she has to have her child.

In London there are clinics where women can be fitted with contraceptives. It is generally true that only when a woman shows a marriage ring will the clinic fit her. The borrowing of a wedding ring, however, is not a crime.

The whole business reminds one of pornographic writing on the walls of a public urinal. It typifies a civilization that deserves the price it pays for its spiteful morality. That price in the end is the ills that flesh is heir to, plus misery and hopelessness.

FOUR

RELIGION AND MORALS

Religion

A recent woman visitor said to me, "Why don't you teach your pupils about the life of Jesus, so that they will be inspired to follow in his steps?" I answered that one learns to live, not by *hearing* of other lives, but by *living;* for words are infinitely less important than acts. Many have called Summerhill a religious place because it gives out love to children.

That may be true; only I dislike the adjective as long as religion means what it generally means today—antagonism to natural life. Religion as I remember it, practiced by men and women in drab clothes, singing mournful hymns of tenth-rate music, asking forgiveness for their sins—this is nothing I wish to be identified with.

I personally have nothing against the man who believes in a God—no matter what God. What I object to is the man who claims that *his* God is the authority for his imposing restrictions on human growth and happiness. The battle is not between believers in theology and nonbelievers in theology; it is between believers in human freedom and believers in the suppression of human freedom.

Some day we will have a new religion. You may gape and exclaim, "What? A *new* religion?" The Christian will be up in arms and protest: "Is not Christianity eternal?" The Jew will be up in arms and protest: "Is not Judaism eternal?"

No, religions are no more eternal than nations are eternal. A religion—*any* religion—has a birth, a youth, an old age, and a death. Hundreds of religions have come and gone. Of all the millions of Egyptians who believed in Amon Ra through the better part of 4,000 years, not a single adherent of that religion can be found today. The idea of God changes as culture changes: in a pastoral land, God was the Gentle Shepherd; in warlike times, He was the God of Battles; when trade flourished, He was the God of Justice, weighing out equity and mercy. Today, when man is so mechanically creative, God is Wells' "Great Absentee," for a creative God is not wanted in an age that can make its own atom bombs.

Some day a new generation will not accept the obsolete religion and myths of today. When the new religion comes, it will refute the idea of man's being born in sin. A new religion will praise God by making men happy.

The new religion will refuse the antithesis of body and spirit. It will recognize that the flesh is not sinful. It will know that a Sunday morning spent in swimming is more holy than a Sunday morning spent in singing hymns—as if God needs hymns to keep Him contented. A new religion will find God on the meadows and not in the skies. Just imagine all that would be accomplished if only ten percent of all the hours spent in prayer and churchgoing were devoted to good deeds and acts of charity and helpfulness.

Every day my newspaper tells me how dead our present religion is. We imprison; we stifle opinion that does not agree with ours; we oppress the poor; we arm for war. As an organization, the church is feeble. It does not stop wars. It does little or nothing to temper our barbarous criminal code. It rarely takes sides against the exploiter.

You cannot serve God and Mammon. To use a modern paraphrase, you cannot go to church on Sunday and practice bayonet fighting on Monday. I know no blasphemy so vile as that of the various churches which, during a war, contend that the Almighty is on their side. God cannot believe both sides are right. God cannot be Love, and at the same time be the patron of a gas attack.

For many, organized conventional religion is an easy way

out for individual problems. If a Roman Catholic sins, he con-
fesses to his priest and the priest absolves the sin.

The religious person casts his burden on the Lord; he believes,
and his path to glory is assured. Thus the emphasis is shifted
from personal worth and individual behavior to credo. "Believe
in the Lord and you shall be saved." This, in effect, says make
a declaration and your spiritual problems are over. You get a
guaranteed ticket to heaven.

Fundamentally, religion is afraid of life. It is a running away
from life. It disparages life here and now as merely the pre-
liminary to a fuller life beyond. Mysticism and religion mean
that life here on this earth is a failure; that independent man
is not good enough to achieve salvation. But free children do
not feel that life is a failure, for no one has taught them to say
nay to life.

Religion and mysticism foster unrealistic thinking and unrealistic behavior. The simple truth is that we, with our TV sets
and jet planes, are farther away from *real* living than the African
native is. True, the aborigine also has his religion born of fear;
but he is not impotent in love, nor homosexual, nor inhibited.
His life is primitive, but he says yes to life in many essentials.

Like the savage, we too seek religion because of fear. But
unlike the savage, we are a castrated people. We can teach our
children religion only after we have unmanned them forever
and broken their spirit through fear.

I have had many a case of a child ruined by religious training.
To quote such cases would not help anyone. On the other hand,
any salvationist, too, can quote cases by the yard, cases that were
"saved" by being "washed in the blood." If one postulates that
man is a sinner and needs to be redeemed, then the religionists
are right.

But I ask parents to take a wider view, a view far outside
their immediate circle. I ask parents to foster a civilization that

will not have sin thrust on it at birth. I ask parents to eliminate any need for redemption, by telling the child that he is born good—*not born bad*. I ask parents to tell children that it is *this world* that can and must be made better, to direct energies to the here and now—not to a mythical eternal life to come.

No child should be invested with religious mysticism. Mysticism offers the child an escape from reality—but in a dangerous form. We all sometimes feel a need to escape from reality, or else we should never read a novel, or go to the movies, or drink a glass of whisky. But we escape with our eyes open, and very soon we come back to reality. The mystic is apt to live a continuously escapist life, putting all his libido into his Theosophy or his Spiritualism or his Catholicism or his Judaism.

No child is naturally a mystic. An incident that occurred at Summerhill during a spontaneous acting class one night emphasizes a child's natural sense of reality if his reactions have not been warped by fear.

One night, I sat down on a chair and said: "I am St. Peter at the Golden Gate. You are to be folks trying to get in. Carry on."

They came up with all sorts of reasons for getting in. One girl even came from the opposite direction and pleaded to get out! But the star turned out to be a boy of fourteen who went by me whistling, hands in his pockets.

"Hi," I cried, "you can't go in there."

He turned and looked at me. "Oh," he said, "you are a new man on the job, aren't you?"

"What do you mean?" I asked.

"You don't know who I am, do you?"

"Who are you?" I asked.

"God," he said, and went whistling into heaven.

Nor do children really want to pray. In children, prayer is a sham. I have asked scores of children, "What do you think about when you say your prayers?" Everyone tells the same tale:

he thinks of other things all the time. A child *must* think of other things, for the prayer means nothing to him. It is an imposition from without.

A million men say grace before meals each day, and probably 999,999 men say it mechanically, just as we say "Beg pardon" when we wish to pass someone in an elevator. But why pass our mechanical prayers and our mechanical manners on to the new generation? It is not honest. Nor is it honest to force religion on a helpless child. He should be left entirely free to make up his mind when he reaches the years of choice.

A greater danger than mysticism is the danger of making a child a hater. If a child is taught that certain things are sinful, his love of life must be changed to hate. When children are free, they never think of another child as being a sinner. In Summerhill, if a child steals and is tried by a jury of his fellows, he is never punished for the theft. All that happens is that he is made to pay back the debt. Children unconsciously realize that stealing is sickness. They are little realists, and are far too sensible to postulate an angry God and a tempting devil. Enslaved man made God in his own image, but free children who face life eagerly and bravely have no need to make any God at all.

If we want to keep our children healthy in soul, we must guard against giving them false values. Many of the people who doubt the theology of Christianity have no hesitation in teaching their children beliefs that they themselves question. How many mothers literally believe in a fiery hell, and literally believe in a golden heaven of harps? Yet these thousands of unbelieving mothers are warping their children's souls by dishing up these antiquated primitive stories.

Religion flourishes because man will not, *cannot,* face his unconscious. Religion makes the unconscious the devil, and warns men to flee from its temptations. But make the unconscious, conscious, and religion will have no function.

Religion to a child most always means only fear. God is a mighty man with holes in his eyelids: He can see you wherever you are. To a child, this often means that God can see what is being done under the bedclothes. And to introduce fear into a child's life is the worst of all crimes. Forever the child says nay to life; forever he is an inferior; forever a coward.

No one who in childhood has been threatened with fear of an afterlife in hell can possibly be free from a neurotic anxiety about security in *this* life. This is so even if such a person rationally understands that a heaven and a hell are infantile fantasies founded on nothing but human hopes and fears. The emotional warping one gets in infancy is almost always fixed for a lifetime. The stern God who rewards you with harps or burns you with fire is the God whom man made in his own image. He is the super-projection. God becomes a wish-fulfillment; Satan a fear-fulfillment.

Thus, what gives pleasure comes to signify what is evil. Playing cards, and going to the theater, and dancing come to belong to the devil. All too often, to be religious is to be joyless. The stiff Sunday clothes that children are compelled to wear in most provincial towns testify to the ascetic and punishing quality of religion. Sacred music, too, is more often than not, mournful in nature. For a great many people it is an effort, a duty, to go to church. For a great many people, to be religious is to look miserable and to be miserable.

The new religion will be based on knowledge of self and acceptance of self. A prerequisite for loving others is a true love of self. How different from being reared under a stigma of original sin—which must result in self-hate and, consequently, hatred of others. "He prayeth best who loveth best all things both great and small." Thus Coleridge, the poet, expressed the *new* religion. In the new religion, man will pray best when he loves all things both great and small—in *himself!*

Moral Instruction

Most parents believe that they fail their child unless they teach him moral values, unless they continually point out what is right and what is wrong. Practically every mother and father consider that, apart from taking care of the physical needs of their child, the inculcation of moral values is their chief duty, and that without such instruction the child would grow up to be a savage, uncontrolled in behavior, and with scant consideration for others. This belief springs to a large extent from the fact that most people in our culture accept, at least passively, the dictum that man is a sinner by birth, that he is naturally bad, and that unless he is trained to be good he will be rapacious, cruel, and even homicidal.

The Christian Church states this belief openly, "We are miserable sinners." The bishop and the schoolmaster believe, therefore, that the child must be led to the light. It does not matter whether the light is the light of the Cross or the light of Ethical Culture. In either case, the purpose is the same—to "uplift."

Since both church and school agree that the child is born in sin, we cannot expect mothers and fathers to disagree with these great authorities. The church says, "If you sin, you shall be punished hereafter." The parent takes his cue from this and says, "If you do that again, I shall punish you *now*." Both strive to elevate by imposing fear.

The Bible says, "The fear of the Lord is the beginning of wisdom." It is much more often the beginning of psychic disorder. For to invest a child with fear in any form is harmful.

Many a time a parent has said to me, "I do not understand why my boy has gone bad. I have punished him severely, and

I am sure we never set a bad example in our home." My work too often has been with damaged children who have been educated through fear of the strap or fear of the Lord—children who have been *coerced* into being good.

The parent rarely realizes what the terrible impact on the child has been of a constant stream of prohibitions, of exhortations, of preachments, and of the imposition of a whole system of moral behavior which the young child was not ready for, did not understand, and therefore did not willingly accept.

The overwrought parent of the problem child never thinks of challenging his own code of morals, being for the most part quite sure that he himself knows exactly what is right and what is wrong, and that the correct standard has been authoritatively stated once and for all in Scripture. The parent rarely thinks of challenging the teachings of his own parents or the teachings of his own schoolmasters or the accepted code of society. He tends to take the entire credo of his culture for granted. To think about these beliefs, to analyze them, involves too much cerebration. To challenge them involves too much shock.

Thus the overwrought parent believes that his boy is at fault. The boy is thought to be wilfully bad. I declare my strong conviction that *the boy is never in the wrong*. Every such boy I have handled has been a case of misguided early education and erroneous early training. Some of the very fundamental principles of psychology are bypassed in the process of the usual early indoctrination of children.

To begin with, almost everyone believes that man is a creature of will—that he can do that which he wills to do. Every psychologist will disagree. Psychiatry has proved that a man's actions are controlled to a large extent by his unconscious. Most people would say that Dillinger could have been a non-murderer if he had only used his will. The criminal law is founded on the erroneous belief that every man is a responsible person capable of willing evil or good. Thus, fairly recently, a man was imprisoned in London for splashing women's dresses with ink. To society, the splasher is an evil scoundrel who could be good if only he would try. To the psychologist, he is a poor, ill neurotic, doing a symbolic act of which he does not know the meaning. An enlightened society would lead him gently to a doctor.

The psychology of the unconscious has shown that most of our actions have a hidden source that we cannot reach except by a long elaborate analysis, and even psychoanalysis cannot reach the deepest parts of the unconscious. We act, but we do not know *why* we act.

Some time ago, I laid aside my many volumes of psychology and took up tile work. I do not know why. If I had taken up ink splashing instead, I would not have known why. Because inlaying tile is a social activity, I am a respected citizen; and because ink splashing is antisocial, the other man is a despised criminal. However, there is one difference between the ink splasher and me; I consciously like handiwork, but the criminal does not consciously like ink splashing. In handiwork, my conscious and my unconscious are working in unison; in ink splashing, the conscious and the unconscious are at odds. The antisocial act is the result of the conflict.

Some years ago, we had a pupil at Summerhill, a boy of eleven—bright, intelligent, lovable. He would be sitting quietly reading. Then suddenly he would jump up, rush from the room, and try to set fire to the house. An impulse seized him, an impulse he could not control.

Many previous teachers had encouraged him, both by counsel and cane, *to use his will* to try to control his impulses. But the unconscious drive to start a fire was too strong to be controlled— it was far stronger than the conscious drive not to be poorly regarded. This boy was not a *bad* boy; he was a *sick* boy. What were the influences that made him sick? What are the influences that turn boys and girls into sick, delinquent children? I shall try to explain.

When we look at an infant, we know there is no wickedness in him—no more than there is wickedness in a cabbage or in a young tiger. The newborn child brings with him a life force; his will, his unconscious urge is to *live*. His life force prompts him to eat, to explore his body, to gratify his wishes. He acts as Nature intended him to act, as he was *made* to act. But, to the adult, the will of God in the child—the will of Nature in the child—is the will of the devil.

Practically every adult believes that the nature of the child must be improved. Hence it happens that every parent begins to teach the young child how to live.

The child soon comes up against a whole system of prohibitions. *This* is naughty and *that* is dirty and *such and such* is selfish. The original voice of the child's natural life force meets the voice of instruction. The church would call the voice of Nature the voice of the devil, and the voice of moral instruction the voice of God. I am convinced that the names should be reversed.

I believe that it is moral instruction that makes the child bad. I find that when I smash the moral instruction a bad boy has received, he becomes a good boy.

There may be a case for the moral instruction of adults, although I doubt it. There is no case whatever for the moral instruction of children. It is psychologically wrong. To ask a child to be unselfish is wrong. Every child is an egoist and the world belongs to him. When he has an apple, his one wish is to eat that apple. The chief result of mother's encouraging him to share it with his little brother is to make him hate the little brother. Altruism comes later—comes naturally—*if the child is not taught to be unselfish*. It probably never comes at all if the child has been forced to be unselfish. By suppressing the child's selfishness, the mother is fixing that selfishness forever.

How does this come about? Psychiatry has demonstrated and proved that an unfulfilled wish lives on in the unconscious. Therefore, the child who is taught to be unselfish will, in order to please Mother, conform to her demands. He will unconsciously bury his real wishes—his selfish wishes—and because of this repression will retain his infantile desires and remain selfish throughout life. Moral instruction thus defeats its own purpose.

So it is also in the sexual sphere. The moral prohibitions of childhood fix the infantile interest in sex. The poor fellows who are arrested for infantile sexual acts—showing schoolgirls obscene postcards, playing with their genitals in public—are men who had moral mothers. The perfectly harmless interest of childhood was labeled a heinous sin. The child repressed the infantile desire. But that same desire lived on in the unconscious, and came out later in its original form, or more often, in a symbolic form. Thus, the woman who lifts handbags in a department store is doing a symbolic act that has its origin in a repression due to moral teaching in childhood. Her behavior actually constitutes the gratification of a forbidden infantile sexual wish.

All these poor people are unhappy people. To steal is to be disliked by one's group, and the group instinct is a strong one. To stand well with our neighbors is a genuine objective in human life. It is not in human nature to be antisocial. Egoism itself is enough to make normal people social. Only a stronger factor than egoism can make a person antisocial.

What is this stronger factor? When the conflict between the two selves—the self that Nature made and the self that moral education fashioned—is too bitter, egoism reverts to the infantile stage. Then the opinion of the crowd takes a subordinate place.

Thus, the kleptomaniac knows the awful shame of appearing in the police court and of being written up in the newspapers, but the fear of public opinion is not so strong as the infantile wish. Kleptomania, in the last analysis, signifies a wish to find happiness; but because symbolic fulfillment can never satisfy the original wish, the victim goes on repeating his attempt.

An illustration will make clearer the process of the unfulfilled wish and its subsequent paths. When little Billie, aged seven, came to Summerhill, his parents told me that he was a thief. He had been a week in the school when one of the staff came to me and said that his gold watch had disappeared from his bedroom table. I asked the housemother if she knew anything about it.

"I saw Billie with the works of a watch," she said. "When I asked him where he got it, he said he found it at home in a very, very deep hole in the garden."

I knew that Billie locked up all his possessions in his trunk. I tried the lock with one of my own keys, and managed to open the trunk. In it lay the wreck of a gold watch, apparently the result of an attack with hammer and chisel. I locked the trunk and called in Billie.

"Did you see Mr. Anderson's watch?" I asked.

He looked up at me with large innocent eyes. "No," he said, and added, "What watch?"

I looked at him for half a minute. "Billie," I said, "do you know where babies come from?"

He looked up with interest. "Yes," he said, "from the sky."

"Oh, no," I smiled. "You grew inside your mommy; and when you were big enough, you came out." Without a word, he walked to his trunk, opened it, and handed me a broken watch. His stealing was cured, for he had been only stealing the truth. His face lost its puzzled, worried look, and he became happier.

The reader may be tempted to think that Billie's dramatic cure was magical. It was not. When a child talks of a deep hole at home, it is likely that he is unconsciously thinking of the deep cavern in which his life began. Again, I knew that the boy's father kept a few dogs. Billie must have known where puppies came from, and he must have put two and two together and made a guess at the origin of babies. Mother's timid lie drove him to repress his theory; and his wish to find out the truth took a form of symbolic gratification. Symbolically, he stole mothers and opened them up to see what was inside them. I had another pupil who kept opening drawers for the same reason.

What parents must understand is that you cannot rush a child into a stage which he is not ready for. People who are not satisfied to let their child develop naturally from the crawling stage to the walking stage, and who set an infant on its two little legs too early in life before he is ready to walk, only achieve the melancholy result of making the child bandy-legged. Since the young limbs are not strong enough to support the child's weight, the demand is premature. The result is disaster. Had the parents waited until the child was *naturally* ready to walk, the child would, of course, have walked perfectly well all by himself. Likewise, untimely efforts to toilet-train the child must produce baleful results.

The same considerations apply to moral instruction. To force a child to adopt values that he is not naturally ready to adopt not alone results in choking off the adoption of such values in due course and in due time, but also induces neuroses.

To ask a boy, aged six, to chin a bar four times is to make an excessive demand on the youngster. His muscles are not strong enough for such exercise. Yet if the same boy is left to develop naturally, he will easily achieve that result at age eighteen. Similarly, one should not attempt to hasten the development of a youngster's moral sense. The parent must exercise patience, secure in the thought that the child has been born good, and that he inevitably will turn out to be a good human being if he is not crippled and thwarted in his natural development by interference.

My experience of many years in handling children at Summerhill convinces me that *there is no need whatsoever to teach children how to behave. A child will learn what is right and what is wrong in good time—provided he is not pressured.*

Learning is a process of acquiring values from the environment. If parents are themselves honest and moral, their children will, in good time, follow the same course.

Influencing the Child

Parents and teachers make it a business to influence children because they think they know what children ought to have, ought to learn, ought to be. I disagree. I never attempt to get children to share my beliefs or my prejudices. I have no religion, but I have never taught one word against religion; nor for that matter against our barbarous criminal code, nor against anti-Semitism, nor against imperialism. I would never consciously influence children to become pacifists, or vegetarians, or reformers, or anything else. I know that preaching cuts no ice with children. I put my trust in the power of freedom to fortify youth against sham, and against fanaticism, and against isms of any kind.

Every opinion forced on a child is a sin against that child. A child is not a little adult, and a child cannot possibly see the adult's point of view.

Let me give an illustration. One night, I said to five boys whose ages ranged from seven to eleven, "Miss Y has influenza and is feeling bad. Try not to make a noise when you are going to bed." They promised to be quiet. Five minutes later, they were having a pillow fight with great noise. Leaving out of consideration the chances of their having an unconscious desire to make life nasty for Miss Y, I contend that the fault lay in their age. It is true that a stern voice and a whip would have secured peace for Miss Y, but peace at the expense of introducing fear into the lives of those children. The universal method of dealing with children is to teach them to adapt themselves to us and our needs. This method is wrong.

Few parents or teachers ever grasp the truth that talking to a young child is wasted breath. No child who ever lived really benefited from the time-honored parental reaction to pulling the cat's tail, "How would *you* like it if someone pulled *your* ear?" Furthermore, no child ever really comprehends what parents mean when they say, "So you stuck a pin in baby? Just to show you that a pin hurts, I'll . . . (*screams*). That will stop you from doing that again." It may stop him—but the ultimate results throng our clinics.

I am trying to convince parents of the fact that a child cannot see cause and effect. To say to a child, "You've been so naughty that you won't get your Saturday nickel," is wrong. For when Saturday comes and he is reminded of his misdeed and its punishment, he simply is genuinely angry and frustrated. Because what happened on, say Monday, is a thing of the long, long past—a thing with no connection with the present Saturday nickel. He does not feel the least bit guilty; but he does feel very hateful against the depriving authority.

A parent should always question whether he is not imposing directives because of his own power drive and his need to satisfy that drive by fashioning someone else. Everyone seeks the good opinion of his neighbors. Unless other forces push him into unsocial behavior, a child will naturally want to do that which will cause him to be well-regarded, but this desire to please others develops at a certain stage in his growth. The attempt by parents and teachers to artificially accelerate this stage does the child irreparable damage.

I once visited a modern school where over a hundred boys and girls assembled in the morning to hear a clergyman address them. He spoke earnestly, advising them to be ready to hear Christ's call. The principal asked me later what I thought of the address. I replied that I thought it criminal. Here were scores of children, each with a conscience about sex and other things; the sermon simply increased each child's sense of guilt.

Another progressive school compels all pupils to listen to Bach for half an hour before breakfast. Now this attempt to elevate by giving a standard of values has psychologically the same effect on the child as the old Calvinistic threat of hell. It makes the child repress what he is told is a lower taste.

When a principal of a school tells me that his pupils love Beethoven and won't have jazz, I am convinced that he has used his influence—because my pupils, by a large majority, favor jazz. I personally hate the noisy, quacking stuff. But I'm sure that principal is wrong, though he may be a good fellow and an honest one.

When a mother teaches a child to be good, she suppresses the child's natural instincts. She is saying to the child, "What you want to do is wrong." This is equivalent to teaching the child to hate himself. To love others while hating yourself is impossible. We can only love others if we love ourselves.

The mother who punishes her child for a small sexual habit is always the woman whose attitude to sex is a dirty one. The exploiter sitting as magistrate on the bench is honestly indignant at the accused man who stole a purse. It is because we haven't the courage to face our own naked souls that we become moralists. Our guidance of children is subjectively a guidance of ourselves. We unconsciously identify ourselves with our children. The child we dislike most is always the child who is most like ourselves. We hate in others what we hate in ourselves. And because each of us is a self-hater, the children get the results in cuffs and scoldings and prohibitions and moral preachments. Why are we self-haters? It is the vicious circle. Our parents tried to improve what nature gave us.

In dealing with malefactors, the parent or teacher or magistrate has to face emotional factors in himself. Is he a moralist, a hater, a sadist, a disciplinarian? Is he a suppressor of sex in the young? Has he any glimmering of depth psychology? Does he act conventionally and through prejudice? In short, how free is he himself?

None of us is entirely free emotionally because we were conditioned in our cradles. Perhaps the right questions to ask are: *Are we free enough to keep from butting in on the life of another, however young that other may be? Are we free enough to be objective?*

Swearing and Cursing

One persistent criticism of Summerhill is that the children swear. It is true that they swear—if saying old English words is swearing. It is true that any new pupil will swear more than is necessary.

At our General School Meeting, a girl of thirteen who came from a convent was always being brought up on charges for shouting out the phrase *son of a bitch* when she went sea bathing. It was impressed upon her that she only swore when bathing at a public beach, with strangers around, and that therefore she was showing off. As one boy put it to her, "You are just a silly little goose. You swear in order to show off in front of people, and you claim to take pride that Summerhill is a free school. But you do just the opposite—you make people look down on the school."

I explained to her that she was really trying to do the school harm because she hated it. "But I don't hate Summerhill," she cried. "It's a terrific place."

"Yes," I said, "it is, as you say, a terrific place, but you aren't in it. You are still living in your convent, and you have brought all your hate of the convent and your hate of the nuns with you. You still identify Summerhill with the hated convent. It isn't really Summerhill you are trying to damage—it's the convent." But she went on shouting out her special phrase until Summerhill became a real place to her and not a symbol. After that, she stopped swearing.

Swearing is of three kinds: sexual, religious, excremental. In Summerhill, the religious type of swearing is no problem because the children are not taught religion. Now most children and most adults swear. The army is famous for what a character of Kipling's called "the adjective." At most universities and clubs, the students use a sexual and an excremental lingo. Schoolboys swear secretly, and they tell dirty stories. The difference between Summerhill and a prep school is that in the one children swear openly; in the other, secretly.

It is always the new pupils who make swearing a problem in Summerhill. Not that the old pupils have saintly tongues, but the old-timers swear at the right time, so to speak. They use conscious control and are careful not to offend outsiders.

Our juniors have an interest in the old English word for feces. They use it a lot, that is, the ones from polite homes do. I mean homes that talk of *No. 2* and *making b.m.'s.* Children like Anglo-Saxon words. More than one child has asked me why it is wrong to say *shit* in public, but right to say *feces* or *excrement.* I'm baffled to know.

Kindergarten children, when free from molding, have a vocabulary that is largely excremental. Summerhill youngsters, aged four to seven, take joy in shouting out *shit* and *piss.* I realize that most of them were rigidly toilet-trained as babies, and that they are therefore likely to have complexes about natural functions. Yet one or two of them were raised in self-regulation, and had no disciplined training in cleanliness, were not subjected to taboos or words like *naughty* or *dirty,* experienced no hiding of adult nakedness, nor big to-do about toilet functions. These self-regulated children seem to have the same delight in using the Saxon words that their disciplined friends have. So it does not seem to be true that freedom to swear automatically takes all attraction away from obscene words. Our little children use such words freely and without proper context; whereas when older boys or grown girls swear, they use the words as an adult would—that is, appropriately.

Sex words are more commonly used than are excremental

words. Our children have no feeling that toilets are funny things. Their lack of repression about excrement makes reference to it rather dull and matter-of-fact. It is different with sex. Sex is such an important part of life that its vocabulary pervades our whole life. In its mentionable form, we see it in practically every song and dance: either *My Red Hot Mamma* or *When I Get You Alone Tonight.*

Children accept swearing as a natural language. Adults condemn it because their own obscenity is greater than that of children. Only an obscene person will condemn obscenity. I imagine that if a parent brought up a baby to believe that the nose was dirty and evil, the child would whisper the word *nose* in dark corners.

Parents must ask themselves the question, "Shall I allow my children to swear openly, or shall I permit them to be obscene in dark dirty corners." There is no halfway. The hush-hush way leads in adulthood to the tiresome stories of traveling salesmen. The open way leads to a clear, clean interest in all life. At a venture, I say that our former pupils have the cleanest minds in England.

Yet the anti-life, disapproving relatives or neighbors who condemn swearing in children have to be met with at one time or another. In the case of Zoë, we have found that she accepts a rational explanation of the behavior of outsiders. Some child taught her the word that the law will not let us print. When we were interviewing a prospective parent—a conventional businessman—she was trying unsuccessfully to fit some toy together and at each failure she exclaimed, "Oh, f— it!" Later, we told her (quite wrongly I think now) that some people did not like that word, and that she should not use it when visitors were present. She said, "Okay."

A week later, she was doing something difficult to accomplish. She looked up and asked a teacher, "Are you a visitor?"

The lady replied, "Of course not!"

Zoë gave a sigh of relief and cried, "Oh, f—it!"

I have seen many a child, who was free at home to say what he liked, ostracized by other homes. *We can't possibly have Tommy to the party because we can't have our children corrupted by his awful language.* To be outlawed is a painful punishment. Therefore one must pay heed to the taboos of the outside world and guide the child accordingly. But the guidance must be without punitive censuring.

Censorship

How much should we censor a child's reading? On my office bookshelves are various books on psychology and sex. Any child is free to borrow them at any time. Yet I doubt if more than one or two have ever shown any interest in them. Not one boy or girl has ever asked for *Lady Chatterley's Lover*, or *Ulysses*, or *Krafft-Ebing*, and only one or two seniors have borrowed the *Encyclopedia of Sex Knowledge*.

One time, however, a new pupil, a girl of fourteen, took *A Young Girl's Diary* from my bookshelf. I saw her sit and snigger over it. Six months later, she read it a second time and told me that it was rather dull. What had been spicy reading to ignorance had become commonplace reading to knowledge. This girl came to Summerhill with a dirty ignorance whispered in classroom corners. Of course, I cleared her up about sex matters. Prohibition always makes children read books on the sly.

In our young days we had our reading censored, so that our great ambition was to get hold of *Tess of the D'Urbervilles*, or *Rabelais*, or translations of French yellowbacks. In other words, censorship was used as a criterion for selecting the most interesting books.

Censorship is feeble inasmuch as it does not protect anyone. Take James Joyce's book *Ulysses*, once forbidden in England and the United States, but then purchasable in Paris or Vienna. It contains words that are usually described as obscene. A naive reader would not understand the words; a sophisticated reader, knowing them already, could not be corrupted. I remember a school principal criticizing me because I introduced *The Prisoner of Zenda* into the school library. Surprised, I asked why.

He said that the opening chapters dealt with illegitimacy. I had read the book twice and had not noticed this fact.

Children's minds seem to be cleaner than those of adults. A boy can read *Tom Jones* and fail to see the obscene passages. If we free the child from ignorance about sex, we destroy the danger in any book. I am strongly against censorship of books at any age.

It is when we leave sex and go to fear that censorship of books becomes a more difficult problem. Such a terrifying book as Bram Stoker's *Dracula* might have a sad effect on a neurotic child, and I would not deliberately leave this book in reach of such a child. Yet because my work is to try to analyze the roots of fears, I would not forbid a child to read it. Rather, I would attack the symptoms raised by reading the book.

As a child, I recall being terrified by the biblical story of the children who were eaten by bears, yet no one advocates the censorship of the Bible. Many children read the Bible searching for obscene passages. As a small boy I knew them all, chapter and verse. It strikes me now that my fear of the bears may have been the result of my conscience pricking me concerning other parts of the Bible.

We are inclined to exaggerate the effect of bloodthirsty stories on children. Most children can enjoy the most sadistic tales. On Sunday nights, when I tell my pupils adventure stories in which they are rescued at the last moment from the cannibal's cauldron, they jump for joy.

It is the supernatural story that is most likely to terrify. Most children fear ghosts, especially children from religious homes. Here, as in sex matters, the proper method is to abolish the fear rather than to censor the book. I grant that it is difficult to lay ghosts in the soul, but the teacher or the doctor must try to lay them. The parent's duty is to see that the ghosts do not enter the child's soul.

No parents should ever read their children stories of cruel giants and wicked witches. Some hesitate to read a story such as *Cinderella* on the ground that this tale has the wrong moral: Be a drudge without the ability to rise above cinders, and a fairy godmother will give you a prince for a husband. But what harmful effect can *Cinderella* have on a healthy child?

The percentage of crime stories on any railway bookstall is high. When a boy of sixteen shoots a policeman, a million or two readers do not see that he is living out the kind of fantasy they read about and enjoy. The thriller denotes our inability to play, to fantasy, to create; fundamentally, it touches our repressed hate and desire to injure and to kill.

Going to the movies and reading books are in different categories. What is written is not so terrifying as what is seen or heard. Some films fill children with terror, and one is never sure where and when something frightening in the movie may arise. There is so much brutality on the screen. Men punch each other in the jaw and sometimes they even hit women. Newsreels display boxing and wrestling contests. To complete the sadistic picture, there are films dealing with bullfighting. I have seen young children afraid of the crocodile or the pirates in *Peter Pan*. *Bambi* is a charming story, so humane and loving that I cannot understand how anyone can shoot a deer for mere sport after seeing the movie. Children love it, although some of them cry in fear when the hunters' dogs attack Bambi. Accordingly, a parent is justified in banning certain films for his young child.

It is questionable whether sex films are harmful to most children. Certainly, such films do not harm free children. My pupils have seen the French film *La Ronde* without much emotion or any bad effects. That is because children see what they want to see.

A film story without sex will not thrive at the box office. Sex movies take more of the national income than books and music.

Cosmetics sell better than concert tickets. But we must remember that, underneath the mentionable form of sex there is always the unmentionable. Behind the bridal carriage, the old shoe, and the rice are the unmentionable things that these symbolize.

The popularity of films is due to the escapist aspect in us all, and that is why producers almost always give us sumptuous sets and magnificent costumes. Amidst all this luxury, the villainous characters get it in the neck and the virtuous ones live happily ever afterward.

Recently, we saw a film about a man who sold his soul to the devil. The children unanimously agreed that the devil looked very much like me. I always become the devil to boys who have been taught that the sex sin is the sin against the Holy Ghost. When I tell them that there is nothing sinful about the body, they look upon me as a tempting devil. To neurotic children I represent both God and the devil. One little chap took up a hammer to kill the devil one day. Helping neurotics can be a dangerous life.

To censor a child's companionship is too difficult in most cases. I think it should be done only when a neighboring child is cruel or bullying. Luckily, most children are naturally selective, and sooner or later they find suitable companions.

FIVE

CHILDREN'S PROBLEMS

Cruelty and Sadism

Cruelty is perverted love; this is why extreme sadism is always perverted sexuality. The cruel person cannot give because giving is a love action.

There is no instinct for cruelty. Animals are not cruel. A cat does not play with a mouse because it is cruel. It is just a game, and there is no consciousness of any cruelty.

In humans, cruelty is due to motives that, for the most part, are unconscious. In my long experience with children at Summerhill, I have rarely had a child who wanted to torture animals. There was one exception some years ago. John, thirteen, was given a puppy as a birthday present. "He loves animals," his mother had written. As John took little Spot around with him, it soon became clear that he was mistreating the dog. I concluded that he was identifying Spot with his younger brother Jim, his mother's favorite.

One day I saw him beating Spot. I went up to the little dog, stroked it, and said, "Hello, Jim." Apparently, I made John conscious that he had been venting his hatred of his rival brother on the poor dog. Thereafter, he ceased being cruel to Spot; but I only touched his symptom; I didn't cure his sadism.

Free, happy children are not likely to be cruel. The cruelty of many children springs from the cruelty that has been practiced on them by adults. You cannot be beaten without wishing to beat someone else. Like the teacher, you select someone who is physically weaker than you. Boys at strict schools are more cruel to each other than are the children at Summerhill.

Cruelty invariably is rationalized: *it hurts me more than it does you.* Few, if any, sadists, say frankly, "I beat people up because I get satisfaction in doing it," although that is the true explanation. They explain away their sadism in moral terms, saying, "I don't want my boy to be soft. I want him to be able to fit into a world that is going to give him many a nasty blow. I thrash my son because I was thrashed when I was a boy, and it did me a hell of a lot of good."

Parents who beat their children are always ready with such glib explanations. I have never yet met a parent who honestly says, "I hit my kid because I hate him, hate myself, my wife, my job, my relations—in fact, I hate life itself. I hit my son because he is small, and he can't hit me back. I hit him because I am afraid of my boss. When my boss jumps on me, I take it out on the kid at home."

If parents were honest enough to say all this, they would feel no need to be cruel to their children. Cruelty is born of ignorance and self-hatred; cruelty protects the sadist from realizing that his own nature is perverted.

In Hitler's Germany, the torture was inflicted by sexual perverts of the Julius Streicher type; his paper *Der Stürmer* was full of vile, perverted sex long before concentration camps were erected. Yet many fathers who berate the sexual perversity of the prison sadist do not apply the same reasoning to their own minor sadisms. To beat a child at home or at school is basically the same thing as torturing a Jew in Belsen. If sadism was sexual in Belsen, it is likely to be sexual in school or family.

I can hear a mother protest, "Nonsense! Do you mean to say that when I slapped Jimmy's hand today because he touched the vase from Granny that I was showing sexual perversion?"

My reply is, "Yes, to a minor degree. If you are happily married and have a fully satisfying sex life, you will not spank Jimmy. Spanking is literally a hatred of the flesh, and the flesh means the body with all its demands and longings. If you love your own flesh, you won't want to make Jimmy's flesh hurt."

Parents can beat their children as much as they please as long as they don't leave welts that can be seen in a magistrate's court. Our criminal code is a long record of cruelty disguised as justice.

Mental cruelty is more difficult to cope with than physical cruelty. A municipal law can abolish corporal punishment in schools, but no law can ever reach the person who practices mental cruelty. A cynical or a spiteful parental tongue can do untold damage to a child. We all know fathers who sneer at their sons. *Butterfingers, you can't do a thing without bungling it*. Such men likewise show their hatred of their wives by constant criticism. And there are wives who rule husbands and children through browbeating and streams of abuse.

A specialized form of mental cruelty is that shown by a father when he takes out his hatred of his wife on the children.

Teachers sometimes show cruelty by being supercilious and sarcastic. Such teachers expect to hear roars of laughter from their pupils when they thus torture some poor, cowering child.

Children will never be cruel unless they have been forced to repress some strong emotion. Free children have little or no self-hate to express. They do not hate others and are not cruel.

Every little bully has had his life warped in some way. Often, he is simply doing to others what has been literally done to him. Every beating makes a child sadistic in desire or practice.

Children under suppression are cruel in their jokes. I have hardly ever seen a practical joke played in Summerhill. The ones I have seen were usually engineered by new arrivals from private schools. Sometimes, at the beginning of a term when the children return from the greater suppression of their homes, there are displays of teasing—hiding bicycles and so on—but these spells do not last more than a week. In the main, the humor of Summerhill is kindly. The reason is that the children enjoy the approval and love of the teachers; for children are good when the necessity to hate and fear is abolished.

Criminality

Many psychologists believe that a child is born neither good nor bad, but with tendencies toward both beneficence and criminality. I believe there is no instinct of criminality nor any natural tendency toward malevolence in the child. Criminality appears in a child as a perverted form of love. It is a radical expression of cruelty. It too springs from lack of love.

One day, one of my pupils, a boy of nine, was playing a game and was pleasantly crooning to himself, "I want to kill my mother." It was unconscious behavior, for he was making a boat, and all his conscious interest was directed toward that activity. The fact is that his mother lives her own life, and seldom sees him. She does not love him, and unconsciously he knows it.

But this boy—one of the most lovable of children—did not start out in life with criminal thoughts. It is simply the old story: *if I can't get love, I can get hate*. Every case of criminality in a child can be traced to lack of love.

Another pupil, also nine, had a phobia of poison; he feared that his mother would poison him. When she arose from the table, he watched her every movement; and often he said, "I know what you are after; you are going to get the poison for my food." I suspected that it was a case of projection. His mother seemed to give more love to his brother; and probably the neurotic son had fantasies of poisoning both his brother and his mother. His fears were probably fears of retribution—*I want to poison her, and perhaps she will poison me in revenge*.

Crime is obviously an expression of hate. The study of criminality in children resolves itself into the study of why a child is led to hate. It is a question of injured ego.

We cannot get away from the fact that a child is primarily an egoist. No one else matters. When the ego is satisfied, we have what we call goodness; when the ego is starved, we have what we call criminality. The criminal revenges himself on society because society has failed to appreciate his ego by showing love for him.

If humans were born with an instinct for criminality, there would be as many criminals from fine middle-class homes as from slum homes. But well-to-do people have more opportunities for expression of the ego. The pleasures money buys, the refined surroundings, culture, and pride of birth all minister to the ego. Among the poor, the ego is starved. Only a very few poor boys attain distinction. To be a criminal, a gangster, even a bully is one way of attaining distinction.

Many people believe that bad films make criminals. It appears to me to be a shortsighted view. I very much doubt that any film ever corrupted anyone. Certainly a film might suggest a method to a youth, but the motive was there before the film came around. The film may make crime more artistic, but it cannot possibly suggest crime to anyone who has not contemplated crime.

Crime is, first of all, a family affair; and second a community affair. Most of us who will be honest will admit that we have killed off our families in fantasy. I had one girl pupil who gave them most horrible deaths—especially her mother.

Authority and jealousy are behind many murderous wishes. No child can stand authority. And since so many children are thwarted from the age of four to sixteen, I marvel that there are not more murderers in the world.

In a child, the will to power is the will to be admired and loved. The child strives to compel admiration and attention. Thus we find criminal thoughts in introverted children—timid children who have no social gifts. The plain, little girl will weave horrible fantasies of sudden death while her pretty sister is dancing solo before guests.

The extrovert has no occasion for hate; he laughs and dances and talks, and the appreciation of his audience satisfies his desire to be admired.

The introvert sits in a corner and dreams of what should be. The most introverted boy in my school takes no part in social evenings. He does not dance; he never sings; he never takes part in a tumble game. In his lessons with me, he tells me of a wonderful magician who serves him. He has only to say the word and the magician will give him a Rolls Royce. I told him a story one day in which all the Summerhill children were wrecked on an island. He did not seem to like the story. I asked him to amend it. "Make it that I was the only one saved," he said.

We are all familiar with this mechanism—the mechanism of climbing up by knocking the other fellow down. It is the psychology of the talebearer. "Please, sir, Tommy was swearing" means *I don't swear; I am a good boy.*

The difference between the person who kills rivals in fantasy and the criminal who kills rivals in reality is one of degree. In so far as we are all more or less starved for love, we are all potential criminals. I used to flatter myself that I cured children of criminal fantasies by my psychological methods, but I now believe that the credit should go to love. To pretend that I love a new pupil would be fatuous; yet the child feels that I love him because I respect his ego.

To allow a child the freedom to be himself is the real cure for criminality. I learned that years ago when I went to see Homer Lane's *Little Commonwealth.* He gave delinquent children the freedom to be themselves, and they became good. In the slums, the only way delinquents have of satisfying their egos is to draw attention to themselves by antisocial behavior. Lane told me that he saw some criminal boys at their trials look proudly

around the court. In a farming community with Lane, these boys found new values, social values—that is, *good* values. To me the demonstration on that Dorset farm was convincing proof that there is no original will to criminality.

I think of the new boy who ran away. Lane chased him and caught him. The boy, accustomed to cuffs, put up a protective arm. Lane smiled and slipped some money into his hand.

"What's this for?" stammered the boy.

"Take the train home, man," said Lane; "don't walk." The boy returned to the Commonwealth that night.

I think of that way, and I think of the stern methods of most reform schools. It is the law that makes the crime. The law at home voiced by father's forbidding commands curbs the ego of the child; and in curbing that ego, makes the child bad. The law of the state merely revives the unconscious memories of the home restraint.

Suppression awakens defiance, and defiance naturally seeks revenge. Criminality is revenge. To abolish crime, we must abolish the things that make a child want vengeance. We must show love and respect for the child.

Stealing

Two kinds of stealing should be distinguished: stealing by a normal child and stealing by a neurotic child.

A natural, normal child will steal. He simply wants to satisfy his acquisitive urge; or with his friends, he wants the adventure. He has not yet made the distinction between *mine* and *thine*. Many Summerhill children engage in this kind of stealing up to a certain age. They are free to live out this stage.

Speaking to a number of schoolmasters about their orchards, I have had them tell me that their pupils take most of the fruit. Now we have a large garden at Summerhill filled with fruit trees and bushes, but our children rarely steal the fruit. Some time ago, two boys were charged at a General School Meeting with pinching fruit. They were new boys. When their consciences were abolished, they had no further interest in fruit stealing.

School thieving is for the most part a communal affair. The communal theft would suggest that adventure plays an important part in stealing; not only adventure, but showing off, enterprise, leadership.

Only occasionally does one see the lone crook—always a sly boy with an angelic innocence all over his face, who gets away with much because at Summerhill there is no gang rat to betray him. No, you can never tell a young thief by his face. Indeed, I have a boy with such an innocent smile and such clear, blue, guileless eyes that I have a good suspicion that he is not entirely ignorant of the whereabouts of a certain can of fruit that disappeared from the school larder last night.

However, I have seen many a child who would steal at the age of thirteen grow up to be an honest citizen. The truth seems to be that children take a much longer time to grow up than we have been accustomed to think. By growing up, I mean becoming a social being.

The child is primarily an egoist—generally until the commencement of puberty, and until then, he generally hasn't the art of identifying himself with others. The concept of *mine* and *thine* is adult: the youngster will develop this sense when he becomes mature.

If children are loved and free, *in time* they will become good and honest. This sounds like a simple dictum, but I am aware of the many snags that crop up in practice.

In Summerhill, I cannot leave the icebox or the money box unlocked. At Summerhill School Meetings, children accuse others of breaking open their trunks. Even one thief can make a community lock-and-key-conscious; and there are few communities of youth that are completely honest. Fifty-five years ago, I dared not leave a book in my overcoat pocket in the students' room of the university; and I have heard rumors that some members of Parliament hesitate to leave valuables in coats and briefcases.

Honesty would appear to be an acquired characteristic that appeared late in man's development with the advent of private property. Possibly the fact which makes most for honesty is fear. It is not abstract honesty that prevents me from cheating on my income tax; it is fear that the game isn't worth the candle, that the disgrace following detection would ruin reputation and work and home.

When there is a law against anything, it must be taken for granted that the law has been made because of a tendency to transgress. In a country with total prohibition, there would be no law against driving a car when under the influence of alcohol. The many laws in all countries against stealing, robbery, swindling, and so on, are based on the belief that people will steal when they can. This is true.

After all, most adults are more or less dishonest. There are few people who will not smuggle something through customs, still fewer who will not cheat on their income tax return. Yet almost anyone is genuinely upset if his son steals a penny.

On the other hand, in their dealings with each other, most people are pretty honest. It would be easy to slip one of your hostess's silver spoons into your pocket if you thought of doing so. You don't think of doing so, but you might think of using a return ticket that the collector forgot to punch and collect. Adults make a distinction between the individual and the organization, whether it be a state organization or a private one. It's all right to cheat the insurance company, but reprehensible to cheat the grocer. Children make no such distinction. They will indiscriminately pinch things from roommates, teachers, shops. Not all children will act in this way, but many will agree to share the stolen product. This means that you find in middle-class children who are free and happy, the same sort of dishonesty that appears among poorer children.

I find that many children will steal when opportunity offers. As a boy I did not steal because I was so thoroughly conditioned. Stealing meant a good walloping when found out, and hell fire for eternity. But children not so thoroughly cowed as I was, will naturally steal. Yet, I insist, that in time and if a child is brought up in love, he will grow out of his stealing stage and mature into an honest man.

The second kind of stealing—habitual, compulsive stealing—is an evidence of neurosis in the child. Stealing by a neurotic child is generally a sign of lack of love. The motive is unconscious. In almost every case of confirmed juvenile stealing, the child feels unloved. His thieving is a symbolic attempt to get something of great value. Whether the theft is one of money or jewelry or what not, the unconscious wish is to steal love. This kind of stealing can be treated only by giving out love to the child. Hence, when I give a boy money for stealing my tobacco, I am aiming at his unconscious feeling, not his conscious thought. He may think that I am a fool, but what he thinks does not matter much; it's what he feels that matters. And he feels that I am his friend, his approver, one who gives him love instead of hate. Sooner or later the stealing ceases, for the love that was symbolically stolen in the form of money or goods is now given freely and therefore need not be stolen.

In this context I mention the case of a boy who was always riding other children's bicycles. Brought up before a General School Meeting, he was charged with "constantly breaking the private property rule by using other kids' bikes." Verdict: "Guilty!" Punishment: "The community is asked to subscribe to buy him a bicycle." The Community subscribed.

However I must qualify the giving of rewards to a thief. If he is of low mentality, or, worse still, if he is emotionally arrested, the reward will not have the desired effect. Or if he has a swelled head, he will not benefit from the symbolic gift. In my work with problem children, I have found that nearly every young thief reacted well to my rewards for stealing. The only failures were the very few who were what one might call conscious crooks, unreachable by therapy or by the disguised therapy of rewards.

The situation becomes complicated, however, when the stealing denotes both a lack of parental love and excessive prohibitions about sex. In this category comes kleptomania, the uncontrollable reaching out of the hand for something forbidden— masturbation. This kind of stealing has the best prognosis when the parents realize their mistake and begin all over again by frankly telling the child that they were wrong in their suppressions. A teacher, unaided by the child's parents, can seldom cure kleptomania. The best person to remove a prohibition is the one who originally set it.

I once had a boy of sixteen sent to my school because he was a bad thief. When he arrived at the station, he gave me the half-fare ticket his father had bought for him in London—a ticket based on understating the boy's age. I would like to impress upon the parents of a habitually dishonest child that they must first examine themselves, trying to find out what treatment of theirs made the child dishonest.

Parents bark up the wrong tree when they blame wicked companions, gangster films, lack of parental control because Daddy was away in the Army, and so on, for their child's habitual dishonesty. By themselves, these factors will have little or no effect on a child who is brought up naturally about sex and who is given love and approval.

I do not know just how much young thieves are benefited by daily or weekly visits to a children's social clinic. I only know that the methods in such clinics are not harsh or hellish and that the social workers try hard to understand the child and treat him without moral judgment or character scolding. The child psychologist and the probation officer are handicapped in their efforts by the home in which the psychically sick child lives. I conjecture that success results only when the psychologist or the probationist persuades the parents to change their treatment of the child. For young thieves are the acne of youth, the outward signs of a sick body, the sick body of our society. No amount of personal therapy can abolish the evil of a bad home, a slum street, a poverty-stricken family.

It is all too true that from the age of five to fifteen, most children are getting an education that goes only to the head. There is hardly any concern with their emotional life. Yet it is the emotional disturbance in a neurotic child that makes him compulsively steal. All his knowledge of school subjects or his lack of knowledge of school subjects plays no part at all in his larceny.

The plain fact is that no happy person steals compulsively and continually. The questions to be asked about a habitual thief are: What is his background? Was his home happy? Did his parents always tell him the truth? Did he feel guilty about masturbation? Did he feel guilty about religion? Why was he disrespectful to his parents? Did he feel they did not love him? There must have been some sort of hell inside him to turn him into a thief. Most surely, the hell some of our judges would send him to will not counteract his inner hell.

A course of therapy would not necessarily solve the young thief's problems. Of course, it could help him a lot, could rid him of some of his fears and hates, could give him some self-respect. But as long as the original hate elements remain in his environment he is likely to regress at any time. The therapy of his parents would lead to more success in the end.

I once had a biggish boy who was psychically three or four. He stole from shops. I considered going down to a shop with him and stealing in his presence (after squaring the shopkeeper first). To that boy I was father and a God. I was inclined to think that his real father's disapproval of him had a lot to do with this stealing. My idea was that if he saw his new Father-God stealing, he would be compelled to revise his conscience about stealing. I fully expected him to protest vigorously.

In curing the neurotic child of his thieving, I see no other possible method than that of approval. Neurosis is the result of a conflict between what one has been told he must not have and what he really wants. I invariably find that the weakening of this false conscience makes the child happier and better. Abolish a boy's conscience and you will cure him of thieving.

Delinquency

In these days of savage assaults with guns and brass knuckles, the authorities are at their wit's end about juvenile delinquency, and apparently will try anything to curb it. The newspapers tell us of a new method for dealing with the problem. It is a hard method: the sentencing of youngsters to reform schools which have a regimen of strenuous drills with strict punishment for defaulters. One picture I saw shows boys drilling with huge logs on their shoulders. At such oppressive places, there seem to be no privileges.

I grant that a few months of this hell may deter some potential delinquents. But such treatment never gets down to root causes, to fundamentals. Much worse, such treatment spells hate to most adolescents, and its harshness is bound to create permanent haters of society.

Over thirty years ago, Homer Lane proved by his work in a reform camp called the *Little Commonwealth* that juvenile delinquents can be cured by love—cured by authority being on the side of the child. Lane took tough boys and girls from the London courts—antisocial, hard-boiled youngsters glorying in their reputation as muggers, thieves, and gangsters. These "incorrigibles" came to the *Little Commonwealth,* and there they found a community with self-government and loving approval. Gradually, these youngsters became decent, honest citizens, many of whom I used to count among my friends.

Lane was a genius in the understanding and handling of delinquent children. He cured them because he constantly gave out love and understanding. He always looked for the hidden motive in any delinquent act, convinced that behind every crime was a wish that originally had been a good one. He found that talking to children was useless, and that only action counted. He held that in order to rid a child of a bad social trait one should let the child live out his desires. Once, when one of his young charges, Jabez, expressed an angry wish to smash up the cups and saucers on the tea table, Lane handed him an iron poker and told him to carry on. Jabez carried on—but the very next day he came to Lane and asked for a more responsible and better paying job than he had been working at. Lane asked why he wanted a better-paying job. "Because I want to pay for them cups and saucers," said Jabez. Lane's explanation was that the action of smashing the cups brought a load of Jabez's inhibitions and conflicts tumbling to the ground. The fact that for the first time in his life he was encouraged by authority to smash something and get rid of his anger must have had a beneficial emotional effect on him.

The delinquents of Homer Lane's *Little Commonwealth* were all from bad city slums, yet I never heard of any of them returning to gangsterdom. I call Lane's way the love way. I call *giving-the-delinquent-hell* the hate way. And since hate never cured anyone of anything, I conclude that the hell way will never help any youngster to be social.

Yet I know very well that if I were a magistrate today and I had a tough, sullen delinquent to deal with, I should be baffled to know what to do with him. For there is no reform school in England today like the *Little Commonwealth* to send him to, and I say so with shame. Lane died in 1925, and our authorities here in England have not learned anything from that remarkable man.

However, in recent years, our fine body of probation officers has shown a sincere desire to try to understand the delinquent. The psychiatrists, too, in spite of much hostility from the legal profession, have gone a long way to teach the public that delinquency is not wickedness but rather a form of sickness that requires sympathy and understanding. The tide is flowing toward love instead of toward hate, toward understanding instead of toward bigoted, moral indignation. It is a slow tide. But even a slow tide carries a little of the contamination away; and in time the tide must grow in volume.

I know of no proof that a person has ever been made good by violence, or by cruelty, or by hate. In my long career, I have dealt with many problem children, many of them delinquents. I have seen how unhappy and hateful they are, how inferior, how emotionally confused. They are arrogant and disrespectful to me because I am a teacher, a father substitute, an enemy. I have lived with their tense hate and suspicion. But here in Summerhill, these potential delinquents govern themselves in a self-governing community; they are free to learn and they are free to play. When they steal, they may even be rewarded. They are never preached at, never made afraid of authority, either earthly or heavenly.

In a few short years, these same haters will go out into the world as happy, social beings. So far as I know, not one delinquent who spent seven years in Summerhill ever was sent to prison, or ever raped, or ever became antisocial. It is not I who cured them. It is the environment that cures them—for the environment of Summerhill gives out trust, security, sympathy, lack of blame, absence of judgment.

Summerhill children do not go on to be criminals and mobsters after they leave the school, because they are allowed to live out their gangsterdom without fear and punishment and moral lectures. They are allowed to grow out of one stage of their development and to pass naturally into the next stage.

I simply do not know how an adult criminal would react to love. I am pretty certain that rewarding a gangster for stealing would not cure him, just as I am pretty certain that a prison sentence does not cure him. Treatment is most hopeful only for the very young. Yet even if given to a child as late in life as fifteen years of age, freedom often turns delinquents into good citizens.

In Summerhill, we once had a boy of twelve who had been expelled from many schools for being antisocial. In our school this same boy became a happy, creative, social boy. The authority of a reform school would have finished him. If freedom can save the far-gone problem child, what could freedom do for the millions of so-called "normal" children who are perverted by the authority of the family?

Tommy, aged thirteen, was a bad problem; he stole and was destructive. During one particular vacation, he could not go home, so we kept him at school. For two months, he was the only child at Summerhill. He was perfectly social. We did not have to lock up food or money. But the moment his gang returned, he led the lads in a raid on the larder—which only proves that a child as an individual and a child in a group are two different people.

Teachers in reform schools tell me that the antisocial youth is often subnormal in intelligence. I would add, subnormal in emotion, too. There was a time when I considered the delinquent child a bright child with creative energy that had to come out in an antisocial way because there was no positive way for him to express this energy. Make him free from inhibitions and discipline, I thought, and he will most likely turn out to be clever, creative, even brilliant. I was wrong, sadly wrong. Years of living and dealing with all sorts of delinquents have shown me that they are, for the most part, inferiors. I can think of only one boy who made his mark in later life. Quite a few were cured of being antisocial and dishonest, and they later went to work at regular jobs. But none rose to become a good scholar, or a fine artist, or a skilled engineer, or a talented actress. When the antisocial drive was abolished, for most of these wayward children there seemed to remain only a dead dullness that knew not ambition.

When a youth has to remain in a bad environment with ignorant parents, he does not have any chance to live out his antisocialness. The abolition of poverty and slums, combined with the ending of parental ignorance, will automatically thin out the population of the reform school.

The ultimate cure for juvenile delinquency lies in curing society of its own moral delinquency, and its concomitant, immoral indifference. We have to take one of two sides, and the two sides are before our eyes. Either we treat delinquent youth in the hateful hell way or we use the method of love.

Allow me the delusion, for a few moments, that I am Secretary of the Interior, with infinite powers in the field of education. Let me draft a general program, a tentative "five-year plan" for schools.

As Secretary I should abolish all so-called reform schools and substitute coeducational colonies throughout the land. I should at once set up special training centers for staffing these with teachers and housemothers. Each colony would be completely self-governing. The staff would have no special privileges. They would have the same food and heating as the pupils. Pupils would be paid for any community work they did. The watchword of the colony would be freedom. No religion, no moralizing, no authority would be tolerated.

I would exclude religion because religion talks, it preaches, it tries to sublimate, it suppresses. Religion postulates sin where sin does not exist. It believes in free will when for some children enslaved by their compulsions, there is no free will.

In the place of religious conditioning, I would advocate that emotions be conditioned by love and by nothing that is cruel and unjust. There would be only one way to reach this ideal in the colony—by letting the young people alone as much as possible, by freeing them from imposed authority, and from hate, and from punishment. I know from experience that this is the only way.

Teachers would be taught to be the equals of pupils, not the superiors. They would retain no protective dignity, no sarcasm. They would inspire no fear. They would have to be men and women of infinite patience, able to see far ahead, willing to trust in ultimate results.

Even though present society would not permit a full love life in this day and age, the mixing of the sexes would lead to much that is valuable, to tenderness, to natural good manners, to a necessary knowledge of the opposite sex, to the lessening of pornography and leering snickers.

The chief characteristic of the staff would be the ability to show trust in the pupils, to treat them as respect-worthy and not as thieves and destroyers. At the same time the staff would have to be realistic and not give the individual too much to chew at one time, such as appointing a thief as treasurer of the colony's Christmas party fund. The staff would have to curb any temptation to lecture by realizing that action counts far more than talk. They would be required to know the history of each delinquent, his *whole* background.

Intelligence tests would have a minor place in the colony. They do not denote potentials that are vital. They do not correctly assess emotions, creativity, originality, and imagination.

The general atmosphere would be that of a hospital rather than that of an institution. Just as no medical man assumes a moral attitude toward a patient with syphilis, so our staff would assume no moral attitude toward the sickness we call delinquency. The colony would differ from a hospital only in that there would usually be no administering of medicines or drugs —even psychological ones. The cure would result only from the presence of genuine love in the environment. The staff would also have to evidence genuine faith in human nature. True, there would be failures and incurables. Society would still have to reckon with them. But they would form a tiny minority, while the majority of delinquents would respond to love and tolerance and trust.

I would keep reminding the cynically-minded of Homer Lane's story of the delinquent boy he interviewed at a London juvenile court. Lane handed him a pound note out of which he was to pay his fare to a nearby town, knowing that the boy would bring him the exact change. He did. [I remind American readers that Lane was born in New England.]

I would keep on reminding such people of the American prison warden who sent a lifer to New York to buy new machinery for the prison shoemaking shop. He returned with a full account of the new machines he had bought. The warden asked, "Why didn't you grab the chance to take off in New York?" The convict scratched his head, "I dunno, warden, I guess it was because you trusted me."

Prisons and punishment can never be a substitute for this wonderful trust in people. Such a trust signifies to the person in trouble that someone is giving him love and not hate.

Curing the Child

Curing depends on the patient more than it does on the therapist. There are so many failures among people who go to therapy because they have been bullied by relatives into going. If, for instance, a man succeeds in sending a reluctant wife to be analyzed, she quite naturally goes with a grudge. *My husband doesn't think me good enough. He wants me to be changed, and I don't like it.*

The same difficulty applies to the young criminal when, under duress, he is compelled to undergo therapy. Therapy for both adolescents and adults must be desired by the patient.

Freedom alone, with no therapy added, will cure most delinquencies in a child. *Freedom*—not license—not sentimentality. Freedom alone will not cure pathological cases. It will barely touch cases of arrested development. But freedom will work when it is practiced in a children's boarding school—provided it is practiced all the time.

Some years ago, I had a youth sent to me who was a real crook who stole cleverly. A week after his arrival, I received a telephone message from Liverpool. "This is Mr. X [a well-known man in England] speaking. I have a nephew at your school. He has written me asking if he can come to Liverpool for a few days. Do you mind?"

"Not a bit," I answered, "but he has no money. Who will pay his fare? Better get in touch with his parents."

The following afternoon the boy's mother called me up and said that she had received a phone call from Uncle Dick. So far as she and her husband were concerned, Arthur could go to Liverpool. They had looked up the fare and it was twenty-eight shillings, and would I give Arthur two pounds ten? Arthur had put through both calls from a local phone booth. His imitation of an old uncle's voice and of his mother's voice was perfect. He had tricked me, and I had given him the money before I was conscious of having been taken.

I talked it over with my wife. We both agreed that the wrong thing to do would be to demand the money back, for he had been subjected to that kind of treatment for years. My wife suggested rewarding him. I agreed. I went up to his bedroom late at night. "You're in luck to-day," I said cheerfully.

"You bet I am," he said.

"Yes, but you are in greater luck than you know," I said.

"What do you mean?"

"Oh, your mother has just telephoned again," I said easily. "She says that she made a mistake about the fare: it isn't twenty-eight shillings—it's thirty-eight shillings. So she asked me to give you another ten." I carelessly threw a ten-shilling note on his bed, and departed before he could say anything.

He went off to Liverpool next morning, leaving a letter to be given to me after the train had gone. It began: "Dear Neill, you are a greater actor than I am." And for weeks he kept asking me why I had given him that ten-shilling note.

One day, I answered him: "How did you feel when I gave it to you?" He thought hard for a minute and then he said slowly: "You know, I got the biggest shock of my life. I said to myself: 'Here is the first man in my life who has been on my side.'" Here was a case of a boy's being conscious of the love that is approval. Usually this consciousness takes a long time in coming. The subject of therapy may only dimly apprehend its effect, and that not until months later.

In past days, when I had much more to do with bad delinquents, I again and again rewarded them for stealing. But it was only after a few years, only after the child was cured, that he had any realization of the fact that my approval had helped.

In dealing with children, one must get down to depth psychology, seek deep motives for behavior. A boy is antisocial. Why? Naturally, his symptoms obtrude and irritate. He may be a bully; perhaps a thief; perhaps a sadist. But why? The teacher's irritation may make him storm and punish and condemn; but after the teacher has expressed all his irritation, the problem remains unsolved. The present trend demanding the revival of strict disciplinary teaching will treat only symptoms and in the end will effect nothing.

Parents bring a girl to Summerhill who is a liar, a thief, a catty creature. They give me a long description of her faults. It would be fatal for me to let the child know that I have been told about her. I must wait until it comes from the girl herself, from her behavior toward me or others here at the school.

Years ago, I had a bad problem child. His parents insisted on his being examined by a psychiatrist, so I took him up to a well-known doctor in Harley Street. I spent half an hour telling the specialist all about the case, and then we had the boy brought in. "Mr. Neill tells me you are a very bad boy," said the doctor sternly. That was *his* version of psychology.

Again and again I have seen similar false and ignorant approaches to children. "You aren't very big for your age," said a visitor to a boy who had an inferiority complex about his size.

Another visitor said to a girl, "Your sister is very clever, isn't she?" The art of dealing with children might be defined as *knowing what not to say*.

On the other hand, it is necessary to show a child that you are not deceived. To let a child go on stealing your stamps is useless; you must always let him know that you know. What is unpardonable is to say, "Your mother told me you steal stamps." This is quite different from saying, "I know you've taken my stamps."

I am always a little nervous in writing to parents about their children, fearing that they may leave my letter lying around when the child is home on vacation. Even more, I fear that they will write their children, saying, "Neill says you are not going to classes and are being a general nuisance this term." If that happens, the child will never have any trust in me. So, usually, I tell as little as possible, unless I know the parents are absolutely trustworthy and aware.

I generally do the right thing with a child because my long experience has shown me the right way. No cleverness about it, no special gift, just practice . . . with possibly a blind eye for the unessentials, the by-products.

Bill, a new boy, has stolen some money from another child. The victim asks me, "Should I charge him in our next General Meeting?"

Without, thinking, I say, "No. Leave it to me." I can reason it out later. Bill is new to freedom, uneasy in his new environment. He has been trying so hard to make himself popular and accepted by his fellows that he has been swaggering and showing off a great deal. To make his theft public would be to give him shame, fear, followed perhaps by defiance and an outbreak of antisocial behavior. Or it might work the other way, for if he had been a gang leader in his last school, proud of secret destructive actions against the staff, a public accusation might make him crow and show off what a tough guy he was.

Another time a child says, "I am going to charge Mary for stealing my crayons," and I am not interested. I do not consciously think of it at the time, but I know that Mary has been in the school for two years and can handle the situation.

A new boy of thirteen, who has been hating lessons all his life, comes to Summerhill and loafs for weeks. Then, bored, he comes to me and says, "Shall I go to lessons?" I answer, "That has nothing to do with me," because he must find his own inner compulsions. But to another child I might reply, "Yes, a good idea," because her home and school life, built on a timetable have made her incapable of deciding anything, and I have to wait until she gradually becomes self-reliant. I do not consciously think of these individual aspects when I reply.

Love is being on the side of the other person. Love is approval. I know that children learn slowly that freedom is something totally different from license. But they can learn this truth and do learn it. In the end, it works—nearly every time.

The Road to Happiness

Freud showed that every neurosis is founded on sex repression. I said, "I'll have a school in which there will be no sex repression." Freud said that the unconscious was infinitely more important and more powerful than the conscious. I said, "In my school we won't censure, punish, moralize. We will allow every child to live according to his deep impulses."

I slowly discovered that most of the Freudians did not understand or believe in freedom for children. They confused freedom with license. They had been treating children who had never had freedom to be themselves, and who had therefore developed no natural respect for the freedom of others. I am convinced that the Freudians founded their theory of child psychology on these warped children.

The Freudians found a great deal of anal eroticism among infants, but I have not found this to be true with self-regulated babies. The antisocial aggression the Freudians found in children does not seem to be there in self-regulated children.

I gradually learned that my territory was prophylaxis—not curing. It took me years to discover the full significance of this, to learn that it was freedom that was helping Summerhill problem children, not therapy. I find that my chief job is to sit still and approve of all the things that a child disapproves of in himself—that is, I try to break down the child's superimposed conscience, his self-hatred.

A new boy swears. I smile and say, "Carry on! Nothing bad about swearing." So with masturbation, lying, stealing, and other socially condemned activities.

Some time ago, I had a small boy who deluged me with questions: "What did you pay for that clock?" "What time is it?" "When does the school term end?" He was full of anxiety and never heard any answer I gave him. I knew he was evading the big question that he wanted to have answered.

One day, he came to my room and asked a string of questions. I made no reply, and went on reading my book. After a dozen questions, I looked up casually and said, "What was that you asked? Where do babies come from?"

He got up, reddening. "I don't want to know where babies come from," he said, as he went out, slamming the door.

Ten minutes later he came back. "Where did you get your typewriter from? What's playing at the movie theater this week? How old are you? (*Pause.*) Well, damn it all, where *do* babies come from?"

I gave him the correct answer. He never came back to ask me any more questions.

Clearing away rubbish is never anything else but toil. Work of this kind is made tolerable only by the delight of seeing an unhappy child become happy and free.

The other side of the picture is the long, tiresome study of a child with no success forthcoming. One will work with a child for a year, and at the end of that year be overjoyed to think that the boy is cured of stealing. Then one day the boy relapses, and the teacher almost despairs. I have patted myself on the back about a particular pupil and then five minutes later have had a teacher rush in and say, "Tommy has been stealing again."

Yet psychology is somewhat like golf: you may go two hundred strokes on a round, you may swear and break your clubs—but on the next sunny morning, you will walk to the first tee with new hope in your heart.

If you tell a child any vital truth or if he confides his troubles to you, he forms a transference—that is, you get all the child's emotions showered on you. When I have cleared up a small child about birth and masturbation, the transference is especially strong. At one stage, it may even take the form of a negative transference, a hate transference. But with a normal child this negative phase does not last long, and the positive love transference soon follows. A child's transference dissolves easily. He soon forgets all about me, and his emotions go out to other children and to things. Since I am a father substitute, girls naturally develop a stronger transference to me than boys do, but I cannot say that a girl always develops a positive transference and a boy always develops a negative transference. On the contrary, I have had girls who showed quite a fierce hatred of me for a time.

At Summerhill, I used to be both teacher and psychologist. Then I slowly discovered that a man cannot play both these roles. I have had to give up being a psychiatrist, for most pupils cannot do much work with the man who is their father confessor. They become irritated and are always in much fear of my criticism. Moreover, if I praise the drawing of any one child, I evoke much jealousy among the other children. The psychic doctor should not really live in the school at all; the children should have no social interest in him.

All schools of psychology recognize the hypothesis of the unconscious, the principle that we all have buried wishes and loves and hates that we are not conscious of. Character is a combination of conscious behavior and unconscious behavior.

The housebreaking youth is conscious that he wants to acquire money or goods, but he does not know the deep motive that makes him choose this way of getting money instead of the social way of earning it. That motive is buried, and that is why moral lectures or punishments never cure him. Scoldings are heard only by his ears, and punishments are felt only by his body. But these preachments and punishments never penetrate to the unconscious motive which controls his behavior.

Because this is so, religion cannot reach a boy's unconscious through preachment. But if some night his curate went out stealing with him, that action would begin to dissolve the self-hatred responsible for the antisocial behavior. That sympathetic kinship would start the boy thinking in different terms. The cure of more than one young thief began when I joined him stealing our neighbor's hens or helped him rob the school's pocket-money drawer. Action touches the unconscious where words cannot. This is why love and approval will so often cure a child's problems. I do not say that love will cure a case of acute claustrophobia or a case of marked sadism; but generally, love will cure most young thieves and liars and destroyers. I have proved in action that freedom and the absence of moral discipline have cured many children whose future had appeared to be a life in prison.

True freedom practiced in community living, as in Summerhill, seems to do for the many what psychoanalysis does for the individual. It releases what is hidden. It is a breath of fresh air blowing through the soul to cleanse it of self-hatred and hatred of others.

The battle for youth is one with the gloves off. None of us can be neutral. We must take one side or the other: authority or freedom; discipline or self-government. No half measures will do. The situation is too urgent.

To be a free soul, happy in work, happy in friendship, and happy in love or to be a miserable bundle of conflicts, hating one's self and hating humanity—one or the other is the legacy that parents and teachers give to every child.

How can happiness be bestowed? My own answer is: *Abolish authority. Let the child be himself. Don't push him around. Don't teach him. Don't lecture him. Don't elevate him. Don't force him to do anything.* It may not be your answer. But if you reject my answer, it is incumbent on you to find a better one.

SIX

PARENTS' PROBLEMS

Love and Hate

The child receives his conscience from his mother, his father, his teacher, his minister—from his environment, in general. His unhappiness is the result of the conflict between conscience and human nature; or in Freudian terms, between his super-ego and his id.

Conscience may win so complete a victory that the boy becomes a monk, and entirely renounces the world and the flesh. In most cases, a compromise takes place—a compromise that is partly expressed in the phrase, "to serve the devil on weekdays and to serve God on Sundays."

Love and hate are not opposites. The opposite of love is indifference. Hate is love that has been changed to the other side of the coin—by thwarting. Hate always contains an ingredient of fear. We see this in the case of the child who hates a younger brother. His hate is caused by fear of losing mother's love, and also by fear of his own revengeful thoughts about his brother.

When Ansi, a rebellious Swedish girl of fourteen, came to Summerhill, she started out by kicking me to make me angry. I was the unfortunate substitute for her father, whom she hated and feared. She had never been allowed to sit on his knee nor had he shown her love in any way. Her love for her father had been changed into hate by his not reacting to her love. At Summerhill, she suddenly found a new father who did not react with sternness, a father whom she did not fear. Then her hate came out. The fact that next day she was exceedingly tender and gentle to me is proof that her hate was merely disguised love.

To understand the full significance of Ansi's attack on me

would mean to know and understand first of all the story of her warped attitude to sex. She came from a girl's school where the pupils discussed sex morbidly and dirtily in dark corners. Her hatred of her father had much in it of the hate that a repressive education in sexual matters had given her. And her hate for a mother who had often punished her was likewise intense.

Few parents realize that by punishing they change their child's love for them into hate. Hate in a child is very difficult to see. Mothers who notice that their children are tender after a spanking do not know that the hate roused by the spanking was immediately repressed. But repressed feelings are not dead; they are only sleeping.

There is a little book called *Morals for the Young* by Marcus. I often try the experiment of reading verses from it to children. One verse runs:

> *"Tommy saw his house on fire,*
> *His mother in the flames expire;*
> *His father killed by falling brick*
> *And Tommy laughed—till he was sick."*

This verse is the favorite. Some children laugh very loudly when they hear it read. Even children who love their parents laugh loudly. They laugh because of their repressed hate for their parents—hate caused by spankings, by criticism, by punishment.

Usually, this kind of hate emerges in fantasies that are seemingly remote from the parents. One young pupil, a boy who loved his father dearly, liked to fantasy that he was shooting a lion. If I asked him to describe this lion, he soon found it had some connection with his father.

One morning, I took each pupil individually and told him the story of my own death. Each face brightened as I told of the funeral. The group was especially cheery that afternoon. Stories of giant killing are always popular with children because the giant is likely to be Daddy.

There should be nothing shocking about a child's hatred of his parents. It always dates from the period when the child was an egoist. The young child seeks love and power. Every angry word, every slap, every injury is a deprivation of love and power. Every scolding word from Mother means to the child, "Mother does not love me." Every "Don't touch that" from Father means, "He stands in my way. If I were only his size!"

Yes, there is hatred of parents in the child, but it is not nearly so dangerous as the hatred of the child in the parents. The naggings, ragings, spankings, and lecturings of parents are hate reactions. Thus the child of parents who do not love each other has a very poor chance for healthy development, for taking it out on the child is a universal habit of such parents.

When a child cannot find love, he seeks hate as a substitute. "Mommy takes no notice of me. She does not love me. She loves my little sister. I'll *make* her take notice of me. I shall!" And he smashes the furniture. All problems of child behavior are basically problems that were begotten by lack of love. All punishment and moral lectures simply increase the hate—they never cure the problem.

Another hate-producing situation is the child whose parents possess him. He hates his bonds, while at the same time he desires those bonds. This conflict sometimes exhibits itself as cruelty. Hate of the possessing mother is repressed; but since an emotion must always find some outlet, the child kicks the cat or strikes his sister, this being an easier way than rebelling against the mother.

It has become a platitude to say that we hate in others what we hate in ourselves. Yet, platitude or no, it is true. The hate we received in our infancy we bestow on our own infants, be we ever so willing to give them our love.

It has been said that if you cannot hate, you cannot love. Maybe. I find it difficult to hate. And I have never been able to give out what might be called personal love to children; and certainly never sentimental love. The word *sentimental* is difficult of definition; I call it bestowing the attributes of a swan on a goose.

When I was treating Robert, an incendiary, a thief, and a potential homicidal character, I naturally had transferred to me his hate and his love of his father. One day, after a talk with me, he ran out and squashed a large snail with his heel. He told me about it and I asked him to describe a snail. He answered, "A long, ugly, slimy brute."

I handed him a piece of paper and asked him to write the word *snail*. He wrote "A Snail."

"Look at what you have written," I said.

Suddenly he burst into laughter. He took his pencil and wrote underneath:

"A Snail"

"A. S. Neill."

"You didn't realize that I was the long, ugly, slimy brute that you wanted to jump on, did you?" I remarked with a smile.

Thus far, there was absolutely no danger to the boy. To make his hate of me conscious was a good thing for him. But suppose I had gone on to say something like this: "Of course I was the snail, but really you do not hate me; you hate the part of yourself that I stand for. You are the slimy brute that must be killed. You were killing a quality in yourself, etc." That, to me, would have been dangerous psychiatry. Robert's job is to play marbles and to fly kites. All that I, or any teacher or doctor, am entitled to do is to free him from conflicts that prevent his flying kites.

Any parent who expects gratitude knows nothing of child nature. Children hate to be indebted to anyone. I have had a long experience of resentment among pupils whom I kept at Summerhill for no fees or for much reduced fees. They expressed more hate against me than twenty paying pupils. Shaw wrote, "We cannot sacrifice ourselves for others without coming to hate those for whom we have sacrificed ourselves."

It is true. And the corollary is true: we cannot sacrifice ourselves for others without coming to be hated by those for whom we have sacrificed ourselves. The cheerful giver does not seek gratitude. Parents who expect their children to be grateful are always doomed to disappointment.

To sum up, every child feels that punishment is hate and of course it is. And every punishment makes the child hate more and more. If you study the diehard who says, "I believe in corporal punishment," you will always find him a hater. I cannot emphasize too strongly that hate breeds hate, and love breeds love. No child was ever cured of hate except through love.

Spoiling the Child

The spoiled child—using the word *spoiled* in any sense we like —is the product of a spoiled society. In such a society, the spoiled child fearsomely clings to life. He has been allowed license instead of freedom. He doesn't know the meaning of true freedom which means *loving* life.

The spoiled child is a nuisance to himself and to society. You see him in trains scrambling over passengers' feet, yelling in the corridors, never paying any attention to his harassed parent's pained request for quiet—a request, indeed, that he has long ceased to hear.

Later in life, as the spoiled brat grows older, he has even a worse time of it than one subjected to too much discipline. The spoiled child is terribly self-centered. He grows up into a man who throws his clothes all over the bedroom, expecting someone to pick them up. Of course, the spoiled child, now grown up, collects many a rebuff.

Often the spoiled child is the only child. Having no one of his own age to play with or to measure himself against, he naturally identifies himself with his parents: he wants to do what they do. Since his parents consider him the world's wonder, they encourage this apparent precociousness, because they fear to lose his love if they thwart him in even the slightest way.

I sometimes find this attitude in teachers who coddle their pupils. Such teachers are in constant dread that they will lose their popularity among the children. That fear is the royal road to spoiling. A good teacher or parent must cultivate being objective. He must keep his own complexes out of his relationship with the child—not an easy thing to do, I grant, for we are so often blind to our own complexes. The unhappy mother, for example, is in danger of having a spoiled son, for she is prone to bestow upon him the wrong type of love.

In Summerhill, a spoiled boy is always a heavy handful. He wears my wife out, for she is the mother substitute. He plagues her with questions: "When will this term end? What time is it? Can I have some money?" Underneath it all, he hates his mother. The questions have the motive of annoying mother. And a spoiled girl is always trying to get a reaction from me, for I am the father substitute. Usually, she seeks not a love reaction but a hate reaction. The spoiled newcomer will hide my pen or tell another girl, "Neill wants you," which really means that she wants Neill to want *her*.

Spoiled boys and spoiled girls have kicked my door, and have stolen my things just to get a reaction out of me. The spoiled child resents suddenly being thrust into a family of many members. He expects the same yielding treatment from me and from my staff that he has received from his fond parents.

The spoiled child usually gets far too much spending money. I often writhe when I see parents send their child a five-dollar bill to spend, and yet I, because of their economic plight, have allowed them to pay low fees or even no fees at all.

A child should not be given everything he asks for. Generally speaking, children today get far too much, so much that they cease having appreciation for a gift. Parents who overdo the giving of presents are often those who do not love their children enough. Such parents have to compensate by making a show of parental love, by showering expensive presents on their children much the same as a man who has been unfaithful to his wife will lavishly buy her a fur coat he can't afford. I make it a rule not to bring my daughter a present each time I go to London; and in consequence, she does not expect a present after every trip. The spoiled child rarely values anything. It is he who gets a new chromium-plated three-speed bicycle, and three weeks later leaves it out in the rain all night.

The spoiled child very often represents for the parents their second chance in life. *I have made little of life because so many people thwarted me; but my son will have every chance to succeed where I failed.* It is this motivation that makes a father who had no musical education insist that his son learn to play the piano. And it makes a mother who gave up a career for marriage send her daughter to ballet lessons even though the child is heavy-footed. And it is parents like these who compel countless boys and girls to take up jobs and studies that, left to themselves, they would never dream of taking up. The poor parent cannot help his feeling. It is very hard for a man who has built up a thriving clothing business to discover that his son wants to be an actor or a musician. But it often happens.

Then there is the spoiled child whose mother does not want him ever to grow up. Motherhood is a job—but not a lifetime job. Most women realize this; yet how often one hears a mother remark about her daughter, "She is growing up too quickly."

A child should not be permitted to violate the personal rights of others. Parents who do not wish to spoil their children *must* distinguish between freedom and license.

Power and Authority

Before psychology discovered the importance of the unconscious, a child was considered a reasonable being with the power to will to do good or evil. His mind was assumed to be a blank slate on which any conscientious teacher had only to write the script.

Now we understand that there is nothing static about a child; he is all dynamic urge. He seeks to express his wishes in action. By nature he is self-interested, and he seeks always to try his power. If there is sex in everything, there is also the drive for power in everything.

The very young child probably finds that noise expresses best of all his power over his environment. The reaction of his adult companions to noise may give him an exaggerated idea of the importance of noise. Or the noise in itself may be important enough.

Noise is often suppressed in the nursery; but before that another suppression takes place—the suppression involved in making the child clean in habits. We can only guess that a child feels himself powerful in his excretory acts. It seems likely that his toilet means much to him, for it is his first act of making. I say we can only guess, for no one can say what a child of one or two years feels and thinks. Certainly one finds children of seven and eight who have a strong feeling of power in their excretory acts.

A normal woman fears a lion; a neurotic woman fears a mouse. The lion is real, but the mouse represents a repressed interest that the woman is afraid to recognize. Now the child's wishes, too, can be converted into phobias by suppression. Many

children have night terrors: they fear ghosts or robbers or bo-
geymen. Often, unknowing parents believe that a story told by a
nursemaid is responsible for these terrors, but the nursemaid's
story merely gives the phobia a form. The root of the terror is the
suppression of sex interest by the parents. The child fears his
own buried interests, just as the woman with the mouse phobia
fears her buried interests.

The suppression need not be primarily one of sex suppression.
The angry father who shouts "Stop that row!" can convert the
child's interest in noise into a fearful interest in father. When a
child's wish is thwarted, he hates. If I take a toy from a bright
boy of three, he would kill me if he could.

One day, I was sitting with Billie. I was in a deck chair
striped black and orange. I, of course, am father substitute to
Billie.

"Tell me a story," he said.

"You tell me one," said I.

No, he insisted, he could not tell me a story; I must tell him
one.

"We'll tell one together," said I. "When I stop, you say something—eh? Well then, there was once a—"

Billie looked at my chair with its stripes. "Tiger," he said,
and I knew I was the animal with stripes.

"And it lay at the roadside outside this school. One day, a boy
went down the road and his name was . . ."

"Donald," said Billie. Donald is his chum.

"Then the tiger sprang out and . . ."

"Ate him up," said Billie promptly.

"Then Derrick said, 'I won't have this tiger eating up my
brother.' So he buckled on his revolver and went down the road.
And the tiger jumped out and . . ."

"Ate him up," said Billie cheerfully.

"Then Neill got wild. 'I simply won't have this tiger eating up all my school,' he said; and he buckled on his two revolvers and went out. The tiger jumped out and . . ."

"Ate him up, of course."

"But then Billie said that this wouldn't do. So he buckled on his two revolvers, his sword, his dagger, and his machine gun and went down the road. And the tiger jumped out and . . ."

"He killed the tiger," said Billie modestly.

"Excellent!" I cried. "He killed the tiger. He dragged its body up to the door and came in and called a General School Meeting. Then one of the staff said, 'Now that Neill is inside the tiger we shall need a new headmaster, and I propose . . .' "

Billie looked down and was silent.

"And I propose . . ."

"You know well enough it was me," he said with annoyance.

"And so Billie became headmaster of Summerhill School," I said. "And what do you think was the first thing he did?"

"Went up to your room and took your turning lathe and typewriter," he said, without hesitation or embarrassment.

I have another story of Billie. One day he said to me, "I know where I can get a bigger dog than the one Father has." His father had two Skye terriers.

"Where?" I asked, but he shook his head, and would not tell me.

"What will you call it, Billie?"

"Hose pipe," he answered.

I handed him a sheet of paper. "Let me see you draw a hose pipe," I said.

He drew a large phallus. I suddenly thought of an old cycle pump I had. I fetched it and showed Billie how to use it as a water squirt.

"Now," said I, "you have a bigger hose pipe than father has," and he laughed loudly. For two days, he went round the school gleefully squirting water. Then he lost interest in his hose pipe.

PHALLUS— *Image of the male organ of generation.*

The question is this: *Is Billie a sex case or a power case?* I think he is a power case. His wish to kill the tiger (me) was the repetition of his wish when he first saw his father. It had nothing directly to do with sex. And his wish to have a phallus bigger than father's was a power wish. Billie's fantasies are power fantasies. I hear him telling the other boys tall stories of the number of airplanes he can drive at one time. There is ego in everything.

The thwarted wish is the beginning of fantasy. Every child wants to be big; every factor in his environment tells him that he is small. The child conquers his environment by fleeing from it; he rises on wings and lives his dream in fantasy. The ambition to be an engine driver is a power motive: to control a train rushing along at great speed is one of the best illustrations of power.

Peter Pan is popular with children—not because he does not grow up—but because he can fly and fight pirates. He is popular with grownups because they want to be children, without responsibilities, without struggles. But no boy really wants to remain a boy. The desire for power urges him on.

Now the suppression of infantile noise and curiosity warps the child's natural love of power. The youths who are called delinquents and who are generally said to be suffering from too much moviegoing are trying to express power that has been suppressed. I have generally found that the antisocial boy, the leader of a gang of window breakers, becomes under freedom a strong supporter of law and order.

Ansi had been a leader of lawbreakers in her school, and the school could not keep her. Two nights after her arrival at Summerhill she began to fight with me playfully, but soon she was no longer playing. For about three hours, she kicked and bit me, saying all the time that she would make me lose my temper. I refused to lose my temper and kept smiling. It was an effort. Finally, one of my teachers sat down and played soft music. Ansi quieted down. Her attack was partly sexual; but on the power side, I stood for law and order. I was headmaster.

Ansi found life rather confusing. At Summerhill she found there were no laws to break, and she felt like a fish out of water. She tried to stir up mischief among the other pupils, but succeeded only with the very young ones. She was trying once more to find her accustomed power in leading a gang against authority. She was really a lover of law and order. But in the domain of law and order that the adults ruled there was no scope to express her power. As second best, she chose the side of rebellion against law and order.

A week after her arrival, we had a General School Meeting. Ansi stood and jeered at everything. "I'll vote for laws," she said, "but only for the fun of having some laws to break."

Our housemother got up. "Ansi shows that she doesn't want laws that everyone will keep," she said. "I propose that we have no laws at all. Let us have chaos."

Ansi shouted "Hurrah!" and led the pupils out of the room. This she easily did because they were younger children, and they had not reached the age of having developed a social conscience. She took them to the workshop, and they all armed themselves with saws. They announced their intention of cutting down all the fruit trees. I, as usual, went to dig in the garden.

Ten minutes later, Ansi came to me. "What do we have to do to stop the chaos and have laws again?" she asked in a mild tone.

"I can't give you any advice," I replied.

"Can we call another General School Meeting?" she asked.

"Of course you can, only I won't come to it. We decided to have chaos." She went away and I continued digging.

In a short time, she returned. "We had a meeting of the children," she said, "and we voted to have a full School Meeting. Will you come?"

"A full meeting?" said I. "Yes, I'll come."

In the meeting, Ansi was serious, and we passed our laws in peace. Total damage done during chaotic period—one clothespole sawed in two.

For years Ansi had found pleasure in leading her school gang against authority. In stirring up rebellion, she was doing something she hated. She hated chaos. Underneath, she was a law-abiding citizen. But Ansi had a great desire for power. She was happy only when she was directing others. In rebelling against her teacher, she was trying to make herself more important than the teacher. She hated laws because she hated the power that made laws. She identified herself with her punishing mother, and was sadistic in her attitude to others. We can only conjecture that her hatred of authority was objectively a hate of her mother's authority; and subjectively, a hate of the bossing mother in herself. I find such power cases much more difficult to cure than sex cases. One can with comparative ease track down the incidents and teachings that give a child a bad conscience about sex, but to track down the thousands of incidents and teachings that have made a child a sadistic power person is difficult indeed.

I think of one of my failures. When I taught in Germany, Maroslava, a Slavic girl of thirteen, was sent to me. She hated her father intensely. For six months, that girl made my school life a little hell. She attacked me in the School Meetings; and on one occasion, she carried a motion that I be put out of the school on the ground that I was useless. I had three days off, and was beginning to enjoy myself writing a book, when unfortunately there was another School Meeting at which it was voted (one dissent, of course) that I should be asked to return. Maroslava was always saying, "I won't have any boss in the school." She was a power person with a tremendous ego. When she left (I had to tell her mother that I could not cure her), I shook hands with her.

"Well," I said pleasantly, "I didn't help you much, did I?"

"Do you know why?" she said with a dry smile. "I'll tell you. The first day I came to your school, I was making a box, and you said I was using too many nails. From that moment, I knew that you were just like every other schoolmaster in the world—a boss. From that moment, you could not possibly help me."

"You are right," I said. "Good-bye."

Hate may be more often thwarted power than thwarted love. The hate that Maroslava radiated was a hate one could feel. To seek power is as much a feminine characteristic as a masculine. Generally, a woman seeks power over people, while a man seeks power over material; and Maroslava and Ansi most certainly sought power over people.

No child under eight is selfish; he is only an egoist. In the case of a boy of six whose father teaches him to be unselfish and beats him when he is selfish, his conscience at first is objective: *I must share my sweets when father is looking*. But a process of identification begins. The boy wants to be as big as father—the power motive. He wants to have as much of mother as father has. He identifies himself with father. And in the process, he takes his father's philosophy. He becomes a little Conservative or a little Liberal. He, as it were, adds his father to his own soul. Conscience, formerly father's voice from without, now becomes father's voice from within. This is the process by which some people become Baptists or Calvinists or Communists.

Girls who were spanked by their mothers grow into spankers themselves. An excellent illustration is the game in which children play school. Teacher whacks all the time.

The child's desire to be grown up is a power wish. The mere size of adults will give a child a sense of inferiority. Why should grownups be allowed to sit up late? Why do they have the best things—typewriters, automobiles, good tools, watches?

My boy pupils delight in soaping their faces when I am shaving. The desire to smoke, too, is mainly a wish to be grown up. Generally, it is the only child whose power is most thwarted; and therefore it is the only child who is most difficult to handle in a school.

I once made the mistake of bringing a young boy to school ten days before the other pupils arrived. He was very happy mixing with the teachers, sitting in the staff room, having a bedroom to himself. But when the other children came, he became very antisocial. Alone he had helped to make and repair many articles; when the others came, he began to destroy things. His pride was injured. He had suddenly to cease being an adult; he had to sleep in a room with four other boys; he had to go to bed early. His violent protest made me decide never again to give a child the opportunity of identifying himself with grownups.

It is only *thwarted* power that works for evil. Human beings are good; they want to do good; they want to love and be loved. Hate and rebellion are only thwarted love and thwarted power.

Jealousy

Jealousy arises from the sense of possession. If sexual love were a genuine transcendence of self, a man would rejoice when he saw his girl kiss another man, because he would rejoice to see her happy. But sexual love is possessive. It is the man with a strong sense of possession who commits a crime of jealousy.

The absence of any visible sexual jealousy among the Trobriand Islanders suggests that jealousy may be a by-product of our more complicated civilization. Jealousy arises from the combination of love with possessiveness about the loved object. It has been often said that a jealous man does not usually shoot the rival who runs away with his wife—he shoots the wife. Probably he kills the woman to put his possession beyond the reach of touch, just as a mother rabbit will eat her young if people handle them too much. The infant ego will have all or nothing: It cannot share.

Jealousy has more to do with power than it has to do with sex. Jealousy is the reaction following an injured ego. "I am not first. I am not the favored one. I am placed in a position of inferiority." This certainly is the psychology of jealousy that we find among, say, professional singers and comedians. In my student days, I used to make friends with stage comedians by the simple method of saying that the other comedian in the cast was rotten.

In jealousy, there is always a definite fear of loss. The opera singer hates another prima donna, dreading that her own applause will suffer in volume and intensity. Indeed by comparison, it is possible that fear of loss of esteem accounts for more jealousy than all the love rivals in the world.

In the family, much depends, therefore, on the elder child's feeling of being appreciated. If self-regulation has given him so much independence that he does not need to be constantly seeking his parents' approval, then his jealousy of the newcomer in the family will be less than if he were an unfree child, one tied forever to his mother's apron strings, and therefore never quite independent. This does not mean that parents of siblings should stand aside and merely observe how the elder child reacts to the younger. From the start, any action that might aggravate jealousy should be avoided, such as a too obvious showing off of the baby to visitors. Children of all ages have a keen sense of justice—or rather of injustice—and wise parents will try to see that the younger child is not in any way favored or given preference over the elder, although this is almost impossible to avoid to some extent.

That baby gets mother's breast may seem an injustice to his older brother. But it may not be so, if the older one feels that he has been allowed to live out naturally his breast-feeding stage. In drawing sound conclusions about this aspect, we need much more evidence. I have had no experience of the self-regulated child's reaction to the arrival of a new baby. Whether jealousy is a permanent trait in human nature, I do not know.

In my long experience with children, I have found that in later life many persons retain with angry emotion some memory of what they considered an injustice they suffered in their kindergarten days. This is especially so with the memory of an incident in which the older child was punished for something that the younger one did. "I always got the blame" is the cry of many an older sibling. In any quarrel where the baby cries, the busy mother's automatic reaction is to storm at the older child.

Jim, aged eight, had a habit of kissing everyone he met. His kisses were more like sucking than kissing. I concluded that Jim had never got over his infantile interest in sucking. I went out and bought him a feeding bottle. Jim had his bottle every night when he went to bed. The other boys, who at first went into screams of derisive laughter (thus hiding their interest in bottles), soon became jealous of Jim. Two of them demanded bottles. Jim suddenly became the little brother who long ago got the monopoly of mother's breast. I bought bottles for all of them. The fact that they wanted bottles proved that these boys still retained their interest in sucking.

Jealousy is something to be particularly guarded against in the dining room. Even some of the staff are jealous when visitors receive any special dish; and if the cook gives one senior pupil asparagus, the others will wax eloquent about kitchen favorites.

Some years ago, the arrival of a tool chest brought trouble into the school. The children whose fathers could not afford to buy them good tools became jealous, and for three weeks they were antisocial. One boy who knew all about handling tools borrowed a plane. He took the iron out of the plane by hammering the cutting edge; and of course, he spoiled the plane. He told me that he had forgotten just how to take an iron out. Whether conscious or unconscious, the destructive act was one of jealousy.

It may be impossible to give each child a room to himself, but each child should have a corner with which he can do what he likes. In Summerhill schoolrooms, each pupil has a table and his own area, and he decorates his corner with joy.

Jealousy sometimes arose out of P.Ls. "Why should Mary get P.Ls. and not me?" Sometimes a girl deliberately and consciously behaved as a problem child merely to be included in the P.L. list. Once, one girl smashed some windows; and when asked what her idea was, she replied, "I want Neill to give me P.Ls." A girl who behaves in this way is usually a girl whose father has not, in her estimation, paid sufficient attention to her.

Since children bring their home problems and jealousies to school with them, what I fear most in my work with them are the letters parents write their children. I once had to write to a father, "Please do not write to your son. Every time a letter comes from you, he goes bad." The father did not answer me but he ceased to write to his son. Then about two months later, I saw the boy receive a letter from his father. I was annoyed but said nothing. That night about twelve, I heard awful screams from the boy's bedroom. I rushed into his room just in time to save our kitten from strangulation. Next day, I went to his room to look for the letter. I found it. "You will be glad to hear," ran a sentence, "that Tom [the younger brother] had his birthday last Monday, and Auntie Lizzie gave him a kitten." The fantasies that arise from jealousy know no bounds in criminality. The jealous child kills off his rivals in fantasy. Two brothers had to travel home from Summerhill for the holidays. The elder got into a state of fear. "I'm frightened I will lose Fred on the way," he kept saying. He was afraid his daydream would come true.

"No," said a boy of eleven to me, referring to his younger brother, "no, I wouldn't exactly like him to die; but if he went away on a long, long journey to India or somewhere and came back when he was a man, I'd like that."

Every pupil new to Summerhill has to endure three months of unconscious hate from the other pupils. For a child's first reaction to a new arrival in the family is a hate reaction. The older child usually believes that mother has eyes only for the newcomer, for the baby sleeps with mother and takes up all mother's attention. The child's repressed hate of his mother is often compensated for by an excess of tenderness to her. It is the older child in a family who hates most. The younger child has never known what it is to be king in the house. When I come to think of it, I see that my worst cases of neurosis are either only children or eldest sons and daughters.

Parents unwittingly feed the hate of an older child. "Why, Tom, your young brother wouldn't make such a fuss about a cut finger."

I remember when I was a boy, another boy was always held up as an example to me. He was a marvelous scholar, was never known to be anywhere but at the top of the class, took all the prizes in a canter. He died. I recall his funeral as being rather a pleasant affair.

Teachers often encounter the jealousy of parents. I have lost pupils more than once because the parents were jealous of the child's affection for Summerhill and for me. It is understandable. In a free school, the children are allowed to do exactly what they like as long as they do not break the social laws which are made by staff and pupils at General School Meetings. Often, a child does not even want to go home for the holidays, for to go home is to be encompassed by restrictive home laws. The parents who do not become jealous of the school or its teachers are those who treat their children at home just the same as we treat their children in Summerhill. They believe in their children and give them the freedom to be themselves. These children delight in going home.

There need be no rivalry between parent and teacher. If the parent turns the child's love into hate by arbitrary orders and rules, he must expect the child to seek love elsewhere. A teacher is merely a father or a mother surrogate. It is the thwarted love for parents that is showered on the teacher only because the teacher is easier to love than the father is.

I couldn't count the number of fathers I have known who hated their sons because of jealousy. These were the Peter Pan fathers who wanted mother love from their wives, hating the young rival and often beating him cruelly. You, Mr. Father, will find your situation complicated by the family triangle. Once your baby is born you are, in some measure, odd man out. Some women lose all desire for a sex life after having a baby. In any case, divided love will characterize the home. You should be conscious of what is happening; otherwise you will find your-

SURROGATE - Substitute

self being jealous of your own child. At Summerhill, we have had scores of children who suffered from either maternal or paternal jealousy, mostly cases in which the father's jealousy had made him stern and even brutal to the son. If a father vies with his children for the love of Mother, his children will be more or less neurotic.

I have seen many a mother who hated to see her daughter show all the freshness and beauty that she, the mother, had lost. Usually, these were mothers who had nothing to do in life, who lived in the past and daydreamed of the conquests they had made at dances many long years ago.

I used to find that I was irritated when two young things fell in love. I would rationalize my emotion by thinking that my irritation was really a fear of awkward consequences. When I realized that it was nothing but a possessive jealousy of the young, all my irritation and fear went away.

Jealousy of youth is a real thing. A girl of seventeen told me that at the private boarding school she had been going to, her teacher considered breasts shameful things that should be hidden by tight lacing. An extreme case, no doubt, yet containing in exaggerated form a truth that we try to forget: age—disappointed and repressed—hates youth because age is jealous of youth.

Divorce

What makes a child neurotic? In many cases it is the fact that his parents do not love each other. The neurotic child craves love, and in his home there is no love. He hears his parents snarl at each other. They may honestly try to keep their secret from their child, but the child can sense an atmosphere. He judges by appearances more than by what he hears. No child is deceived by words like *dearest* and *darling*.

I have had, among others, the following cases:

Girl of fifteen, thief. Mother disloyal to father. Girl knew.

Girl of fourteen, unhappy dreamer. Neurosis said to date from a day when she saw her father with his lover.

Girl of twelve, hated everyone. Father impotent; mother soured.

Boy of eight, thief. Father and mother quarreled openly.

Boy of nine; lived in fantasy (anal-erotic mostly). Parents furtively hostile to each other.

Girl of fourteen, bed-wetter. Parents living apart.

Boy of nine; impossible at home owing to ill temper; lived in fantasy of grandeur. Mother unhappily married.

I realize how difficult it is to cure a child when the home remains a place of lovelessness. Often I have answered a mother's question, "What shall I do about my child?" with the reply, "Go and get yourself analyzed."

Fathers and mothers have often said to me that they would separate were it not for the children. It would often be better for the children if unloving parents *did* separate. A thousand times better! Unloving matrimonial life means an unhappy home; and an unhappy atmosphere is always psychic death to a child.

I have sometimes found that the young son of an unhappily married mother reacts to his mother in terms of hate. He torments his mother in a sadistic manner. One boy used to bite and scratch his mother. Less extreme cases torture the mother by continually demanding her attention. According to the Oedipus complex theory, it should be the other way around. The little boy looks upon his father as a rival for mother's love. One would naturally suppose that in a case where the father is manifestly out of the running, the son would, as the successful suitor, show increased tenderness to his mother. I often find him instead showing an extraordinary cruelty to his mother.

The unhappily married mother will always show favoritism. The marital outlet for love being closed, she will concentrate her love on one child. The essential thing in a child's life is love, but the unhappily married parent cannot give love in the proper proportion. Either he gives too little or too much love. It is difficult to say which is the greater evil.

The child starved for love becomes a hating individual, antisocial and critical. The child overwhelmed with love becomes a mother's darling, a timid, feminine soul, always seeking the safety of the mother. The mother may be symbolized by a house (as in agoraphobia), by Mother Church, or by Mother Country.

I have no concern with divorce laws. It is not my business to advise adults. It is my concern, however, to study children; and it is important to suggest to parents that the home must be changed if the neurotic child is to have any chance of recovery. Parents must be courageous enough, if necessary, to realize that their influence is bad for their children. One mother said to me, "But if I do not see my child for two years, I shall lose him."

"You have lost him already," I answered; and she *had* lost him, for he was unhappy at home.

Parental Anxiety

It might be said that the anxious parent is the one who cannot give—give love, give honor, give respect, give trust.

Recently, the mother of a new boy came to visit Summerhill. For a weekend, she made the boy's life miserable. He wasn't hungry, but she stood over him and made him eat his lunch. He was grubby after making a tree house, and she ran him off the grounds and into the house to scrub him clean. He had spent his pocket money on ice cream, and she gave him a lecture about how bad ice cream was for his stomach. She corrected him when he addressed me as Neill, and she demanded that he call me *Mr.* Neill.

I said to her, "Why the devil did you enroll him in this school when you have such a fussy, anxious attitude toward him?"

She answered innocently, "Why? Because I want him to be free and happy. I want him to become an independent man, unspoiled by outside influence."

I said, "Oh," and lit a cigarette. The woman had no suspicion that she was treating her boy cruelly and stupidly, that she was transferring to him all the anxiety that her own frustrated life gave her.

I ask: What can be done about it? Nothing! Nothing but to give a few illustrations of the damage done by parental anxiety and to hope for the best, hope that perhaps one parent in a million will say, "I never thought of that! I thought I was doing right. Maybe I was wrong."

In one case a distracted mother writes, "I am at my wits' end to know what to do with my son of twelve who has suddenly begun to steal things from Woolworth's. Please, please tell me what to do." It is just as though a man wrote to complain that after consuming a bottle of whisky every day for twenty years, he finds that his liver is dead. It would probably do no good to advise him to cut out the drinking at that stage. And so I usually advise a frantic mother who has a serious child behavior problem to consult a child psychologist or to look up the address of the nearest children's clinic.

I could, of course, answer the distracted mother, "My dear woman, your son has begun to steal because his home is unsatisfactory and unhappy. Why not set about making his home a good home?" If I were to do this, I might give her a bad conscience. Even if she had the best will in the world, she could not change her son's environment because she doesn't know how. What's more, even if she knew how, she wouldn't have the emotional capacity to carry out the program.

Certainly, with the guidance of a child psychologist a willing woman could bring about quite a change. A psychologist might recommend a separation from an unloved or unloving husband, or moving the mother-in-law out of the home. What a psychologist is unlikely to alter is the inner woman, the moralist, the anxious, frightened mother, the sex antagonist, the nag. Merely changing the external conditions too often has its limitations.

I have mentioned the frightened mother. I recall an interview with another kind of parent. She was the mother of a prospective pupil, a girl of seven. Every question she asked was an anxious one: "Does someone see that their teeth are brushed twice a day? Will she be watched so that she doesn't walk on the highway? Will she get lessons every day? Will someone give her her medicine each night?" Anxious mothers unconsciously make their children a part of their own unsolved problems. One mother was always in a state of fear concerning her daughter's health. She was continually writing me long letters of instructions regarding what the girl should eat or, rather, not eat, how she should be clothed, and so on. I have had many children of anxious parents. Invariably, the child acquires the parental anxiety; hypochondria is a frequent result.

Martha had a small brother. The parents are both anxious people. I hear Martha in the garden shouting to her brother. "Don't go into the pool—you'll get your feet wet." Or "Don't play with that sand—you'll soil your new pants." I say I hear Martha, but I should have said that I heard Martha—when she first came to school. Nowadays, she doesn't care if her brother looks like a chimney sweep. It is only during the last week of the term that her old anxiety returns, for then she realizes she is returning home to an atmosphere of constant anxiety.

I sometimes think that strict schools owe part of their popularity to the fact that the pupils delight in going home for holidays. Parents see in the happy faces of their children a love of home, whereas it is just as often hatred of the school. The hate of the child has been bestowed on the stern teachers; the love of the child is thrown lavishly upon the parents. This is the same psychological mechanism used by a mother when she shifts a child's hate to his father by saying, "Wait till your father comes home tonight. He'll give it to you!"

Often, I hear doctors and other professional men say, "I send my boys to a good private school so that they will get a good accent and will meet people who will be useful to them later on." They take it for granted that our social values will continue just as they have for generations. Fear of the future is a very real thing in parents.

Parents want disciplined schools when the home is a center of strict parental authority. The strict school carries on the tradition of keeping the child down, keeping him quiet, respectful, castrated. Moreover, the school does excellent work in treating only the head of the child. It restrains his emotional life, his creative urge. It trains him to be obedient to all the dictators and bosses of life. The fear that began in the nursery is increased by stern teachers whose rigid discipline grows out of their own power drives. The average parent, seeing only the exterior child with his school blazer, with his superficial manners, with his worship of football games, is pleased to see how successfully his dear son is being schooled. It is tragic to see young life sacrificed on this antediluvian altar of so-called education. The strict school demands only power—and the fearful parent is satisfied.

Like every ego-seeking power, the ego of the teacher will strive to draw the children to himself. Think what a tin god a teacher really is. He is the center of the picture; he commands and he is obeyed; he metes out justice; he does nearly all the talking. In the free school, the power element is eliminated. In Summerhill, there is no chance of a teacher's showing off his ego. He cannot compete with the more vocal egoism of the children. Thus, instead of respecting me, the children often call me a fool or a silly ass. Generally, these are terms of endearment. In a free school, the love element becomes the important one. The words used are secondary.

A boy comes to Summerhill from a more or less strict, anxious home. He is allowed freedom to do what he likes. No one criticizes him. No one tells him to mind his manners. No one asks him to be seen and not heard. The school is naturally a paradise to a boy. For paradise to a boy is a place where he can express his whole ego. His delight in being free to express himself soon becomes linked up with me. I am the man who allows him to be free. I am the Daddy that Daddy should have been. The boy is not really loving me. A child does not love—he just wants to be loved. His unspoken thought is: *I am happy here. Old Neill is a pretty decent guy. He never butts in and all that. He must be very fond of me or he would order me about.*

Vacation comes. He goes home. At home, he borrows father's searchlight, and no doubt leaves it lying on the piano. Father protests. The boy realizes that home is not a free place. One boy often said to me, "My people aren't up-to-date, you know. I'm not free at home like I am here. When I go home, I'm going to teach my father and mother." I suppose he carried out his threat, for he was sent to another school.

Many of my pupils suffer badly from "relationitis." At present, I have a strong desire to have an acrimonious talk with the following relatives of my pupils: two grandfathers (religious), four aunts (religious and prudish), two uncles (irreligious and moralizing). I sternly forbade the parents of one of my boys to allow him to visit his hellfire-loving grandfather, but they answered that it would be impossible to take such a drastic step. Woe to the boy!

At a free school, the child is safe from relatives. Nowadays, I warn them off. Two years ago, an uncle came and took his nephew, aged nine, for a stroll. The boy came back and began to throw bread about the dining room. "Your outing seems to have upset you," I said. "What did your uncle talk about?"

"Oh," he said lightly, "he talked about God all the time, God and the Bible."

"Didn't happen to quote the text about casting your bread upon the waters, did he?" I asked, and he began laughing. Incidentally, he gave up bread-throwing. When that uncle returns here, his nephew will simply be "temporarily unavailable."

In general, though, I cannot complain about most parents of my pupils. We get along splendidly together. Most of them are with me all the way. One or two timorously doubt, but continue to trust. I always tell the parents quite frankly what my methods are. I always tell them to take it or leave it. The ones who are with me all the way have no occasion to be jealous. The children feel just as free at home as at school, and they like going home.

Pupils whose parents do not completely believe in Summerhill do not want to go home for holidays. The parents demand too much of them. They do not realize that a child of eight is interested mainly in himself. He has no social sense, no real idea of duty. At Summerhill, he is living out his selfishness and he will get rid of it by expressing it. One day he will become social, because his respect for the rights and opinions of others will modify his selfishness. From the child's point of view, disagreement between school and home is disastrous. He begins to have a conflict: Which is right, home or school? It is essential for a child's growth and happiness that home and school should have a single purpose, a combined point of view.

One of the chief causes of disagreement between parent and teacher, I find, is jealousy. A girl pupil of fifteen said to me, "If I want to make Daddy roaring mad, I just say to him, 'Mr. Neill says so-and-so!'" Anxious parents are often jealous of any teacher that a child loves. That is natural. Children are, after all, possessions; they are property; they are a part of the parent's ego.

The teacher, too, is equally and frailly human. Many teachers have no children of their own; and so unconsciously they adopt their pupils. They strive, without realizing what they are doing, to steal the child from the parents. It is really necessary that a teacher be analyzed. Analysis is no panacea for all ills; it has a limited scope, but it clears the ground. I think that the chief merit of analysis is that it makes one understand others more easily, makes one more charitable. For this reason alone, I strongly recommend it for teachers; for after all, their work is to understand others. The analyzed teacher will cheerfully face his own attitude to children, and by facing it, improve it.

If a home yields fears and conflicts, it is a bad home. A child who has been pushed ahead too fast by his anxious parents is likely to become resentful. Unconsciously, he is determined that his parents shall not win. A child who has not been reared with anxiety and conflict will meet life in the spirit of adventure.

Parental Awareness

Being aware means being free from prejudices, from infantile attitudes—rather, as free as possible, for who can ever get free of early conditionings? Awareness implies getting under the surface of things, discounting the superficial. Because of their emotional attachment this is not easy for parents. *What a mess I have made of my kids!* is the cry in scores of letters I have received. The teacher, not handicapped by a strong emotional attachment to his pupils, has a far better chance than the parent to practice constant awareness in guiding the child to freedom.

Many a time I have had to write to a father that his problem son didn't stand a chance unless he, the father, changed some of his methods. I have had to point out, for instance, that it is an impossible situation wherein Tommy is free to smoke at Summerhill while he gets a beating for smoking at home. For smoking, substitute *bathing, washing, not learning, swearing,* and so on.

I have never put a child against his home. It was freedom that did the job, and of course, the unaware home simply could not take the challenge, could not understand the workings of freedom.

I would like to illustrate the wrong kind of parent-child relationship with several examples. The children I am going to write about are not abnormal in any way. They are simply victims of an environment in which there is no awareness of the child's real needs.

There is Mildred. When she returns after every vacation, she is spiteful, quarrelsome, dishonest; she bangs doors, complains about her room, complains about her bed, and so on. It takes more than half a term before she is once again easy to live with. She has spent her vacation nagging and being nagged by her mother, a woman who married the wrong man. All the school freedom in the world cannot give that child lasting contentment. As a matter of fact, an exceptionally bad vacation at home is followed up by petty thievery at school. Making her conscious of the situation does not change the home environment of unawareness, of hate, of constant interference with her life. Even at Summerhill, a child sometimes cannot get away from the home influence—the bad home influence that has no values, no knowledge of what a child thinks and feels. Alas! One cannot easily teach people values.

Johnny, aged eight, returns to school with a nasty look. He teases and bullies weaker children. His mother believes in Summerhill, but his father is a disciplinarian. The boy must jump to his father's command, and the child tells me that he is sometimes slapped. What can be done about him? I don't know.

I write to a father, "It is fatal for you to criticize your boy in any way. Do not rage at him. Above all, never punish him." When the boy goes home on vacation, his father meets him at the station. And the first thing he says to the boy is, "Keep your head up, man. Don't slouch!"

Peter's mother promised to give him a penny every morning that his bed was dry. I countered by offering him three cents every time he wet the bed. But in order to prevent a conflict between the mother and myself in the child's mind, I persuaded her to cut out her reward before I began mine. Now Peter more often wets the bed at home than he does at school. One element in his neurosis is that he wants to remain a baby; he is jealous of his baby brother. He vaguely senses that his mother is trying to cure him. What I am trying to do is to show him that wetting the bed doesn't matter a bit. In short, my three cents reward is encouraging him to remain a baby until he has lived it all out and he is ready to *give it up naturally*. A habit means that something has not been lived out. To discipline or bribe it out of existence means making the child feel guilty and giving him hateful morals. It is better to wet the bed than to become a moral prig.

Little Jimmy returns after a vacation saying, "I'm not going to skip a single lesson this term." His parents have been urging him to pass his high-school entrance exams. He goes to lessons for a week and then he doesn't show up at classes for a month. Another proof that mere talking is always useless. Worse than that, talk can be hampering.

As I said, these cases are not problem children at all. Under a rational environment and with parental understanding, these youngsters would be normal children.

I once had a problem boy who had suffered under the wrong teaching methods, and I told his mother that she must undo the mischief. She promised she would. She brought him back after the summer vacation, and I said, "Well, did you take off the prohibition?"

"Yes," she said, "I did."

"Good! What did you say to him?"

"I said, 'Playing with your penis is not wrong, but it is a silly thing to do.'"

She took off one prohibition and she put on another. And of course, the poor boy continued to be antisocial, dishonest, hateful, and full of anxiety.

My case against the parent is that he will not learn. Most of my work seems to consist of correcting parental mistakes. I feel both sympathy and admiration for the parents who honestly see the mistakes they have made in the past and who try to learn how best to treat their child. But other parents, strangely enough, would rather stick to a code that is useless and dangerous than to try to adapt themselves to the child. Even stranger, they seem to be jealous of the child's love for me.

The children do not love me so much as they love my non-interference in their affairs. I am the father they daydreamed about when their real father shouted "Stop that row!" I never demand good manners nor polite language. I never ask if faces have been washed. I never ask for obedience or respect or honor. In short, I treat children with the dignity that adults expect to be treated with. I realize, after all, that there can be no real competition between the father and me. His work is to earn an income for his family. My work is to study children and to give all my time and interest to children. If parents refuse to study child psychology in order to become more aware of their children's development, they must expect to be left behind. And parents *are* left behind.

I have had a parent write to a child in my school, "If you can't spell better than you do, I'd rather you not write me." That was written to a girl of whom we were not quite sure whether she was mentally defective or not!

More than once I have had to roar at a complaining parent, "Your boy is a thief, a bed-wetter. He is antisocial, unhappy, inferior. And you come to me and grouse because he met you at the station with a dirty face and dirty hands!" I am a man slow to wrath, but when I meet a father or mother who will not or cannot acquire a sense of values about what is important and what is trifling in a child's behavior, I get angry. Perhaps that is why I am thought to be anti-parent. On the other hand, what a joy it is when a mother comes for a visit, meets her muddy, tattered child in the garden, beams, and says to me, "Isn't he looking well and happy?"

Yet, I know how difficult it is. We all have our own standards of values and we measure others by our personal yardstick. Possibly I should apologize for being a man who is fanatic about children, impatient of parents who do not see children with my eyes. But if I did apologize, I would be a hypocrite. The truth is that I know I am right about values—as far as children are concerned.

The parent who genuinely wants to change his poor relationship with his child can start by asking himself certain down-to-earth questions. I can think of a score of pertinent questions. *Am I angry with my child because I had a row with my husband (or wife) this morning? Is it because our intercourse last night did not give me enough pleasure? Or because the woman next door says I spoil my brat? Or because my marriage is a failure? Or because the boss told me off at the office?* It can help very much to ask oneself questions like these.

The really deep questions, the lifetime-conditioned ones, alas, are beyond consciousness. It is very unlikely that an irate father will pause and ask himself this complicated question: *Am I angry with my son for swearing because I was brought up strictly, with whippings and moral lectures, with fear of God, with respect for meaningless social conventions, with intense sexual repression?* The answer would mean a degree of self-analysis that is beyond the capability of most of us. Too bad, for that answer would save many a child from neurosis and unhappiness.

The biblical phrase about visiting the iniquities of the fathers on the children has been understood in its physical context for generations. And even the uneducated can learn the moral of Ibsen's *Ghosts,* where the son is ruined because of the syphilis of the father. What is not understood is the much more frequent ruination of the children by the psychological sins of the fathers. For the child, there can be only one escape from this destructive cycle of character distortion—early guidance toward self-regulation on the part of the aware parent.

It must be emphasized that self-regulation demands more giving than a set system of rules does. The parents will have to sacrifice more of their time and self-interest for at least two years. They must not play a game to gain the baby's love or gratitude. They must not look on baby as a show piece to give smiles and perform tricks when relatives come visiting. Self-regulation implies much parental selflessness. I emphasize this aspect because I have seen young couples who thought that they were using self-regulation when they were making the baby adapt himself to their own convenience, trying to make the child accept a bedtime that fitted in with their desire to go to the movies of an evening. Or later on, giving the child soft, noiseless toys so that Daddy won't be disturbed during his forty winks.

"But stop," cries the parent, "you can't *do* that to us! We have our own rights in life!" I say no, not during the first two years —or maybe four years of a child's life. The first years must be years of the most careful watchfulness, because the whole of the surroundings are against self-regulation, and one is forced to fight for a child with a conscious intensity.

I have several other bits of advice for parents who are in earnest about giving their children a good start toward self-regulation and freedom.

Parking a baby in a baby carriage in the garden, perhaps for hours at a time, is a dangerous practice. No one can know what agonizing feelings of fear and loneliness a baby can experience on waking up suddenly to find himself alone in a strange place. Those who have heard a baby's screams on such occasions have some idea of the cruelty of this stupid custom.

If you want your child to grow up without being neurotic, you must not—*dare* not—stand aloof from him. You must play with him, not only at his games, but play *with* him in the sense that you are a child too, able to enter into his life and accept his interests. If you have any silly dignity, you will not be able to do this.

It is always better, if possible, for grandparents to live separately—and not with the children. What usually happens is that the grandparents insist on laying down the law about the upbringing of children, or that the grandparents spoil them by seeing only the good or the bad in them. In wrong homes the children have four bosses instead of two. Even in good homes there is a strain because most of the time the grandparents keep trying to bring in their own antiquated views on childhood. Grandparents are often inclined to spoil a child by a too possessive love. This usually happens when Grandma has no real interest in life after her own family has grown. The third generation gives her a chance to begin her job anew. Under the notion that her daughter or daughter-in-law is incompetent as a mother, Grandma takes over, and the child is pulled both ways —and is apt to withdraw from *both* sides. To a child, squabbling means a loveless home, whether it be between Mother and Granny or between man and wife. And even if the squabbling is subtly hidden from the child, he is never deceived. He *feels,* without being conscious of it, that there is no love in his house.

The question of school may also be difficult. Your wife may wish to send the child to a coed progressive school, and you may wish to send the child to a public school. There may be a clash. Possibly the worst result may occur if either you or your wife is a Roman Catholic. I have no advice to offer here. Ideological or religious gulfs are too often unbridgeable. I can only say that some of my most difficult pupils were the result of the parents' differences of opinion on schools. A boy whose father was against Summerhill but gave way for the sake of peace never made substantial progress here because he knew his father really disapproved. It is a tragic situation for any child to be in. He never finds any security of tenure, fearing that any day his father will decide to transfer him to a disciplined school.

However, some antagonism between parent and teacher is to be expected. Teachers are aware of this, and some of them work hard in order to bring the staff and parents into closer contact through parent-teacher meetings in the school. Excellent! It should be done everywhere. Teachers should realize that they can never be as important an influence on children as the parents are. That is why it is hopeless to try to cure a problem child when the home retains the atmosphere that made the child a problem.

Parents must face the fact that, sooner or later, it is necessary for children to break away from them. Naturally I do not mean that children should leave their parents and never see them again. I mean breaking away *psychically;* ridding themselves of the infant's dependence on home. It is natural for a mother to try to keep her children dependent on her. I know many homes where a daughter has remained at home to comfort her parents in their old age. In most of the cases, I realize, the home is an unhappy one.

One part of the daughter's psyche is urging her to go out into the world and live her own life. The other part, the dutiful part, compels her to remain with her parents. She must always have an inner conflict, and this conflict usually shows itself in irritation: *Of course, I love mother, but she is so tiresome at times!*

Today, thousands of women have the dullest jobs on earth—preparing meals, doing dishes, washing clothes, ironing, dusting. They are unpaid housekeepers, and their lives are drab. When the family leaves the nest, the mother's job is finished. The nest from which the fledglings have flown is a lonely nest, and the mother should be sympathized with rather than condemned. Her maternal tendency is to keep her job as long as possible—even though she may unintentionally cause her child suffering in the process. All this should point to the obvious fact that every married woman should have a trade or profession that she can take up again once her maternal responsibilities are over.

The parent is God, and a jealous God. The parent has the legal right to say, *I shall mold my child thus!* A mother and father can beat their child, terrorize him, make his life miserable. The law can interfere only if too much bodily damage is done. It cannot interfere at all, however, no matter how much psychical damage is done. The tragedy is that the parent believes that he is always acting for the best.

Humanity's great hope is that parents *will* act for the best, if they have awareness and are on the side of the child in his development toward freedom in work, and knowledge, and love. If this book has helped even one parent to realize the tremendous influence for good or evil that a parent exerts, it will not have been written in vain.

SEVEN

QUESTIONS AND ANSWERS

In General

You call humanity anti-life. What do you mean? I am not anti-life, nor are my friends anti-life.

In my lifetime I have seen two horrible wars, and I may live to see a much more horrible third one. Many millions of youths died in those two wars. When I was a boy, men died in an imperialist cause in South Africa. From 1914 to 1918, they died in the "war to end all wars." From 1939 to 1945, they died to crush Fascism. Tomorrow, many may die to crush or to further Communism. That means that the great masses of people are willing to give up their lives and their children's lives at the command of central authorities for causes that do not touch their individual lives.

We are anti-life and pro-death if we are pawns of politicians, merchants, or exploiters. We are pawns because we were trained to seek life negatively, humbly fitting ourselves into an authoritative society, and ready to die for the ideals of our masters. Only in romantic novels do people die for love; in reality, they die for hate.

That is the crowd aspect. But the individual is anti-life in his everyday existence. His love-making is in the main unsatisfactory; his pleasures are mostly tawdry, cheap, escapist. He is a moralist, that is, one who considers natural living to be wrong or at the best inadequate, and he trains his children accordingly.

No pro-life child would ever be given a conscience about sex or lessons or God or manners or nice behavior. No pro-life parent or teacher would ever strike a child. No pro-life citizen would tolerate our penal code, our hangings, our punishment of homosexuals, our attitude toward bastardy. No pro-life person would sit in a church and claim to be a miserable sinner.

Let me make it clear that I do not advocate libertinism. The test is always this: *Is what Mr. X is doing really harmful to anyone else?* If the answer is no, then objectors to Mr. X are acting anti-life.

One can argue the other way and point to the pro-life of young people when they dance, hike, play games, go to films, concerts, plays. And there is something in that argument, too, for youth craves for what is pro-life, and is so brightly alive and optimistic that it finds its pleasure even when it is suppressed by authority. Later this craving persists, so that man is ambivalent, seeking pleasure and at the same time fearing it.

When I use the word *anti-life,* I do not mean death-seeking. I mean fearing life more than fearing death. To be anti-life does not mean to be pro-death. To be anti-life is to be pro-authority, pro-church religion, pro-repression, pro-oppression, or at least subservient to these.

Let me summarize: Pro-life equals fun, games, love, interesting work, hobbies, laughter, music, dance, consideration for others, and faith in men. Anti-life equals duty, obedience, profit, and power. Throughout history anti-life has won, and will continue to win as long as youth is trained to fit into present-day adult conceptions.

Don't you believe that most of humanity's ills will be solved when the economic problems of the world's millions have been solved?

It is not very satisfying to realize that our home and school training lead to drab lives for the majority of people. Oh, yes, dull jobs in shops and offices are necessary; what is unnecessary is the deadness of people who hate their desks and sales counters, who have to seek relief for their starved emotions in trite films, dog racing, picture magazines, and newspaper accounts of sensation and crime.

Millionaires with Cadillacs are no happier in their inner lives than are railway porters. The answer is that no man can enjoy economic comfort or security if his soul is anti-life and anti-love. The rich man and the poor man have this in common: they have both been reared in a world that disapproves of love, fears love, makes love an obscene joke.

Many who agree that most people are unhappy will say that when all economic problems are solved, then life will be full and satisfying and free. For myself, I cannot believe this. The little we have seen of economic freedom has not been encouraging. The economic freedom that makes possible an electric kitchen does not lead to any greater happiness or wisdom; all it does is to allow more comfort, and this soon becomes accepted automatically and loses its emotional value.

Our character-forming methods have made England a successful country in material things; they have given us a high standard of living. But that's as far as the success goes. By and large, people are still unhappy. No, the economic solution alone will never free the world from its hate and misery, its crime and scandal, its neuroses and diseases.

What can we do about an unhappy marriage?

Some middle-class parents seek a solution in psychoanalysis, which very often results in a breakup of the marriage. But even if analysis were more successful than it usually is, we cannot analyze the world. Curative work with individuals is a piddling business which cannot sufficiently affect the masses.

The solution for humanity lies in proper rearing of the young, not curing the neurotic. I must confess that I have nothing to say that will solve the marriage question of today. It is a hard thought, but if Mr. and Mrs. Brown are living together unhappily because they were reared in an anti-life atmosphere, there is nothing one can do about it.

That sounds like rank pessimism. We can be optimistic only if we strive to treat the children in such a way that they will not hate sex and life. Every time I see a child spanked, a child lied to, a child made ashamed of its nakedness, I see with misery that such a child will grow up to be a hateful husband or wife.

Do you deem it important that both persons in a marriage should be on the same intellectual level?

The intellectual side of marriage is a minor one. A marriage of heads is a dull, cold affair; whereas a marriage of hearts is one of warmth and giving. Nature does not make a man or a woman fall in love because of the intellectual prowess of the partner. Later, however, when the sex urge weakens, a common intellectual interest will tend to make a couple happy. The same brand of humor is perhaps the best prognosis for a long happy marriage.

What is the cause of excessive worry about work, and why do so many young people commit suicide nowadays?

I question if any child has ever worried about work. The apparent worry has a deeper source; almost invariably, it arises from a sense of sin about masturbation. Children without guilt about masturbation are usually bright and keen in their work.

Stekel said, "Suicide is the last sexual act." The masturbation prohibition is one that causes a child to hate his body and his soul, and suicide is a logical reaction. If the body is so vile, the sooner it is got rid of the better.

What is your opinion of social workers?

I have great respect for the social workers who enter the slum homes of problem children. They are doing fine work. But does their work go deep enough?

No one expects them to psychoanalyze the mothers and fathers. Everyone knows that their labor is uphill. They cannot abolish the slums that make children anti-social. Nor can they change ignorant parents—parents who stunt growth by bad feeding and make sex a matter of sordid adventures in dark closets.

The welfare workers are heroes and heroines. They endeavor to help youth overcome the evils of a poor home life. Even if a social worker had a complete belief in freedom, how could he apply such principles in a slum home? Could one say to a mother, "Mrs. Green, your son is stealing because his drunken father beats him, because you spanked him at the age of two for touching his penis, because you have never showed him any love"? Would Mrs. Green understand?

I do not say that the woman cannot be re-educated. But I do say that she cannot be re-educated by the talk of a social worker, nor of anyone else. Here the problem is partly economic. At least a start should be made by abolishing the slum.

About Summerhill

Under the Summerhill system, how does a child's will power develop? If he is allowed to do what he pleases, how can he develop self-control?

In Summerhill, a child is *not* allowed to do as he pleases. His own laws hedge him in on all sides. He is allowed to do as he pleases only in things that affect *him*—and only him. He can play all day if he wants to, because work and study are matters that concern him alone. But he is not allowed to play a cornet in the schoolroom because his playing would interfere with others.

What, after all, is will power? I can will myself to give up tobacco, but I cannot will myself to fall in love, nor can I will myself to like botany. No man can will himself to be good, or for that matter, to be bad.

You cannot train a person to have a strong will. If you educate children in freedom, they will be more conscious of themselves, for freedom allows more and more of the unconscious to become conscious. That is why most Summerhill children have few doubts about life. They *know* what they want. And I guess they will get it, too.

Remember that what is called a weak will is usually a sign of lack of interest. The weak person who is easily persuaded to play tennis when he has no desire to play tennis is a person who has no idea of what his interests really are. A slave discipline system encourages such a person to remain weak-willed and futile.

If a child is doing something dangerous at Summerhill, do you allow him to do it?

Of course not. People so often fail to understand that freedom for children does not mean being a fool. We do not allow our little children to decide when they shall go to bed. We guard them against dangers from machinery, automobiles, broken glass, or deep water.

You should never give a child responsibility that he is not ready for. But remember that half the dangers that children encounter are due to bad education. The child who is dangerous with fire is one who was forbidden to know the truth about fire.

Do the children in Summerhill suffer from homesickness?

I notice that when an unhappy mother brings a new child to Summerhill, the child clings to her in tears, screaming to be taken home. I also notice that if the child does not scream enough, the mother is annoyed. She *wants* her child to be homesick; the greater the homesickness, the more the child loves her. Often the wretched child is playing happily five minutes after the mother's train has departed.

Why the child of an unhappy home is homesick when he starts school is difficult to say. It is likely that his unhappy home gives him acute anxiety. What, he wonders, is happening at home this minute? The most probable explanation lies in the fact that an unhappy mother, thwarted in her love of her mate, transfers too much of her love and of her hate to her children.

Homesickness is usually the sign of a bad home, a home in which there is much hate. The homesick child longs not for the love of home, but for the strife and for the protection of home. That sounds paradoxical, but it isn't when we reflect that the more unhappy the home is, the more the child seeks protection. He has no anchor in life, and he exaggerates the anchorage he calls home. Absent from it, he idealizes it. He longs not for the home he knows, but for the home he would *like* to have.

Do you accept backward children at Summerhill?

Sure. It all depends on what you mean by backward. We do not take mentally defective children, but a child who is backward at school is a different story. Many children are backward at school because the school is too dull for them.

Summerhill's criterion of backwardness has nothing to do with tests and sums and marks. In many cases, backwardness simply means that the child has an unconscious conflict and a guilty conscience. How can he take an interest in arithmetic or history if his unconscious problem is, "Am I wicked or not?"

I speak with personal feeling about this question of backwardness, for as a boy I simply couldn't learn. My pockets were full of bits of scrap iron and brass; and when my eyes were on my textbook, my thoughts wandered to my gadgets.

I have seldom seen a backward boy or girl who has not the potentialities of creative work; and to judge any child by his or her progress in school subjects is futile and fatal.

Suppose a child refuses to pay the fine imposed by a General School Meeting?

Children never do. But I expect they would refuse if they felt they had been treated unjustly. Our appeal system overcomes any sense of injustice.

You say that the children in Summerhill have clean minds. What do you mean?

A clean mind is one that cannot be shocked. To be shocked is to show that you have repressions that make you interested in what shocks you.

Victorian women were shocked at the word *leg* because they had an abnormal interest in things leggy. Leggy things were sexual things, repressed things. So that in an atmosphere like Summerhill, where there is no taboo about sex and no connecting of sex with sin, children have no need to make sex unclean by whispering and leering. They are sincere about sex just as they are sincere about everything else.

After Willie, seven, returned from his first term at Summerhill, his language was so strong that the neighbors wouldn't let him play with their children. What should I do about it?

Unfortunate, sad, and painful for Willie, but what is the alternative? If your neighbors are shocked by a few *damns* and *hells,* they are repressed people who ought not to be in touch with your Willie.

What do Summerhill children think of the movies?

They see all kinds of films. We have no censorship. The result is that by the time they leave school, they have acquired a good judgment of films. Quite often, an older child will stay away from the movies on the ground that the film doesn't sound interesting. The older pupils who have seen the great films of France, Italy, and Germany are very critical of the average

Hollywood production. Boys below the age of puberty are bored by love films. To them, Kim Novak is nobody.

What do you do with a child who answers back?

No child in Summerhill ever answers back. A child answers back only when he is treated as an inferior by someone who is dignified. In Summerhill, we speak the language of the children. If a teacher complained of being answered back, I should know that he or she was a dud.

What do you do with a child who won't take its medicine?

I don't know. In Summerhill, we never have a child who won't take his medicine. Our feeding is so balanced that illness is not one of our school problems.

Do the older children at Summerhill look after the smaller children?

No, the younger ones don't need to be looked after. They are too busy on their own important affairs.

Have you ever had colored pupils at Summerhill?

Yes, we have had two colored pupils in Summerhill; and so far as I could see, the other children were unconscious of their color. One colored boy was a bully and was disliked; the other was a likable fellow and was exceptionally popular.

Have you any Boy Scouts in Summerhill?

No, I don't think our boys would stomach the one good deed per day. To do a good deed a day consciously savors of priggishness. There is much that is good in the Boy Scout movement, but to me it is marred by its moral uplift and its bourgeois ideas of right and wrong and purity.

In my school, I have never expressed any opinion about the Boy Scouts. On the other hand, I have never heard one of our boys evince any interest in the movement.

What is your policy with a child brought up in a sincerely religious home? Do you allow such a child to practice religion in Summerhill?

Yes, the child can practice religion, without fear of any adverse comments by the teaching staff or the pupils. But I find that no child wants to practice religion when he is free.

Some new pupils go to church for a few Sundays and then they cease going. Church is too dull. I find no indication that worship is a natural thing in children. When the sense of sin is washed out, prayer is never used.

Generally, children from a religious home are insincere and repressed. That is inevitable under a religious system that has lost its original love of life and concentrates on its fear of death. You can instill in a child a fear of the Lord but not a love of the Lord. Free children do not need a religion because their life is spiritually creative.

Are the children at Summerhill interested in politics?

No. That may be because they are middle-class children who have never had the experience of poverty. I make it a rule to keep the teaching staff from trying to influence the children politically. Politics, like religion, is a matter for personal choice to be made later on in life as the child grows up.

Do any Summerhill pupils join the army later?

So far only one has joined the forces—the RAF. It is possible that the army is too uncreative to attract free children. Fighting, after all, is destruction. Summerhill children would fight for their country just as readily as any other children, but they would probably want to know exactly what they were fighting for.

Our old pupils fought in the Second World War and a few died.

Why do you have your boys and girls sleeping in separate rooms?

Well, Summerhill is a school in England, and we have to be mindful of the mores and laws of England.

About Child Rearing

Do you think that every parent who reads your books or hears you lecture will treat her child differently and better—once she knows? Does the cure for damaged children lie in getting knowledge to the parents?

A possessive mother, reading this book, may get a very bad conscience and cry in defense, "I can't help myself. I don't want to ruin my child. It's all very well for you to diagnose, but what is the remedy?"

She is right. What *is* the remedy? Or, indeed, *is* there a remedy? The question asks so much.

What cure is there for a woman whose life is dull and full of fears? What cure is there for a man who thinks that his cheeky son is the cat's whiskers? Worst of all, what remedy is there when the parents are ignorant of what they are doing and become indignant at even the slightest suggestion that they are doing the wrong thing?

No, knowledge in itself won't help unless a parent is *emotionally ready* to receive the knowledge and has the inner capacity to act on what new knowledge comes his way.

Why do you say so much about the necessity of a child's being happy? Is anybody happy?

Not an easy question to answer because words confuse. Of course none of us is happy all the time; we have toothaches, unfortunate love affairs, boring work.

If the word happiness means anything, it means an inner feeling of well-being, a sense of balance, a feeling of being contented with life. These can exist only when one feels free.

Free children have open, fearless faces; disciplined children look cowed, miserable, fearful.

Happiness might be defined as the state of having minimal repression. The happy family lives in a home where love abides; the unhappy family, in a tense home.

I place happiness first because I place growth first. It is better to be free and contented and be ignorant of what a decimal fraction is, than to pass school exams and have your face covered with acne. I have never seen acne on the face of a happy and free adolescent.

If a child is given absolute freedom, how soon will he realize that self-discipline is an essential of living, or will he ever realize that?

There isn't such a thing as absolute freedom. Anyone who allows a child to get all his own way is following a dangerous path.

No one can have social freedom, for the rights of others must be respected. But everyone should have individual freedom.

To put it concretely: no one has the right to make a boy learn Latin, because learning is a matter for individual choice; but if in a Latin class, a boy fools all the time, the class should throw him out, because he interferes with the freedom of others.

As for self-discipline, it is an indefinite thing. Too often it means a discipline of self that has been instilled by the moral ideas of adults. True self-discipline does *not* involve repression or acceptance. It considers the rights and happiness of others. It leads the individual to deliberately seek to live at peace with others by conceding something to their point of view.

Do you honestly think it is right to allow a boy, naturally lazy, to go his own easy way doing as he chooses, wasting time? How do you set him to work when work is distasteful to him?

Laziness doesn't exist. The lazy boy is either physically ill or he has no interest in the things that adults think he ought to do.

I have never seen a child who came to Summerhill before the age of twelve who was lazy. Many a "lazy" lad has been sent to Summerhill from a strict school. Such a boy remains "lazy" for quite a long time; that is, until he recovers from his education. I do not set him to do work that is distasteful to him, because he isn't ready for it. Like you and me, he will have many things to do later that he will hate doing; but if he is left free to live through his play period now, he will be able, later on, to face any difficulty. To my knowledge, no ex-Summerhillian has ever been accused of laziness.

Do you believe in fondling children?

Once when my daughter Zoë was young, she started and cried at the banging of a door. My wife picked her up and hugged her warmly and then held her in such a way that she could kick her limbs freely.

At any sign of stiffening, the parent should play with the child in such a way that the child can freely move his muscles. I find a sham fight effective with children of four or five, a fight I must always lose. Laughter is a great releaser of emotion and bodily tightness, and a healthy baby laughs and chuckles a lot. Tickling the ribs will often start a bout of happy laughter, and . . . oh, here, I should mention a school of child psychology that disapproves of touching a child in case one gives it a father or mother fixation. I am sure that that is nonsense. There is no reason at all why parents should not fondle their children, tickle them, stroke them, pat them.

One should ignore those life-shy psychologists who tell you never to have the baby in bed with you, never to tickle it. The unconscious idea behind the prohibition is that any bodily contact might arouse sexual emotions in the baby. There might be a danger but only if the parent were so neurotic as to find self-centered pleasure in physical contact with the baby; but I am writing for more or less normal people—not parents who are still infants themselves.

What can a progressive parent do about the aggressiveness of other children?

If parents send self-regulated Willie to public school where he is bound to meet cruelty and aggression and spitefulness among other children, are his parents to let Willie find out for himself that he can be hurt by hate and violence?

When Peter was three, his father told me he would teach him how to box, so that he could fight against the hate coming out in others. Living in a so-called Christian world in which turning the other cheek is a sign not of love and charity but of cowardice, that father was right. If we do not do something positive, our self-regulated children will be heavily handicapped.

What is your opinion of corporal punishment?

Corporal punishment is evil because it is cruel and hateful. It makes both the giver and the recipient hate. It is an unconscious sexual perversion. In communities where masturbation is suppressed, the punishment is given on the hand—the means of masturbation. In segregated boys' schools where homosexuality is suppressed, the caning is given on the bottom—the object of desire. The religious hate of the vile flesh makes corporal punishment popular in religious regions.

Corporal punishment is always a projected act. The giver hates himself and projects his hate on to the child. The mother who spanks her child hates herself; and in consequence, hates her child.

In the case of a teacher with a large class, the use of the strap is not so much a matter of hate as one of convenience. It is the easy way. The best way to abolish it would be to abolish large classes. If a school were a place for play, with freedom to learn or not to learn, whipping would automatically die out. In a school in which the teachers know their jobs, corporal punishment is never resorted to.

Do you seriously believe that the way to break bad habits is to let children continue their vices?

Vices? In whose opinion are they vices?

Bad habits? You mean masturbation, possibly.

By forcibly breaking a habit, you do not cure it. The only cure for any habit is to allow the child to outlive his interest in that habit. Children who are allowed to masturbate indulge much less than children who have been forbidden to masturbate.

Beating always prolongs trouser-messing. Tying up the hands makes an infant a perverted masturbator for life. So-called bad habits are not bad habits at all; they are natural tendencies. The designation "bad habits" is the result of parental ignorance and hate.

Does correct home rearing counteract the wrong teaching of a school?

In the main, yes. The voice of the home is more powerful than the voice of the school. If the home is free from fear and punishment, the child will not come to believe that the school is right.

Parents should tell their children what they think of a wrong school. Too often parents have an absurd sense of loyalty to even the most stupid of school teachers.

What is your attitude toward fairy tales and Santa Claus?

Children love fairy tales and that in itself is enough to sanction them.

As for Santa Claus, I don't think we need be troubled by him, for children soon learn the truth about him. But there is an odd connection between him and the stork story. The parents who want their children to believe in Santa Claus are usually those who tell their children lies about birth.

Personally, I never tell children about Santa Claus. If I did, I guess our four-year-olds would laugh me to scorn.

You say that creation is better than possession, yet when you allow a child to create, the thing he makes becomes a possession and he will overvalue it. What about it?

The fact of the matter is that he doesn't. A child values what he makes for about a day or a week. A child's natural sense of possession is weak; he will leave his new bicycle out in the rain, and he will leave his clothes lying about anywhere. The joy is in the making. The true artist has no interest in his work when it is finished. No work of art ever pleases its creator, because his aim is perfection.

What would you do with a child who won't stick to anything? He is interested in music for a short period, then he changes to dancing, and so on.

I'd do nothing. Such is life. In my time, I have changed from photography to bookbinding, then to woodwork, then brass-work. Life is full of fragments of interests. For many years I sketched in ink; when I realized that I was a tenth-rate artist, I gave it up.

A child is always eclectic in his tastes. He tries all things; that's how he learns. Our boys spend days making boats; but if an aviator happens to visit us, the same boys will leave half-made boats and begin to make airplanes. We never suggest that a child should finish his work; if his interest has gone, it is wrong to pressure him to finish it.

Should one ever be sarcastic to children? Do you think this would help to develop a sense of humor in a child?

No. Sarcasm and humor have no connection. Humor is an affair of love, sarcasm of hate. To be sarcastic to a child is to make the child feel inferior and degraded. Only a nasty teacher or parent will ever be sarcastic.

Eclective - Selective - choosing - to pick out

My child is always asking me what to do, and what to play. What shall I answer? Is it wrong to give the child play ideas?

It is good for a child to have someone to give him exciting things to do, but it is not necessary. The things that a child finds to do by himself are best for him. Thus, no Summerhill teacher will ever advise a child what to do. A teacher will only assist a child who asks for technical information about *how* a thing is done.

Do you approve of gifts to a child to show one's love?

No. Love doesn't need outward tokens. But children should have gifts at the usual times—birthdays, Christmas, and so on. Only, no gratitude should be expected or demanded.

My boy plays truant from school. What can I do about it?

My guess is that the school is dull, and your boy is active.

Speaking broadly, truancy means that the school is not good enough. If possible, try to send your boy to a school in which there is more freedom, more creativity, more love.

Should I teach my child to save by giving her a little bank?

No. A child cannot see beyond the horizon of today. Later on, if she sincerely desires to buy something costing a lot of money, she will save without being trained to save.

Let me emphasize again that a child must be left to grow at its own rate. Many parents made dreadful mistakes in trying to force the pace.

Never help a child if he can do something alone. When a child tries to climb up on a chair, doting parents help it up, thereby spoiling the greatest joy in childhood—conquering a difficulty.

What shall I do when my boy of nine hammers nails into my furniture?

Take the hammer from him and tell him it is your furniture and you won't have him damaging what doesn't belong to him.

And if he doesn't stop hammering then, dear woman, then sell your furniture and with the proceeds go to some psychologist who will help you realize how you made your boy a problem child. No happy, free child will want to damage furniture, unless of course the furniture is the only thing in the home that can be used for hammering nails into.

The first step to stop such damage is to provide wood and nails, preferably in a room other than the living room. If sonny refuses the wood and still wants to put nails into the furniture, then he hates you and is trying to anger you.

What do you do with a child who is obstinate and sulks?

I don't know. I hardly ever see one at Summerhill. There is no occasion for obstinacy when a child is free. Defiance in a child is always the fault of adults. If your attitude to a child is one of love, you will do nothing to make him obstinate. An obstinate child has a grievance. My job would be to find out what is at the root of his grievance. I should guess it's a feeling that he has been treated unjustly.

What should I do with my child of six who draws obscene pictures?

Encourage him, of course; but at the same time clean your house, for any obscenity in the home must come from you. A child of six has no natural obscenity.

You see obscenity in his drawings because you yourself have an obscene attitude to life. I can only imagine that the obscene drawings deal with toilets and sexual organs. Treat these things naturally without any idea of right and wrong and your child will pass through this temporary childish interest, just as he will pass through other childish interests.

Why does my small son tell so many lies?

Possibly in imitation of his parents.

If two children, brother and sister five and seven years old, continually squabble, what method should I adopt to get them to stop? They are very fond of each other.

Are they? Is one getting more love from Mother than the other? Are they imitating Father and Mother? Have they been given guilty consciences about their bodies? Are they punished? If the answer is no to all these questions, then the squabbling is the normal desire to exercise power.

However, brother and sister should be with other children who have no emotional attachment to them. A child must measure himself against other children. He cannot measure himself against his own brothers and sisters because all sorts of emotional factors enter into the relationship—jealousies, favoritism, etc.

How can I stop my child from sucking his thumb?

Don't try. If you succeed, you'll probably drive the child back to a pre-sucking interest. What does it matter? Lots of efficient persons have sucked their thumbs.

Thumb-sucking shows that the interest in the mother's breast has not been lived out. Since you cannot give a child of eight the breast, all you can do is to see that the child is provided with as much opportunity for creative interest as possible. But that does not always cure. I have had creative pupils who sucked their thumbs up to the age of puberty.

Leave your child alone.

Why does my child of two always destroy toys?

Most probably because he is a wise child. Toys are usually com- pletely uncreative. The destruction has the aim of finding out what is inside.

But then, I do not know the circumstances of this case. If the child is being made into a self-hater by spankings and lectures, he will naturally destroy anything that comes his way.

What can be done to cure a child's untidiness?

But why cure it? Most creative people are untidy. It is usually a dull man whose room and desk are models of neatness. I find that children up to nine are in the main tidy; between nine and fifteen, these same children may be untidy. Boys and girls simply do not see untidiness. Later on, they become as tidy as they need be.

Our boy of twelve won't wash before coming to table. What should we do?

Why do you attach so much importance to washing? Have you considered that washing may be a symbol to you? Are you sure that your concern about his being clean is not covering your fear that he is morally unclean?

Don't nag the boy. Take my word for it that your dirt complex is a subjective personal interest. If you feel unclean, you will attach an exaggerated importance to cleanliness.

If you must have him appear at table clean—I mean if Aunt Mary sits at table with you and there is a prospect of her leaving her clean nephew a fortune—well, the best way is to forbid him to wash.

How can one keep a child of fifteen months away from a stove?

Put up a fireguard. But allow the child to learn the truth about stoves by getting his fingers burnt ever so slightly.

If I criticize my little daughter about trifles, you may say I hate her, but really, I don't, you know.

But you must hate yourself. Trifles are symbols of big things. If you criticize for trifles, you are an unhappy woman.

At what age should a parent allow a child to drink alcohol?

I am on unsure ground here because I have a complex about alcohol. I personally like my pint of beer, my glass of whisky;

I like wines and liqueurs. I certainly am no rabid abstainer. Yet I fear alcohol because I saw it do so much damage in my youth. Hence, I am not inclined to give alcohol to children.

When my young daughter wanted to taste my Pilsener or my whisky, I allowed her to do so. Over the beer she made a wry face, and said, "Nasty!" Of the whisky she said, "Lovely," but did not ask for more.

In Denmark, I saw self-regulated babies ask for curaçao; they were each given a glass which they drank to the dregs, but they did not ask for more. I recall a farmer who used to come in his gig to pick up his children from school on a wet, cold day. He always brought a flask of whisky and gave each one a dram. My father shook his head sadly. "Mark my words," he said, "they will all be drunkards later." When they grew up, all of them were teetotalers.

Sooner or later, every child will come up against the question of alcohol, and only the ones who cannot cope with life will be likely to drink too much.

When my old pupils come back to Summerhill, they go down to the local bar and have a wet reunion, yet I never heard of one who drank to excess.

Quite illogically, I forbid strong drink in my school, although some may think that children ought to be allowed to find out the truth about drinking for themselves.

What do you do with a child who won't eat?

I don't know. We have never had one at Summerhill. If we had, I should at once suspect him of showing a defiant attitude to his parents. We have had one or two children who were sent to Summerhill because they wouldn't eat; but they never fasted in the school.

In a difficult case, I should consider the possibility of the child's having remained emotionally at the breast stage, and would try feeding with a bottle. I should also suspect that the parents had been fussy and insistent about food, giving the child food that he did not want.

About Sex

What exactly does pornography mean?

This is not an easy question to answer. I should define pornography as an obscene attitude toward sex and other natural functions, a guilty attitude similar to that of repressed schoolboys who leer and snigger in dark corners and write sex words on walls.

Most sex stories are pornographic; and often the teller rationalizes when he says that it isn't the smut that makes it a good story, but the wit or humor. Like most men, I have told and listened to a thousand sex stories; but looking back now, I can think of only one or two that I would consider worth telling again.

I find that usually the raconteur of sex stories is one who does not have a satisfactory sex life. It would be too sweeping to say that every sex story is the result of repression, for that would suggest that all humor is so. I roared when I saw Charlie Chaplin in a bathing suit dive into two inches of water, but I have no repressions about diving. Humor exists in any ludicrous situation whether it is sexual or nonsexual.

In our present society, none of us is free to draw a firm line between what is pornographic and what is not. Many a so-called "commercial traveler" story appealed to me when I was a student, whereas today I think that ninety-nine per cent of them are simply crudely obscene.

By and large, pornography is simply sex plus guilt. The audiences that cackle at comedians who make suggestive cracks are composed of people who have been given a sick attitude toward sex. When adults tell sex stories to children, they are themselves at the leering, smutty stage of development.

If all children were free and oriented about sex, adult obscenity would cut no ice; but since millions of children are ignorant and guilty about sex, the pornographic adult merely adds to their ignorance and guilt.

Are certain forms of sex behavior improper?

Every form of sex behavior is proper if both persons find delight in it. Sex is abnormal and perverted only when it is used in a way that does not afford the highest enjoyment to *both* participants.

Matrimony is associated with decent sex—that is, restrained sex. Even youths of both sexes who accept the sexual life of their parents would be apt to be shocked if they imagined that father and mother enjoyed all sorts of sex play.

The authoritarian pillars of society have relegated sex play to the realm of pornography and obscenity, as have their followers who are afraid to indulge in sex play. If they did, they would most probably experience strong feelings of aggression and wallow in a lust-excitement induced primarily from doing what is prohibited.

When sex is tender and bathed in love, nothing is improper.

Why do children masturbate and how should we stop them?

We must distinguish between infantile masturbation and adult masturbation. Infantile masturbation is really not masturbation at all. It begins with curiosity. The infant discovers his hands and nose and toes, and mother crows with delight. But when he discovers his sexual apparatus, mother hastily takes his hand away. The main effect is to make the sexual organs the most interesting parts of the body.

The infant's erotic zone is the mouth, and when small children are not given moral prohibitions about masturbation, they have very little interest in their sexual organs. If a small child is a masturbator, the cure is to approve of the habit, for then the child has no morbid compulsion to indulge.

With older children who have reached puberty, approval will lessen the habit. But remember that sex must find some outlet, and because marriage is always late, owing to the fact that the young cannot marry until they can afford to set up a house, the sexually ripe are faced with two alternatives—masturbation or clandestine sexual intercourse. The moralists condemn both, but they offer no substitute. Oh, yes, of course, they advocate chastity, which means the crucifixion of the flesh. But since only a few monastics can apparently crucify the flesh indefinitely, the rest of us cannot get away from affording sex an outlet.

Until marriage is made independent of the financial element, the masturbation problem will continue to be a big one. Our films and novels rouse sex in the young and lead to masturbation, because proper sex is denied to youth. The fact that everyone has masturbated doesn't help much. The companionate marriage seems about the only way out. But so long as sin is attached to sex, this is not a likely social solution.

But to return to the question: Tell the child that there is nothing sinful about masturbation. If you have already told him lies about its alleged consequences—disease, madness, etc., be brave enough to tell him you were a liar. Then and only then will masturbation become of less importance to him.

My daughter of twelve likes to read smutty books. What shall I do about it?

I should provide her with all the smutty books I could afford to buy. Then she would live out her interest.

But why is she so interested in smut? Is she looking for the truth about sex you never told her?

Would you reprove a boy of fourteen for telling sex stories?

Of course not. I should tell him better ones than he knew. Most adults tell sex stories. As a student, I got some of my best ones from a clergyman. To condemn an interest in sex is sheer hypocrisy and cant.

The sex story is the direct result of sexual repression. It lets off the steam that is bottled up by the doctrine of sin. Under freedom, the sex story would almost die a natural death. *Almost—* not quite—because sex is a fundamental interest.

Who should give sex instruction—teachers or parents?

Parents, of course.

About Religion

Why are you opposed to religious training?

Well, among other reasons, in my years of dealing with children I have found that the most neurotic children are those who have had a rigid religious upbringing. It is a rigid religious upbringing that gives to sex an exaggerated importance.

Religious instruction is damaging to the child's psyche because religious adherents, for the most part, accept the idea of original sin. Both the Jewish and Christian religions hate the flesh. Conventional Christianity all too often gives the child a feeling of dissatisfaction with self. As a boy in Scotland, I was taught from my earliest years that I was in danger of hell-fire.

Once, a boy aged nine, of good English middle-class parentage, came to Summerhill. This was my conversation with him.

"Who is God?"

"Don't know; but if you're good you go to heaven, and if you're bad you go to hell."

"And what sort of place is hell?"

"All dark. The devil is bad."

"I see. And what sort of people go to hell?"

"Bad people: them that swear and murder people."

When are we to realize the absurdity of teaching children stuff like that, of equating profanity with murder and making each of them worthy of unremitting punishment?

When I asked the boy to describe God to me, he said he had no idea of God's appearance. But, he assured me, he loved God. When he said that he loved a God whom he could not describe and whom he had never seen, he was merely using a meaningless, conventional tag. The real truth is that he *fears* God.

Do you believe in Christ?

Some years ago, we had in Summerhill the child of a lay preacher. One Sunday night when we were all dancing, the preacher shook his head. "Neill," he said, "it's a wonderful place, this, but why, oh why, are you such pagans?"

"Brown," I answered, "you spend your life standing on soap boxes telling people how to be saved. You *talk* about salvation. We *live* salvation."

No, we do not consciously follow Christianity, but from a broad point of view, Summerhill is about the only school in England that treats children in a way that Jesus would have approved of. Calvinist ministers in South Africa beat their children, just as Roman Catholic priests beat their children. In Summerhill, we give children love and approval.

How should children get their first ideas about God?

Who is God? I don't know. God to me means the good in each one of us. If you try to teach a child about a being whom you yourself are vague about, you will do more harm than good.

Wouldn't you say that swearing is taking God's name in vain?

Children's swearing deals with sex and natural functions—not God. It is difficult to argue with a religious person who makes God a sacred personage and accepts the Bible as literal fact. If God were represented as a being of love and not as a being of fear, no one would think of taking His name in vain. The cure for blasphemy is to make our gods loving and human.

About Psychology

Isn't it inevitable that every person will grow up to be a neurotic?

Self-regulation is the answer to the arresting questions arising out of Freud's discoveries. Every analyst must feel, even if dimly, that the hours spent in analyzing a patient would never have been necessary if the patient had been self-regulated as a baby. I say dimly, because we cannot be really sure of anything.

My daughter, reared in freedom, may have to go to an analyst one day and say: "Doctor, I need treatment. I am suffering from a father complex. I am fed up with being introduced as the daughter of A. S. Neill. People expect far too much of me; they seem to think I should be perfect. The old man is dead now, but I can't forgive him for parading me in his books. And now, do I lie down on this sofa?" . . . One never knows.

How does self-hate manifest itself?

In a child, self-hate is shown by antisocial behavior, quarreling, spitefulness, bad temper, destructiveness. All self-hate tends to be projected, that is, transferred to others.

The mother of an illegitimate child will condemn sexual looseness in others. The teacher who has tried for years to conquer masturbation will cane children. The old maid who has sublimated sex, that is, repressed it, will show her self-hate in scandal-mongering and bitterness. All hate is self-hate.

The persecution of Jews is done by people who hate themselves. You see this also in colored communities. The Cape Colored, like the Eurasian, is much more intolerant to the true native than the white is.

When you are on the child's side, isn't that your way of getting possession of the child?

What if it is? If it helps the child, what does it matter what my motive is?

I know a girl of eight who stammers in her mother's presence. Why?

Stammering is very often an attempt to gain time in order to avoid betraying oneself in speech. When I get a difficult question in lecturing, I try to hide my ignorance and confusion by beginning with "Well . . . er . . . hm . . ."

The child in question appears to be afraid of her mother. I suspect the mother of being a moralist.

I found that one small boy's stutter was due to his trying to hide the fact that he had masturbated and felt guilty about it. The cure was to convince him that masturbation is not a sin. But the psychology of stammering is almost unexplored territory.

Can a husband analyze his wife, or can a wife analyze her husband?

On no account should relatives ever attempt to deal with each other psychologically. I have known cases in which a husband analyzed his wife, or the wife analyzed her husband. These analyses were always unsuccessful, sometimes positively harmful.

No parent dare treat his own child analytically, whatever the school of treatment.

Why do so many adults express gratitude to a strict teacher of their childhood?

Conceit, mostly. The man who gets up at a meeting and says, "I was thrashed as a kid and it did me a hell of a lot of good," is virtually saying, "Look at me. I'm a success in spite of—even because of—my early thrashings."

A slave does not really want freedom. He is incapable of appreciating freedom. Outside discipline makes men slaves, inferiors, masochists. They hug their chains.

Can an ordinary teacher do psychoanalysis?

I'm afraid not. He should first of all be analyzed himself; for if his own unconscious is an unknown territory, he won't get far in exploring the unknown land of a child's soul.

About Learning

You don't approve of Latin or mathematics; how, then, do you suggest a child's mind should be developed?

I don't know what "mind" is. If the experts in mathematics and Latin have great minds, I have never been aware of it.

Does your disapproval of advanced mathematics influence Summerhill children not to study mathematics?

I never speak to children about mathematics. I myself like mathematics so much that I often do geometrical and algebraic problems just for fun.

My case against mathematics is that the study is too abstract for children. Nearly every child hates mathematics. Though every boy understands *two* apples, few boys can understand *x* apples.

Moreover, I make the same point against mathematics that I make against Latin and Greek: What is the use of teaching quadratic equations to boys who are going to repair cars or sell stockings? It is madness.

Do you believe in homework?

I don't even believe in school lessons unless they are voluntarily chosen. The homework habit is disgraceful. Children loathe homework, and that is enough to condemn it.

Why do some boys learn only when made to feel physical pain?

I expect that I could learn to recite the Koran if I knew I'd be flogged if I didn't. One result, of course, would be that I should forever hate the Koran, and the flogger, and myself.

What should a teacher do when a boy plays with his pencil when she is trying to teach a lesson?

Pencil equals penis. The boy has been forbidden to play with his penis. Cure: get the parents to take off the masturbation prohibition.

Index

abilities and aptitudes, 4-6, 27
abnormal child, 272-275, 276-282, 285, 289
abnormal mothers, 95, 108
abnormal parents, 108
abortion, 237-238
acne, 356
acting, 15, 31, 66-70, 111, 196
activities at Summerhill, 13
actors, jealousy of, 317
adolescents, 23, 56-58, 208-211, 216, 287, 289, 371
adopted children, 150
"adoption" of child by teacher, 330
adults, and conflict with children, 8, 18-19, 108, 138-145, 177-181, 303, 330; consideration for child's wishes, 108; as criminals, 284-285; desire for power, 155; dishonesty, 277-288; fears, 309; gratitude for childhood thrashings, 98, 169, 377; rights, 108, 144, 186, 193, 336, 339; starved emotions, 345; therapy for, 289; values, 112, 113, 130, 138, 140, 142, 143, 332; views not those of child, 255; work and drudgery, 338, 345, 348. *See also* Parents
aggressiveness, 20, 113, 358
air guns, rule against, 53
alcohol, 366-367
Aldeburgh, town of, 14
allowances, 164, 186, 198-199, 307
altruism, 60, 181, 250-251
American in Paris, An, George Gershwin, 71
analysis, *see* Psychoanalysis
anger, 122, 167
animal dung, 175

animals, cruelty to, 269; fear of, 104 and humans, 100, 160, 207, 269
answering back, 352
"anti-life," 343-344
anti-Semitism, 24, 255, 352
antisocialness, *see* Criminality; Delinquency; Stealing
anxiety, about child's unhappy home, 349-350; and fear, 127, 131; about money, 198; of parents, 187, 325-330; and suicides of young, 346-347
approval, 117-123, 194, 281, 282, 290, 318
aptitudes, natural, 4-6, 27
arithmetic studies, 5, 12, 26, 40, 350, 378
armed services, Summerhill pupils in, 85, 354
army system, 103, 156-157
arrested development, 289
art, 13-15, 26
athletics, 62, 73
atomic bomb, 103, 131, 211
attendance at classes, 4-5, 13, 30-31
authoritarian morality, 8, 112, 114
authority, 52, 53, 118, 120, 153-156, 210, 216, 226, 273, 287, 297, 314, 327, 328

babies, interest in origin of, 36, 38, 43, 97, 149, 151, 205, 206, 209, 219, 220, 225, 252-253, 295; and parents, 25, 63, 101, 318, 336
baby, cuddling, 63, 101, 357-358; discomfort of, 96; feeding, 95, 96, 177-181; left alone in carriage, 336; left to cry, 122, 178; natural functions, 96, 101; playing with, 63, 101, 122,

336, 357-358; self-regulated, 104, 105, 177, 178, 336; thumb sucking, 96, 101; unkindness to, 25, 63, 122, 336

Bach, 72, 97, 257

backward children, 359

bad habits of child, 96, 101, 359

bad home conditions, 323, 329-339, 347, 349-350

bad-tempered children, 275, 323

Bambi, Felix Salten, 265

Barrie, James, *Peter Pan,* 69, 265

bastardy, 24, 212, 236-237, 344

bathing, 20, 46, 73, 103

bathing suits, 113, 115, 229

beating of children, 98, 100, 115, 129, 157, 158, 160, 165-170, 269-270, 302, 315, 359, 377

bedtime rules, 45-47, 182-183

bed-wetting, 332-333

Beethoven, 72, 97, 192, 257

behavior, *see* Emotions; Manners; Moralizing

Bergen-Belsen concentration camp, 270

Bible, 247, 264, 329, 374

bicycle, borrowed, 49, 51, 52, 279

bicycle shed built by children, 59

birth control, *see* Contraceptives

birth question, *see* Babies

bomb-throwing experience, 125

books, 18, 21-22, 69, 213, 263-266

boring of walls and wood by children, 139-140

"boss-schoolmaster" and Slavic girl, 314-315

bottles for big boys, 319

boxing lessons, 358

Boy Scouts, 353

boys, and girls compared, 15, 40-41, 62-67, 139, 184, 186, 201, 234, 315; at play, 13, 15

bread-throwing boy, 329

breakfast at Summerhill, 13

breast feeding, 95, 179, 206, 318

bribery, 164

British Government Inspectors' Report, 75-85; notes on, 86-88

bullying, 48, 271

candy for children, 186

capital punishment, 112, 343

careers, of Summerhill graduates, *see* Vocations; for women, 339

castration, 219

"castration complex," 126

censorship, 114, 153, 263-266, 351-352, 372

Chaplin, Charlie, 369

character, 100, 113, 296, 335

chastity, 371

cheating, adult, 277, 278, 280

Chekhov, Anton, 69

chemical laboratory classes, 13

child, asking what to do, 362; conscience of, 301; an egoist, 42, 114, 181, 250, 251, 272-277; ever-changing interests of, 361; fears of, 210; feeding, 177-181; and growth pace, 362-363; in group, 285; labor of, 61; and parents, 130; phobias of, 127-128, 131, 272, 309-310; problems of, 268-297; refusing to eat, 367-368

childbirth, questions about, *see* Babies

child guidance, 331

child's side, being on, 117, 119, 120, 282, 290, 339, 376

chores, 60, 61, 164

Christ, 241, 374

Christianity, 240-248

Cinderella, 265

civilization and society, 23, 28, 102, 104

class attendance, 4-5, 13, 30-31

class consciousness, 65, 111, 327

claustrophobia, 297

cleanliness, personal, 101, 140, 152, 184-185, 366

clever boy crook, 289-290

climbing trees, 20-21

clothes complex, 186
clothing, 3, 101, 115, 153, 185-187
coal-heaver boy, 185
coeducation, 56-58, 286
Coleridge, 246
college entrance exams, 7-8, 30-32, 61, 64, 110
colored communities, 376
colored pupils at Summerhill, 352
Communism, 65, 343
community spirit, 55
compelling attention, 162, 164, 170, 308
compulsive stealing, 276, 278, 280-281
compulsory work by pupils, 59
conflict, between children and adults, 8, 18-19, 108, 143, 177-181, 303, 330-339; between school and home, 17, 157, 303, 330, 338
conformist, 12
conscience of child, 301
consideration, 108, 192
contentment, 356
contraceptives, 209, 215, 238
controlled parenthood, see Contraceptives
convent, girls from, 5, 15, 260
Conway, Sir Martin, The Crowd in Peace and War, 112
Cook, Caldwell, The Play Way, 27
coprophilic child, 174
corporal punishment, 157, 168, 271, 343, 358-359
correction, 166-167
correction system, 286-288
corruption of youth, 113
cosmetics industry, 209, 213, 214, 266
courses of study, 5, 13, 24, 25, 350
Coward, Noel, The Vortex, 69
cowardice, 125, 126, 129
creative child, 360-361
creative play, 15
creative toys, 189
crime films, 265, 273, 280
crime stories, 213, 265
criminal and society, 121

criminal code, 98, 112, 121, 242, 248, 255, 270, 343
criminality, 272-275
criticism, by child, 146-147; by parent, 118, 122, 271, 332, 366
crook, story of clever boy, 289 290
crowd, 112, 343
Crowd in Peace and War, The, Sir Martin Conway, 112
cruelty, 269-271
cup-smasher boy, 283
curing child, 38, 40, 118, 211, 279-286, 289-293, 359
curriculum, see Courses of study; School subjects
cursing, 259-262

damage to property, see Destructiveness
dancing, 14, 60, 71-72, 344, 374
dangerous weapons rule, 53
death, child's idea of, 129
defecation, 172-176
defiance, 363
delinquency, juvenile, 250, 272-275, 278, 283-288, 289, 312
delinquent boy (Jabez), story of, 288
democracy, school, 46, 55
destructiveness of child, 106, 138-145, 165, 319, 365, 375
Dickens, Charles, 69
diet, see Food; Vegetarianism
dignity, 146, 334
Dillinger, 248
disapproval, 118, 122, 271
discipline, 16, 53, 95, 107, 109, 118, 155-161, 198, 291
disease, 24
dishonesty, 148, 277, 278
disobedience, 167
divorce, 323-324
docile children, 4
doctors, 96, 101, 149, 182, 287, 291
dolls, see Toys
double standard, 98
Douglas, George, The House with the

Green Shutters, 191
Dracula, Bram Stoker, 264
dramatics, 15, 66-70, 196
"dressing up," *see* Cleanliness; Clothing
drinking, alcoholic, 366-367
drugs, 149, 287
dung, 175
duty, 152, 153, 338, 344

eating, 181, 367-368
economic problems, 347
education and society, 91, 92, 103, 113, 114, 116, 147, 170, 286-288, 328
egoism, 42, 114, 181, 250, 251, 272-277, 309, 315, 317, 328, 330
Ellington, Duke, 72
emotions, 25-26, 71, 100, 280, 286, 327, 345
Encyclopedia of Sex Knowledge, 263
English studies, 13, 27
environment, 17, 18, 286, 323, 329-339, 349-350
equals, children as, 8, 11, 21, 107, 160, 287
etiquette, 148, 192. *See also* Manners
examinations, 6-7, 8, 25, 30-33, 61, 64, 88, 110, 115-116, 159, 356
excrement, 172-176
exhibitionist, 127-128, 169
extrovert, 274

failures among pupils, 15, 31-32, 54, 279, 295, 314
faith in children, 117, 159, 287-288
family authority, *see* Parents' authority
fantasy and make-believe, 60-65, 69, 128-129, 133-139, 146-149, 151, 199, 265, 273-274, 302, 304, 310, 313, 320, 323
Fascism, 343
father, cruelty to child, 271; identification with, 315; jealous, 321-322; punishing, 97, 98, 119, 122, 126-132, 158, 159, 161, 167, 169, 226, 270, 271, 301, 315, 327, 331, 332; respect for, 132, 146; show-off, 356; substitute for, 130, 296, 301-307, 310, 328, 330, 334; symbol, 40, 130
favoritism, 21, 47, 324, 304
fear, 97, 161, 168, 169, 264, 328; of animals, 104; anxiety and, 127; goodness dependent upon, 129-130, 159, 248; and hate, 4, 9, 39, 95, 113, 118, 124-131, 170, 198, 225; and honesty, 277, 278; persuasion through, 114-115; in the soldier, 125, 157; of spiders, 127; of thunder, 131, 146; of the young, 112
fears, of adult, 309; of child, 104, 105, 124-132, 310; of father, unconfessed, 146; present-day and primitive, 124; religious, 124-132, 223, 245-248, 353, 373; about sex, 126-128, 223; of women, 309, 310
feces, 96, 172-176
feeding, 95, 96, 177-181, 367-368
Fielding, Henry, *Tom Jones,* 264
fights, 8, 20, 113
films, 213, 265-266, 273, 280, 351-352, 371
fines, automatic, 50-51, 350
food, 13, 47, 156, 175-182, 367-368
football, 46, 65
force and coercion, 114
forcing opinions on children, 255
foreign countries, Summerhill influence in, 91
free child, 4, 92, 104-116, 118, 161, 285, 294, 321, 339, 349, 356
freedom, absolute, 356; to attend classes, 5, 13, 31, 34; in boarding school, 289; child's first reaction to, 5, 13, 31, 34, 110-116, 121-122, 161, 181, 194, 195, 271, 292, 328; clever and dull children's reaction to, 113, 116; for children, 4, 92, 103-116, 118, 285, 294, 321, 339, 349, 356; for juvenile delinquents, 285, 289; no cure for pathological delin-

quency, 289; to play, 284; and license, 53, 107, 289, 294, 306, 308, 344; for school staff members, 21; of speech, 35, 47-48, 50, 115, 158, 259-262, 294, 351, 374

French, teaching of, 24

Freud, Sigmund, 20, 89, 126, 205, 206, 220, 225, 231, 263, 294

friendships, boy and girl, 23, 56-58, 208-210, 212, 215, 216, 287

fruit stealing at school, 276

fun, sense of, 200-201

furniture and child, 138, 139

Galsworthy, John, 69

games, 62-65, 73-74

gangs, see Criminality; Delinquency

gangster films, 265, 273, 280

gangster play, 13, 14, 52, 62-65, 66, 139, 265, 282, 284

gardening, 8, 59-60, 65, 120-121, 163, 183

General School Meeting, 7, 14, 15, 18, 45, 55, 74, 155, 230, 276-279, 292, 313, 314, 321, 350

geography instruction, 7, 13, 26, 31, 74

geometry studies, 26, 378

Germany, teaching in, 314

George Gershwin, *An American in Paris,* 71-72

ghosts, fear of, 127, 264, 310

Ghosts, Henrik Ibsen, 335

gifts for children, 307, 362

girl who wouldn't wash, 184

girls, and boys compared, 15, 40-41, 62-67, 139, 184, 186, 201, 234, 315; from convent, 5, 15; friendships of, 208-211, 216; inferior status in society, 99; at play, 14, 15; use of lipstick, 186

God, child's idea of, 244, 246, 373, 374; identifying with, 167

God-fearing training, 124, 127, 132, 223, 246-248, 353, 373-374

Gone with the Wind, Margaret Mitchell, 213

Government Inspectors, Report of British, 75-85

grandparents and children, 337

gratitude to parents, 61, 305

Greek studies, 378

grief of child, 69

growth of child, 277, 362-363

guilt fantasy, 129

gymnastics, 62, 73

habits of child, 333

habitual thief, see Compulsive stealing

hair styles of girls, 186

Hamlet, 7

hammering nails, 140, 143, 144, 363

handiwork, 14, 25, 31

happiness, 24, 92, 111, 117, 182, 183, 294-297, 345, 346, 356

hate reaction, 8, 20, 40, 48, 92, 101-103, 119, 129, 144-145, 157-160, 165-166, 170, 198, 207, 269, 271, 282, 301, 307, 314, 315, 320, 321, 359, 375

health and sleep, 182-183

hell fire, threat of, 126-128, 131, 223, 245, 278, 329, 373

heterosexual play in childhood, 208, 210, 224, 227

history, teaching of, 13, 24, 26, 31, 350

Hitler, Adolf, 100, 270

hobbies, 361

hockey, 73, 74

Holmes, Sherlock, 67

home, going, 321, 327-339; letters from, 36; versus school, 17, 157, 329, 330, 338

homesickness, 8, 349-350

homosexuality, 165, 208, 219, 222, 234-235, 344, 359

honesty, 277, 278

Hope, Anthony, *The Prisoner of Zenda,* 263

hose-pipe story, boy's, 311

House with the Green Shutters, The, George Douglas, 191

Howard, Sidney, *The Silver Cord,* 69
humor, 7, 200-201, 346, 361, 369
hunting, 24, 212
huts, sleeping (Summerhill), 3
hypochondria, 327

Ibsen, Henrik, *Ghosts,* 69, 335
identification, with father, 315; with God, 167; of parent with child, 257, 306, 308
illegitimate child, 24, 38, 99, 150, 236-238, 264, 375
impotency, 158
incendiary, child, 223-224, 249
indoor games, 73
infant, *see* Baby; Feeding
infantile sex repression, 96, 101, 210, 225, 251
infantile sexual interest, 97, 126
inferiority, sense of, 12, 37, 68, 126, 133, 136-137, 160, 201, 291, 315, 317
ink-splasher in London, 249
insolence, 167, 194
Inspectors, Report of British Government, 75-85
Instructions for Expectant Mothers, 100
intelligence tests, 287
interest, compelling, 162, 164, 170
intolerance, race, 376
introverted child, 273-274
Israel, community centers in, 64-65

Jabez, story of, 283
Jacobs, W. W., 67
Japan, Summerhill influence in, 91
jazz, 31, 71, 72, 257
jealousy, of daughter, 322; destructiveness caused by, 319; of father, 321-322; of free child, 105, 303; of grownups, 316; of new pupil, 320; of parents, 16, 187, 321, 329, 330, 334; of younger brother, 36, 144, 162, 173, 250-251, 269, 272, 274,

301, 317, 320, 332, 364; of youth, 321, 322
Jesus, 241, 374
Jews, 111, 376
joking with child, 200-201
Joyce, James, *Ulysses,* 263
Judaism, 241, 244, 373
justice and punishment, 164-165, 256-257
juvenile delinquency, 250, 272-275, 278, 282-289

killing, in fantasy, 128-129, 273-274, 302-304, 310-312, 320; in war, 98
Kingsley, Charles, *Westward Ho!,* 69
Kipling, Rudyard, 260
kitchen, raiding, 47, 51
kleptomania, 251-252, 279-280
Koran, 379
Krafft-Ebing, 263

Lady Chatterley's Lover, D. H. Lawrence, 263
Lamb's Essays, 6
Lane, Homer, 89, 121, 274-275, 282-283
La Ronde, 265
Latin studies, 115, 378
laughter, 357-358
law, 103, 112, 157
lawbreaker girl, 312-314
Lawrence, D. H., *Lady Chatterley's Lover,* 213-214, 263
laws at Summerhill, 313-314
laziness, 59-60, 337
learning, 4, 6, 25, 115, 378
Leiston, town of, 3, 14, 22, 47, 50
lessons, optional, 5, 13, 30-31, 73, 284, 378
letters, from home, 36, 319-320; to parents, 292; writing, 117, 153
liar, child, 35, 146-151, 364
libertinism, 113, 344
license, 107, 306-308, 344
lifer on machinery-buying trip, 288
lipstick, use of, 186

literature, classes in, 26
Little Commonwealth, Homer Lane, 121, 274, 282-283
living out interest, 172-175
living standards, high, 345
locked doors, freedom and, 141 142
love affairs of adolescents, 23, 56-58, 215-216, 287, 371
love, and approval, 117-123; as cure for neurosis, 38, 40, 118, 161, 272, 278-279, 282, 287, 297; and hate, 301-305; lack of, 8, 40, 54, 92, 117-122, 130-131, 145, 149, 151, 272, 278-279, 282, 287, 288, 301, 303, 323-324, 328, 356; and marriage, 343; for others, 257; perverted, 269; too much, 324
love interest in films, 213
love parts in school plays, 68
love stories, 213
love therapy, 283, 284
luncheon at Summerville, 13
lying, 146-151, 364; child's romantic, 150-151; of parents, 97, 101-102, 146-151, 220, 371; to parents, 216
lynching of Negroes, 24

magician fantasy, boy's, 274
Malinowski, 211, 215
manners, 3, 47-53, 97, 107, 110, 118, 148, 181, 192-197
manual labor, *see* Work
Marcus, *Morals for the Young,* 302
marriage, 96, 98, 99, 152, 212, 216-217, 343, 345-346, 371
masturbation, 16, 22, 37, 38, 101, 103, 126, 133, 158, 164, 182, 207-214, 222-228, 235, 279, 281, 294, 347, 359, 370-371, 376
maternity, rooming-in care, 177
mathematics studies, 13, 26, 27, 31, 40, 60, 378
mechanics, aptitude in, 27, 30
medicine, 24, 287
Meistersinger, Die, 72
mental cruelty, 271, 335

mentally defective children, 350
metalwork, 31
Mitchell, Margaret, *Gone with the Wind,* 213
money, 4, 187, 198-199, 363
Montessori system, 27, 172, 174
moral sense, child's, 254
morality, authoritarian, 8, 98, 118, 166, 169, 220
moralizing, 58, 120, 130, 144, 169, 174, 182, 207, 218, 248-258, 280, 284, 287, 293-297
Morals for the Young, Marcus, 302
mother, anxious, 325-327; jealous, 322; and sex instruction, 151, 218-219; of spoiled child, 307; substitute for, 307; symbol of, 40; unhappy, 323-332
mouth activities, 223, 225
moving pictures, 14, 51, 265-266, 351-352
mud, playing with, 28, 63, 74, 174, 185
muggers, child, 282
music instruction, 12
music preferences, 31, 71-72
mysticism, 244, 245

nagging, 37, 40, 171, 271, 325, 332, 366
nakedness, 229-230
natural functions of child, 96, 101, 172-176
nature of the child, 250
needlework, 27
Negroes, 24, 352, 376
neurosis, 38, 40, 118, 161, 281, 289, 294
neurotic adults, 375
neurotic child, 280-281, 323, 324
Nijinsky, 26
noise, 45-47, 63, 189-191, 255, 309, 312, 364
Notes on British Government Inspectors' Report, 86-88

nudity, 229-230
nursery, training in, 95-96, 100-101, 172-176

obedience, 102, 107, 155-161, 327-328
obscenity, 260, 364, 369-370
obstinate child, 363
Oedipus complex, 324
old age, 89, 90, 112-113
only child, 306, 316, 320
optional lessons, 5, 13, 30-31, 284
oral activities of child, 6, 223, 225
"original sin," 104, 149, 244, 247, 344, 373
originality, 6, 31-33

pageantry, 65
painting at Summerhill, 14, 31
parent-child relationships, 331-339
parent-teacher rivalry, 321, 338
parental responsibility, 339
parents, abnormal, 37-38, 95; anxious, 325-330; attitudes toward school, 16, 17, 157, 333-339; authority of, 210, 216, 226, 327, 328; child's criticism of, 146-147, 329; commandments for, 118-123; criticism and disapproval, 118, 122, 271, 332; divorced, 323, 324; educating of, 356; hypocrisy of, 146; identification with child, 257, 306, 308; jealousy, 16, 187, 321, 329, 334; letters from, 36, 319-320, 334; lying, 97, 101-102, 146-151, 220, 371; mistakes, 333; money complex of, 187; nagging by, 37, 40, 171, 271, 325, 327, 332; of problem children, 15, 36-38, 103, 303, 323, 326, 331; problems of, 300-339; self-analysis of, 335; show-off, 122, 307, 318, 336; of spoiled children, 306; treatment of child, 152-154, 308; tyranny of, 339; unhappy, 125-126, 270, 303, 307, 323, 332; unloving, 323, 324; visiting, 16, 22, 187, 325, 334, 349; writing to, 292

pastimes, Summerhill, 13, 31
pathological juvenile delinquency, 289
penal code, 343
persecution of Jews, 111, 270, 370
personality and character, 6
perversion, sexual, 270, 358-359
perverted love, 269
Peter Pan, James Barrie, 265, 309, 321
phobia, 131, 272, 309-310; drowning, 129; earthworms, 127-128; poisoning, 272
play, 3, 5, 14-15, 25, 62-65, 185, 190-191, 232, 348, 363
Play Way, The, Caldwell Cook, 27
play writing, 15, 66-70
playing gangsters, 13
playing school, 315
playing truant, 362
plays, children's, 66-70, 196
P.Ls., see "Private Lessons"
pleasure seeking, 344
pocket money, 164, 198-199, 307
poisoning phobia, 272
policeman, fear of, 120, 146, 151
politics, 24, 91-92, 111, 354
pornography, 210, 221, 231-233, 287, 369-370
possessiveness, 19, 142, 143, 317, 322, 360-361
pottery making, 14, 15
poverty and crime, 273, 274, 286. See also Slums
power, adult desire for, 151; and authority, 309-316; child's sense of, 309; fantasies of, 312; seeking, 315; and strict school, 328
practical jokes, 271
praising the child, 122
prayer, of child, 244; for child, 171
preaching to children, 255, 286, 297 See also Moralizing
pregnancy, fear of, 56, 58, 99
prenatal influences, 125-126, 131
Presley, Elvis, 72, 97

priggishness, 52

primitive Africans, 211, 215, 243, 318

primitive man, 124

prison for juvenile delinquents, 284, 288. *See also* Reform schools

prison system, 103, 113, 121

Prisoner of Zenda, The, Anthony Hope, 263

"Private Lessons" (P.Ls.), 19, 36-44, 173, 319

private property and child, 138, 139

prize-giving, 25, 74

probation officer, 280, 283

problem child, 53-54, 101; parents of, 15, 37-38, 103, 118-119, 144, 161, 173, 179, 272-279, 284-289, 294, 319, 326-333, 347, 359, 363

problem parents, 37-38, 103, 323, 326, 331, 333

prohibition laws, 277

prohibitions, 20-21, 248, 250, 251, 348, 349. *See also* Censorship

"pro-life," 343-344

promiscuity, 236-237

property, disregard for, 138, 139; respect for, 138, 139, 142, 166-167

prostitution, 210

prudery, 113-115, 207

psychiatrists, 283, 291. *See also* Social work

psychic damage to child, 95, 169, 205. *See also* Neurosis

psychoanalysis, 330, 345

psychological attention, 35-44, 48, 291, 294. *See also* Curing the child; "Private Lessons"

psychology, 4, 20, 296, 309, 375-377; talks on, at Summerhill, 12, 14

public recognition, 89-91

public speaking by children, 55

punishment, 129, 155-161, 248, 256, 270, 286, 287, 302, 305, 315, 359; for child's sexual offenses, 205, 206, 257, 282; criminal, 103, 112, 121, 149; and rewards, 162-171; voted at General School Meeting, 7, 50, 245

questions of small boy, 294-295

Rabelais, 263

Ravel, 72

reaction of child to freedom, 5, 13, 31, 34, 110-116, 121-122, 161, 181, 194, 195, 271, 292, 328

reading of stories, 21-22, 69, 153-154, 263-266, 360. *See also* Censorship

reading instruction, 27, 29, 30, 40, 137

reading preferences, 31, 69, 264, 360, 372

rebel, schoolgirl, 313-314

reform schools, 121, 275, 285-288

regimentation, 112

Reich, Wilhelm, 131, 159, 207

religion, 22, 24, 103, 111, 114, 118, 149, 158-159, 169, 206, 207, 211, 215, 223, 240-247, 250, 255, 280, 288, 344, 359, 373-374

religious fears, 124, 126-128, 131-132, 223, 245-248, 353, 373, 374

religious home, child from, 353

religious training, 256, 329

repression, 99-100, 158, 176, 182, 190, 205, 210, 214, 217, 218, 224-225, 235, 251, 294, 309, 312, 316, 344

required subjects, 7-8, 164

respect for property, 108, 138, 139, 142, 166-167

responsibility, 152-154, 339, 349

retarded child, 281, 289, 350

revenge, criminality as, 275

rewards, 129-130, 162-171, 279, 284, 285, 290

rights of adult, 108, 144, 186, 193, 336, 339

rod theory, Solomon's, 168

room of child, 3

rooming-in maternity care, 177

Rosenkavalier, Der, 72

rules at Summerhill, bathing and swimming, 20, 46; bedtime, 45-47, 182-183; dangerous weapons, 53

sacrifice, 305

sadism, 145, 212, 269-271, 297, 314, 324

safeguards in care of children, 20-21, 53, 106, 153-154

Salten, Felix, *Bambi*, 205

Santa Claus, 360

sarcasm, 360-361

savages, African, 211, 215, 243, 317

saving money, 362

saw, borrowed and damaged, 166-167. *See also* Tools

school, built by children, 61; choice of, 337

School Meeting, *see* General School Meeting

school subjects, 24, 350

school versus home, 17, 157, 329, 330, 338

schoolboy playing with pencil, 379

schoolroom jealousy, 320

schools and sex education, 151, 218-219

science, teaching of, 13, 26

Scott, Sir Walter, 69

self-analysis of parents, 335

self-approval, 19, 257

self-assurance, 154

self-confidence, 6

self-discipline, 19, 109-110, 114, 356

self-government, 50-54, 153, 195. *See also* General School Meeting

self-hate, 375-376. *See also* Hate

self-interest of child, 59, 60, 114, 163, 164

self-regulated child, 104, 105, 155, 166, 177, 185, 220-221, 260, 318, 359. *See also* Free child

self-regulation, 116, 185, 188, 220, 294, 318, 335-336, 375

self-reliance, 152-154, 159

selfishness, of adult, 193; of child, 114, 193, 250-251, 315

selling by child of articles of clothing, 50

sense of humor, 200-201

sense of justice, 50

separate rooms, 3, 354

sex, answering child's questions about, 151, 205, 206, 218-222, 225, 295; attitudes, 24, 96, 115, 205-217, 220, 221, 257, 371; behavior, 376; crimes, 209, 211; education, 151, 218-222, 372; fears, 126-128, 205; instruction, 218-222, 372; interest in books and films, 263-266, 371; morality, 205; repression, 205, 223, 294; suppression in children, 207-208, 223; suppression in infants, 96, 101, 210, 225, 251, 370-371; stories about, 373; taboo, 205, 206, 209, 212, 222, 231, 351; words, 260-261

sexual affairs of adolescents, 23, 56-58, 215, 287

sexual interest of child, 97, 126, 133, 135, 205, 220, 226, 227, 232, 233, 295

sexual offenses of child, 205-207, 223, 257

sexual perversion, 270, 358-359

Shakespeare, 67

Shaw, George Bernard, 69, 305

Shimoda, Seishi, 91

show-off parents, 122, 307, 318, 336, 356

Silver Cord, The, Sidney Howard, 69

sincerity, 111, 113, 117, 120, 149, 194, 195

sister and brother squabbling, 363

Slavic girl at Summerhill, 315

sleep and health, 182-183

sleeping, in huts at Summerhill, 3; one or more in a room, 3, 354; in parents' room, 127

slums, 273, 274, 280, 286, 347

smoking, 35, 45, 113, 331

smutty stories, 96, 158, 205, 212, 232, 233, 261, 369, 370

snail-drawing boy, 304

social approval, 159, 256, 262

social clinic, 280

social laws, 108

social sense, 330
social uniformity, 112
social values, 65, 111, 327
social work, 280, 347
society, 23, 28, 98, 99, 102-104, 112, 121, 248, 280, 286, 306, 343, 345
sodomy, 235. See also Homosexuality
soldier, destructiveness of, 144; fear in, 125, 157, 169
Solomon's rod theory, 168
spanking, 101-103, 165-167, 198, 315. See also Beating of children; Punishment
spending money, 164, 198-199, 307
spiders, fear of, 127
spoiling child, 107, 108, 195, 198, 199, 306-308
spontaneous acting, 70
sports, 73, 74, 328. See also Games
sportsmanship, 74
staff, school, 9, 17, 19, 21, 47
stammering, 376
standard of living, 345
standard education, 24, 55
stealing, 12, 35-36, 48-49, 148, 149, 187, 245, 252, 276-281, 289, 296-297, 325-326
Stekel, Wilhelm, 347
Stoker, Bram, Dracula, 264
stories and reading, 21-22, 69, 360
Stravinsky, 72
Streicher, Julius, 270
Strindberg, August, 69
stuttering, 376
subjects, school, 24. See also Courses of study
subservience, 193
success, 4, 29, 345
sucking, big boys' interest in, 319
suicides of young, 346-347
sulky child, 363
Summerhill, activities, 13; age groups, 3; benefactors, 17; food, 13, 47, 180-182; finances, 17, 87; founding, 3; health at, 182-183, 352; idea behind, 3, 91; influence abroad, 91; location, 3; management, 47; no religious affiliation, 22; number of pupils, 87; questions and answers about, 348-354; Report of Government Inspectors, 75-85; rooming arrangements, 3; rules and prohibitions, 20-21, 348, 349; selection of pupils, 91; self-government, 45, 52-53, 350 (see also General School Meeting); social features, 47, 194, 195; staff, 9, 17, 19; typical day, 13
sunbathing at Summerhill, 230
Sunday clothes, 97, 101, 186, 246
suppression, 173, 175. See also Repression
swearing, 35, 47-48, 50, 115, 158, 259-262, 294, 351, 374
swimming, 20, 73

table manners, 97, 181, 192, 194
taboo, sex, 205, 206, 209, 212, 222, 231, 351
tantrums, 166
teacher, "adoption" of child by, 330; cruel, 165, 168, 170, 271, 375; ego of, 328, 330; emotionally free to guide child, 33; giving sex information, 151, 218-219; popular, 307; power of, 328; psychoanalysis of, 330; respect for, 194
teaching methods, 5, 25, 114, 116, 130
teamwork, 155
teasing, 20
tennis, 73, 74
terrorizing boy, 167
terrors of child, see Fears
Tess of the D'Urbervilles, Thomas Hardy, 263
Thackeray, 69
theater, school, 66-70, 196
theology, see Religion
therapy, 35, 40, 281, 289-293, 294. See also "Private Lessons"
thief, child, see Stealing
thievery, see Stealing

thumb-sucking, 96, 101, 115, 164, 179, 223, 365
thunder, fear of, 131, 146
tidiness, 140, 184-185, 306, 365
tiger, boy's story about, 310-311
tile work hobby, 219
timetable feeding, 95, 96, 177, 178
toilets, 96, 172-176, 253, 260, 309
toleration, 123
Tom Jones, Henry Fielding, 264
tool chest gift, jealousy over, 319
tools, care of, 18, 19, 140-143, 152, 166-167. *See also* Workshop
totalitarianism, 177
toys, 14, 25, 188-189, 365
transference by child, 295-296
trials for offenses, 49-50. *See also* General School Meeting
truancy, 362
trust, 117, 288
truthfulness about sex, 151
truthtelling, unwise, 219-220
tyranny of parents, 339

Ulysses, James Joyce, 263
unconscious destructiveness of child, 138
unconscious, influence of, 245, 248-250, 279, 294, 296, 309, 348; religion and, 245
understanding the child, 118, 156, 282, 339
unfree child, 95-103
unhappiness, 345
unhappy home, 323, 324, 332, 349-350
unhappy marriage, 345-346
unhappy mother, 125-126, 270, 323, 324, 349, 356
unhappy parents, 323, 324, 332, 337, 338
uniformity and social regimentation, 112
university entrance exams, 7-8, 30, 31, 32, 61, 64, 110, 115, 116, 159

unselfishness, 315
untidiness, 140, 184-185, 306, 365
unwanted child, 125-126
urination, 172

values, of adult, 112, 113, 130, 144, 327, 332; of individual, 18, 138, 140-143, 327, 334-335, 361
vegetarianism, 180-181, 255, 315
"vices" of child, 359
visiting parents, 16, 22, 187, 325, 334, 349
visitors at Summerhill, 11, 12, 18, 122, 141, 142, 172, 182, 190, 195, 196, 201, 220, 261-262
vocations of Summerhill graduates, 5-6, 7, 30, 32-34, 43-44, 61, 72, 88, 109-110, 116, 195-196, 285
Vortex, The, Noel Coward, 69

walking, 183
walls, damage to, 139
war, 24, 98, 103, 111, 112, 131, 161, 212, 242, 343, 354
washing, 184, 366. *See also* Cleanliness
watch stolen by boy, 252
wayward children, *see* Delinquency; Stealing
weapons, rule against dangerous, 53
weeding, 59, 120-121
welfare workers, 347. *See also* Social work
Wells, H. G., 242
Westward Ho!, Charles Kingsley, 69
"Where do babies come from?" *see* Babies
whipping of child, *see* Beating of children; Punishment; Spanking
window-breaking, 10-11, 150, 312
women, clothing of, 214; fears of, 309, 310; household duties, 338; role of, in society, 99
wood and metal workshop, 14, 140-142

woodwork, 31
work, of adults, 114, 338, 345; and child, 59, 60, 120-121, 163, 164; by women, 338-339
workshop, private, 141, 142
worries of child, 346-347
Wren, Sir Christopher, 136
writing to parents, 292
writings and lectures, 25, 28, 89, 102, 183

young, fear of, 112
Young Girl's Diary, A (Preface by Sigmund Freud), 263
younger children at Summerhill, 352
youthful offenders, *see* Juvenile delinquency; Stealing

Zoë, 104, 105, 108, 156, 157, 172, 180, 185, 188, 212, 220, 229, 261-262, 307, 357, 375